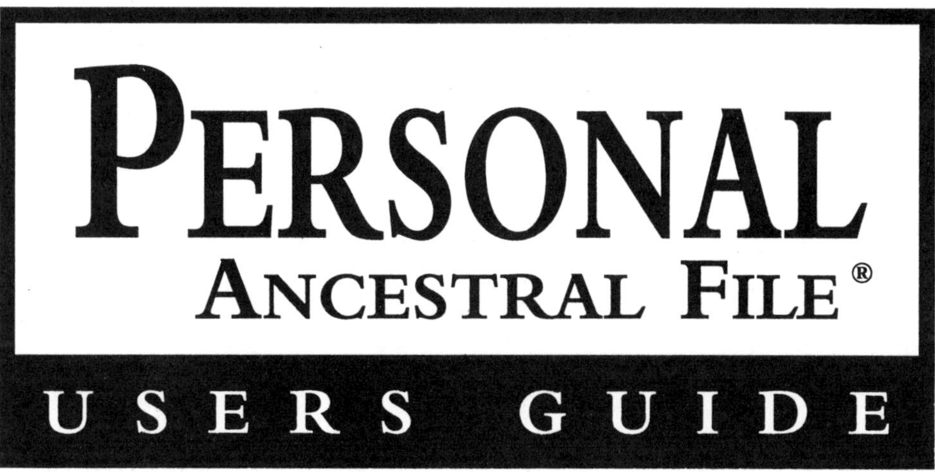

AN AUTHORIZED GUIDE FROM

THE HOPE FOUNDATION

PUBLISHED BY

Ancestry®

copyright page

Trademarks

About The Hope Foundation

The Hope Foundation was established to illuminate personal nobility through family history research. The Hope Foundation, as a non-profit organization, engages in charitable activities that focus on genealogy as a tool to bond individuals in a common brotherhood. The Foundation is involved in family history research centers in prisons and conducts genealogy research and training in youth detention centers, youth clubs, and community centers.

The Hope Foundation is the author of several genealogy training manuals and is the author of several widely-used genealogy software programs.

The Hope Foundation has created a special Jewish edition of its Ancestral Quest genealogy software to assist living heirs to easily create and document their family trees. This sophisticated software will assist them in proving and documenting their lineage as legal heirs to Holocaust victims in recovering confiscated assets.

About Ancestry.com

Ancestry.com is an award-winning publisher of major family history products, both in print and electronic formats. For the past fifteen years, Ancestry.com has provided outstanding products and services aimed at those interested in researching their family. The company's hard-earned reputation for excellence is acknowledged through numerous organizations such as The American Library Association, The National Genealogical Society, The Federation of Genealogical Societies, and other leading groups involved in family history research.

Ancestry.com continues to maintain its leading-edge position with essential reference works; informative and entertaining periodicals; easily-accessible reference material on CD-ROM; and a vital genealogical presence on the Internet. In all aspects of Ancestry.com's business, focus is on connecting and strengthening families.

Table of Contents

Chapter 1

Getting Started with Personal Ancestral File 4.0®

NOTE: BEFORE DOWNLOADING, VERIFY THE FOLLOWING MINIMUM SYSTEM REQUIREMENTS.

System Requirements:

- Windows 95/98/NT
- IBM compatible 486/66 processor (Pentium recommended)
- 16 to 32 MB memory
- 20 MB hard disk space
- 256-color display adapter supporting 640 x 480 screen resolution or better
- Internet access
- Optional printer, mouse

Downloading Personal Ancestral File 4.0®

Personal Ancestral File (PAF) 4.0 can be downloaded at no charge from the Internet. The address where PAF is located is **www.familysearch.com**. When you reach the FamilySearch site, your browser will display **FamilySearch Internet Genealogy Service**.

NOTE: THE FOLLOWING FIGURES DISPLAY THE NETSCAPE BROWSER. YOUR BROWSER MAY BE DIFFERENT, BUT IT SHOULD DISPLAY THE SAME INFORMATION FROM THE FAMILYSEARCH SITE.

Click on **What's New** in the top left-hand corner (Fig. 1)

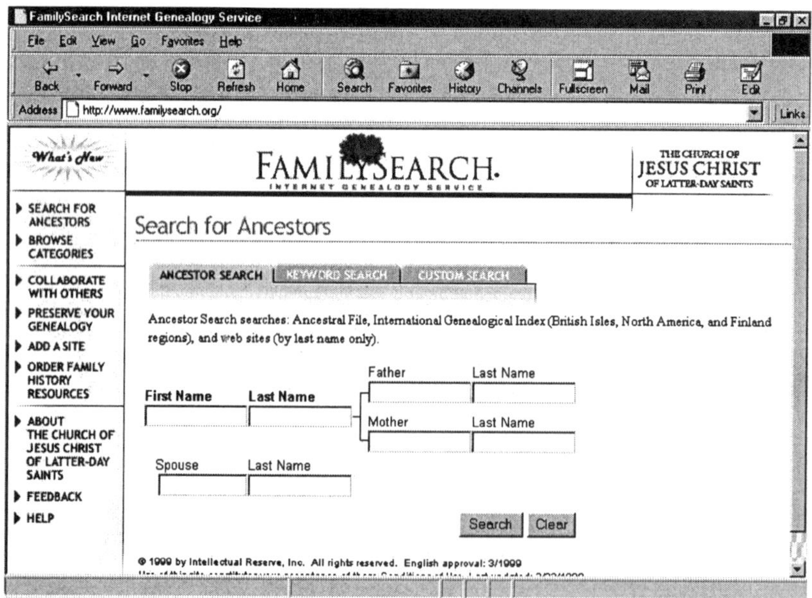

Figure 1

The browser window will now be titled **What's New - Feedback page**. (Fig. 2) Under **What's New**, click on **free download of Personal Ancestral File 4.0®**.

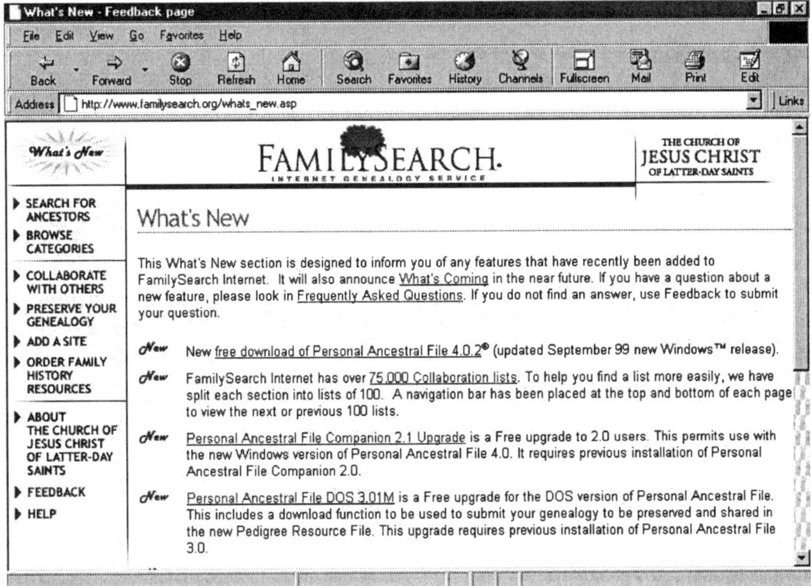

Figure 2

The new window displayed is **Other Family History Resources**. (Fig. 3) At the new window, you will see a section called **Downloadable Family History Products**.

Click on **Personal Ancestral File 4.0 (New Windows release)**.

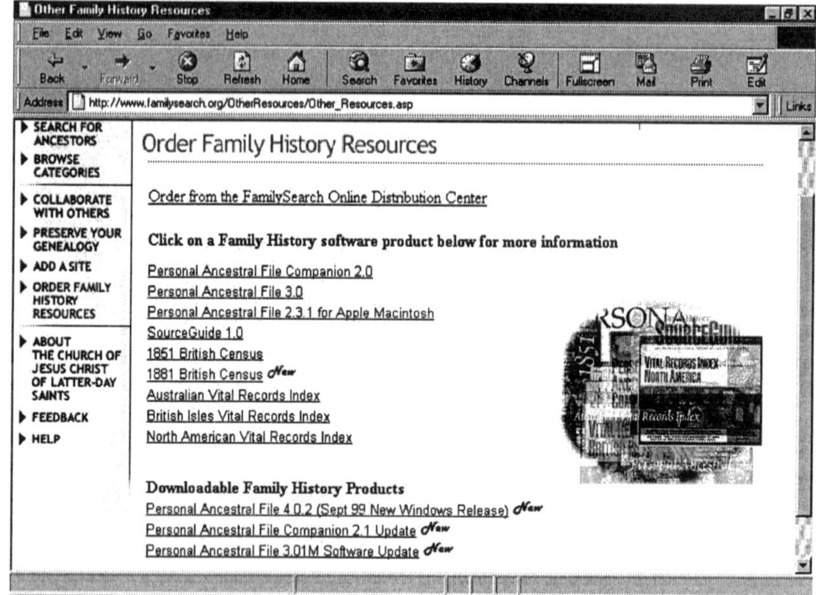

Figure 3

The browser will display **PAF 4.0 page.** (Fig. 4)

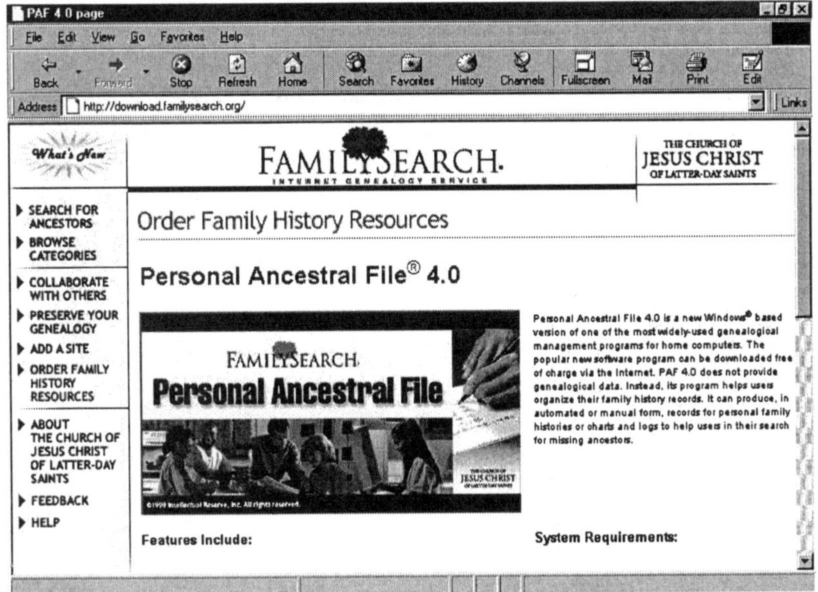

Figure 4

As you scroll down this page, you will see **System Requirements, Steps to download and install Personal Ancestral File**, and **Click here to read the license agreement**. Click on the **license agreement**. (Fig. 5)

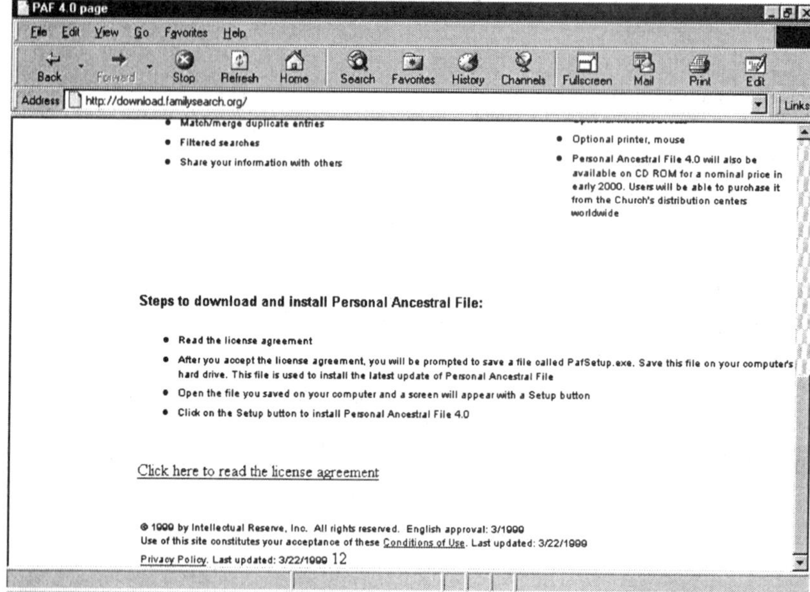

Figure 5

The **License Agreement** will appear on your monitor. (Fig. 6) Read through the agreement. At the bottom of the agreement you will see two boxes: **I accept** and **Cancel**. Select **I accept** to continue.

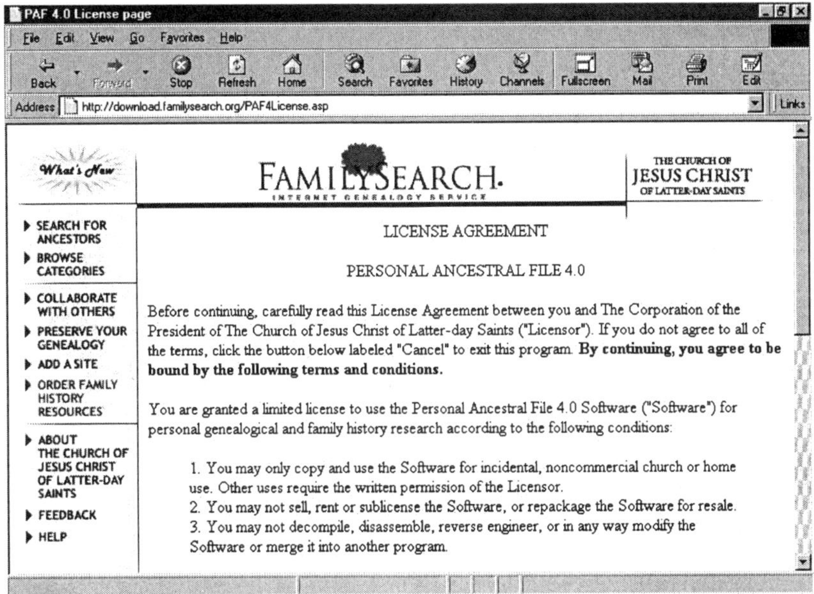

Figure 6

This will bring up a window titled **PAF 4.0 Form page**. To continue the download you must complete this registration form. (Fig. 7)

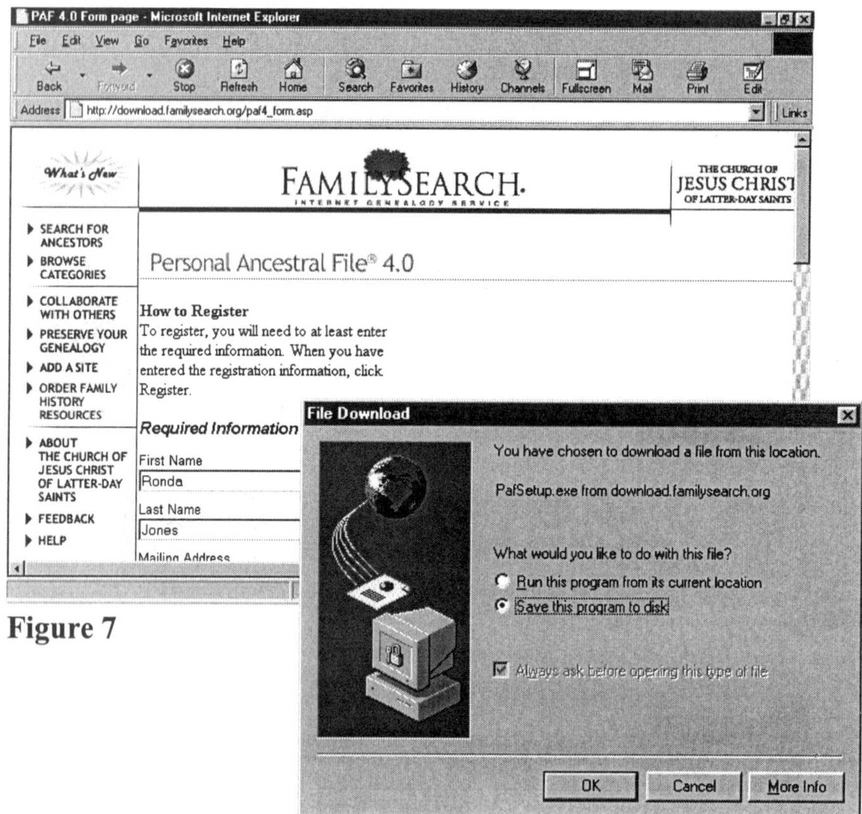

Figure 7

Figure 8

When you have completed your registration select **Register** at the bottom of the screen. A pop-up **Security Information** window may be displayed. (Fig. 8) If so, click **Continue**.

The next window, **Other Family History Resources Download Complete page**, will display for a few seconds. (Fig. 9)

The computer will display the **Save as** window. (Fig. 10) In the **File name** field, enter the name of your file.

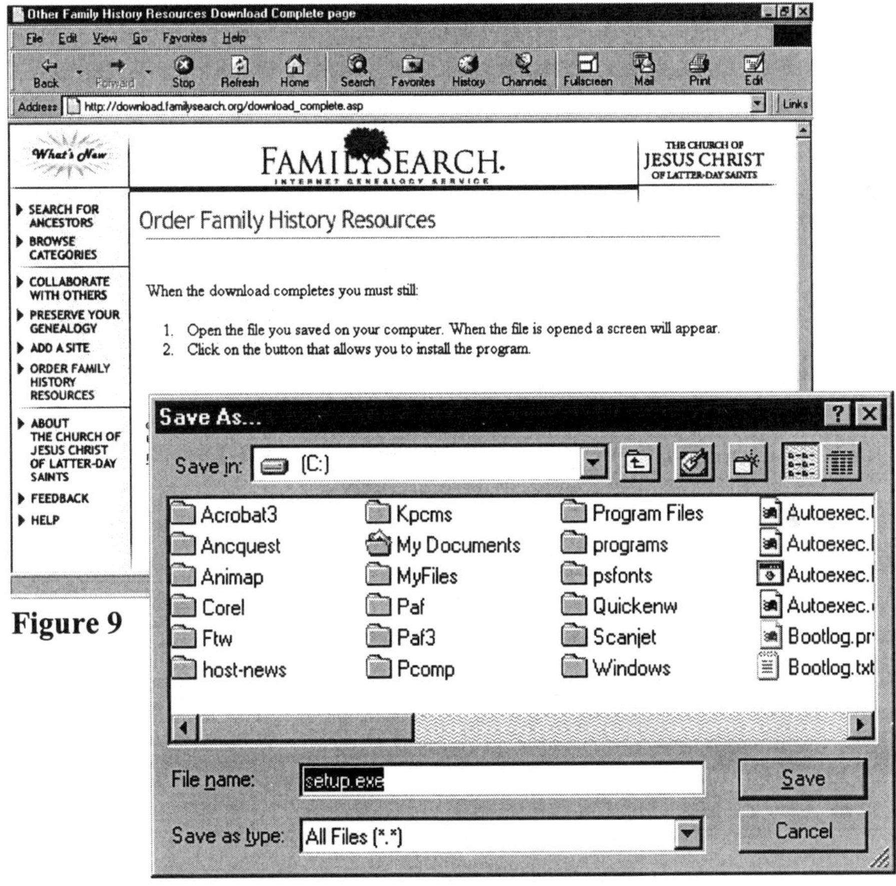

Figure 9

Figure 10

For example, in Figure 10, the file name is **setup.exe** and will be saved on the (C:) drive, which is shown in the **Save in** field. After you enter the **Save in** and **File name**, click **Save**. PAF will return to **Other Family History Resources Download Complete page**.

At this window, **Other Family History Resources Download Complete page**, you will see the following message:

> When the download is complete you must still:
> - Open the file you saved on your computer. When the file is opened a new window will appear.
> - Click on the button which begins installation of PAF 4.0.

Close the window **Other Family History Resources Download Complete page** and terminate the Internet connection if you have a dial-up connection. Locate the setup file, double click on the icon. (Fig. 11)

Figure 11

The next window displayed is **Personal Ancestral File® - Welcome**. Click **Finish** to continue.

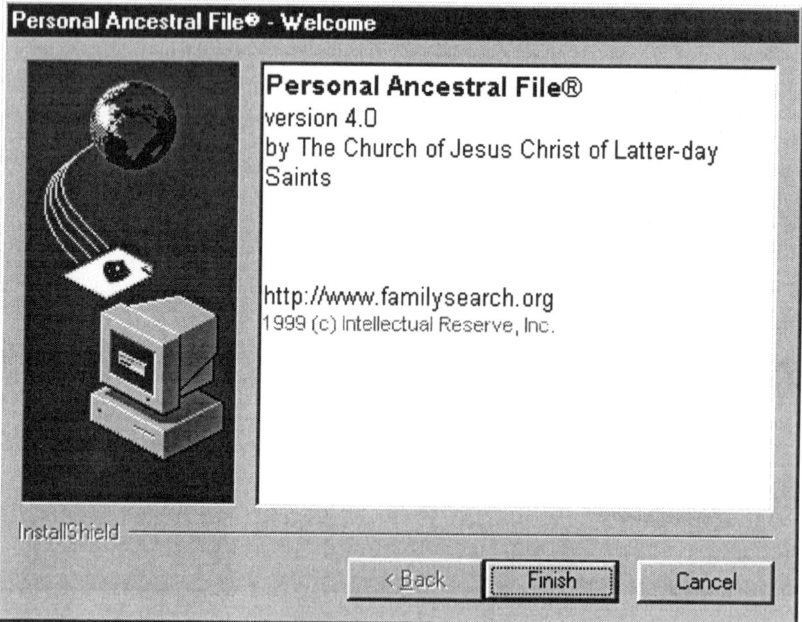

Figure 12

PAF 4.0 will continue with set up. You will see a screen **Unpacking** and also a pop-up **Personal Ancestral File** window that is visible for a few seconds, depending on your computer configuration.

You next window is **Welcome**. (Fig. 13) Select **Next** to continue. The new window is the **Software License Agreement**. Click **Yes** to continue with the installation of PAF 4.0.

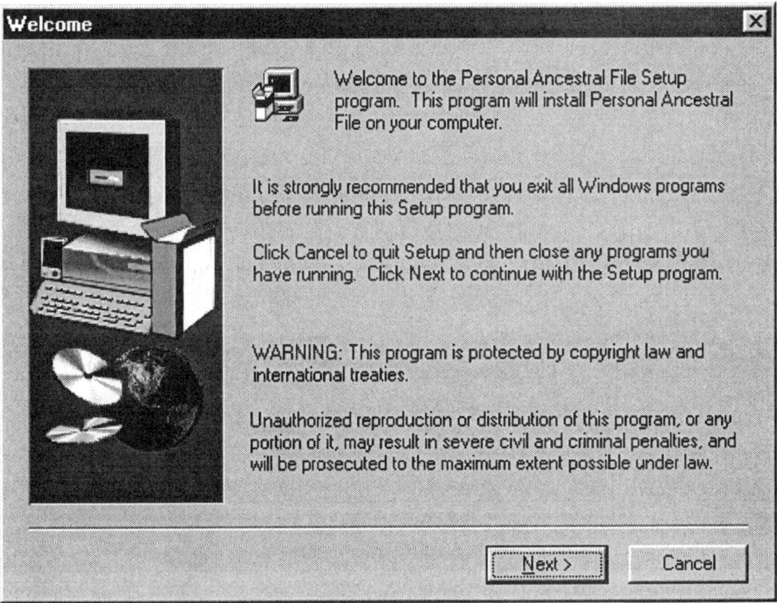

Figure 13

The new window, **Choose Destination Location** (Fig. 14), will ask for the location where you want to save PAF 4.0. If you aren't sure where, or don't care where it resides, click the **Next** button. You can select **Browse** to view the path of where PAF will reside.

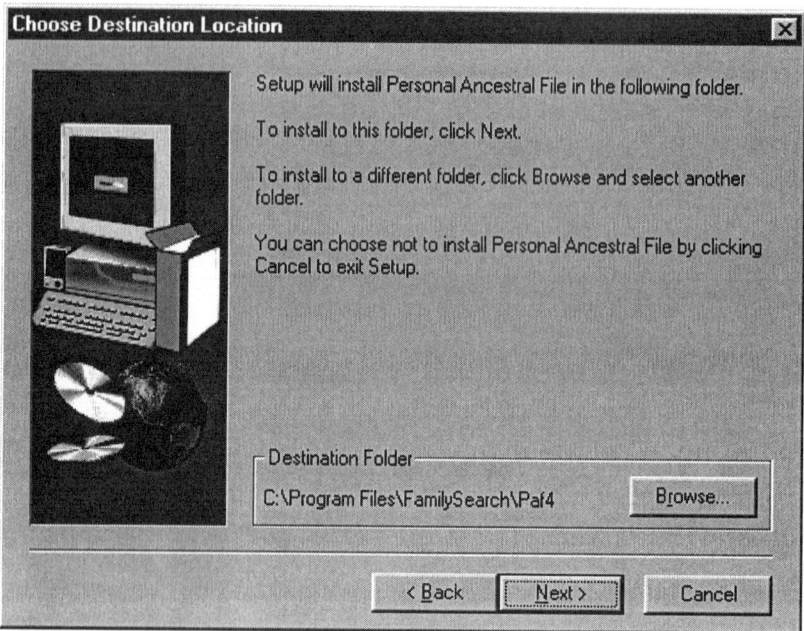

Figure 14

At this point another window will appear, **Select Program Folder**. (Fig. 15) The new window displays the applications resident on your computer and has created a new folder **FamilySearch.** Select **Next** to continue. PAF 4.0 will continue to install.

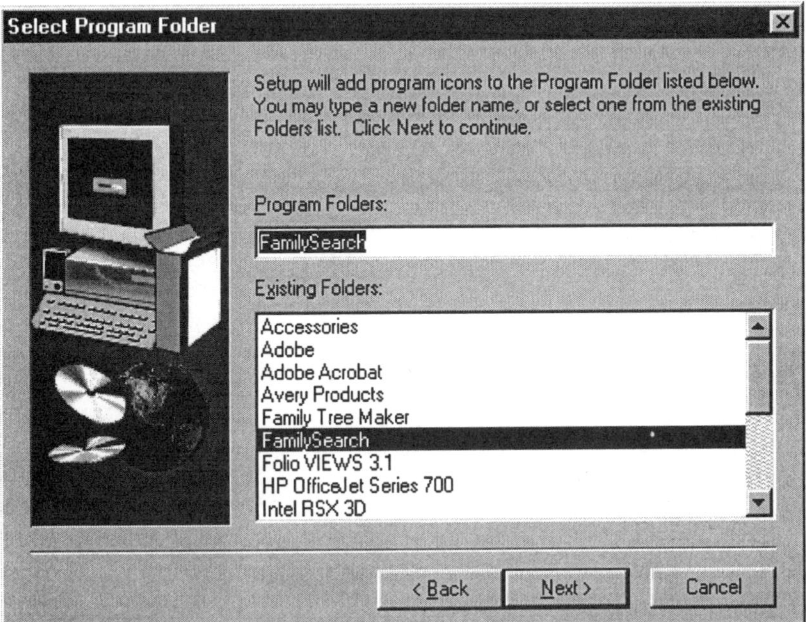

Figure 15

PAF set up is now complete. (Fig. 16) If you would like to see basic instruction and information, select **View Getting Started now**. If you want a shortcut on PAF on your desktop, select **Place a shortcut on your desktop** click **Finish**.

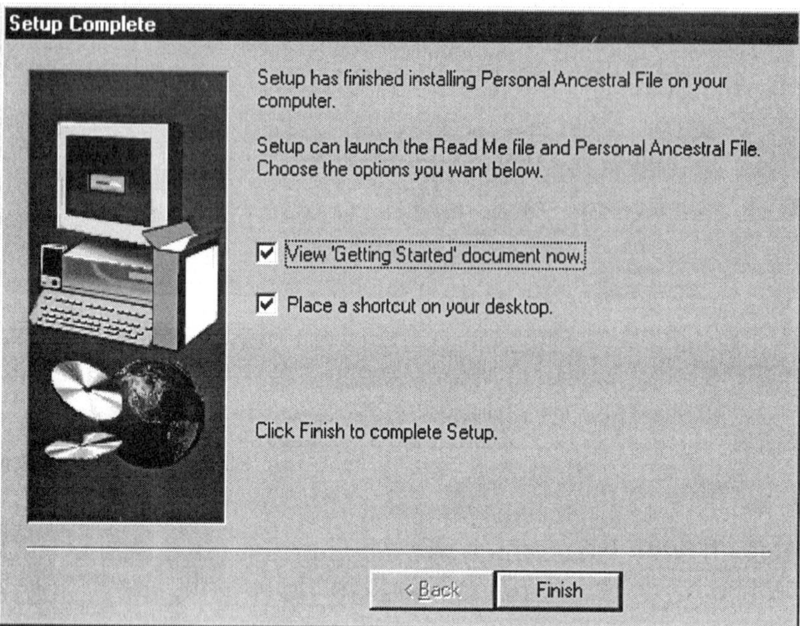

Figure 16

If you checked **View 'Getting Started' document now** your next window will be a WordPad display with the information you selected. This document can be printed and/or saved for future use. You will need to exit this window.

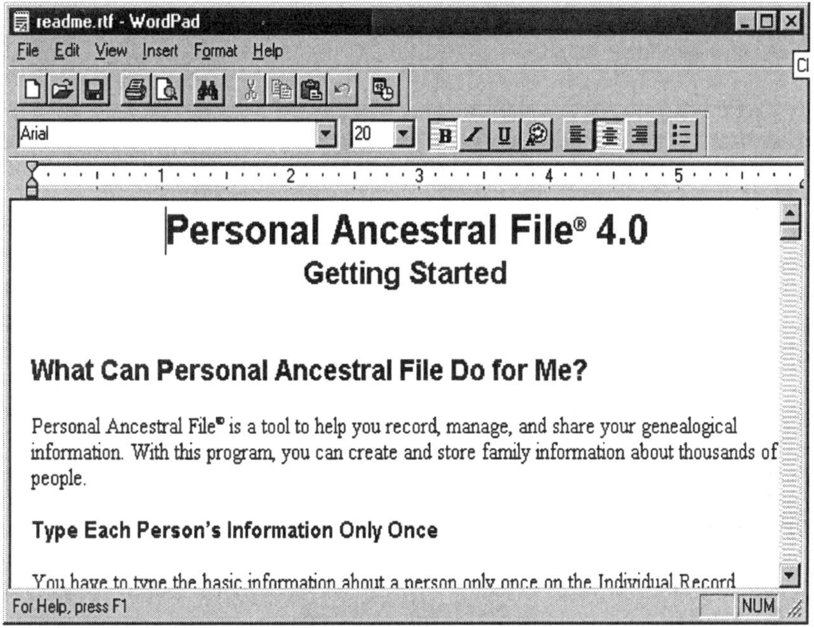

Figure 17

PAF 4.0 is ready to use. Click on the icon **Personal Ancestral File** and begin.

NOTE: PERSONAL ANCESTRAL FILE 4.0 WILL ALSO BE AVAILABLE ON CD-ROM IN EARLY 2000. USERS WILL BE ABLE TO PURCHASE IT FROM THE CHURCH OF JESUS CHRIST OF LATTER-DAY SAINTS DISTRIBUTION CENTERS WORLDWIDE.

Where to Start

How you begin using PAF 4.0 will depend on what you have done.

If you:

- are just beginning to create your family tree, you must create a new file and begin entering information about you and then your family. (see chapter 4; **Start Personal Ancestral File 4.0**)

- have used PAF 3.0 or higher, version 4.0 can utilize the database you have already created.

- have used PAF 2.31 you must convert your databases before using them. To convert your databases, open the file INDIV2.DAT in Personal Ancestral File. **Backup your data file and keep the backup until you are sure the converted file is correct.** See Appendix B for more detailed information.

- are transferring files from any other GEDCOM compatible program, you have to create a GEDCOM file and import into the version 4.0.

Hint: Press F1 to view **Topics**.

"How do I"

Open an existing database
Create a new database
Have the computer search for existing databases

"Tell me more about"

Adding and linking individuals
Importing GEDCOM files
Converting files from earlier versions of Personal Ancestral File
Closing databases
Deleting databases
Making backup copies
Restoring backup copies
Checking and repairing databases

Chapter 2

What, Where and How

What If You Have Problems Using PAF 4.0

1. PAF 4.0 has a built in **Help** file. Press F1 from anywhere in PAF 4.0 and a pop-up screen will appear to help with the function you are presently using. You can also access the **Help** file by using your mouse to click on **Help**. You can then search for the topic for which you need help, or use the index to locate the topic with which you need help. In addition, the **Help** file has two other options called **Tell me more about** and **How do I**.

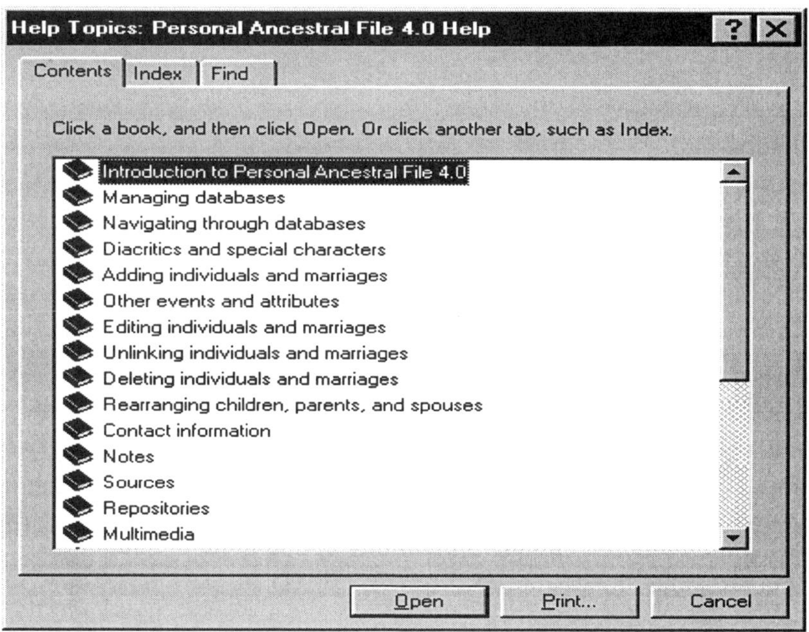

Figure 18

2. The Family History Department of The LDS Church is not able to give personal assistance with PAF 4.0 due to the large volume of new users. However, the **Help** file has been incorporated into PAF 4.0 along with a website with frequently asked questions. That site location is found on the Internet at ***www.familysearch.org/paf/paf_faq.asp***.

3. If you are unable to find your answer, use the **Feedback** option to submit your question, report a problem or any suggestions you may have.

4. You may find help from any local Family History Center or a PAF users group.

What If You Have Used PAF Companion in the Past?

A patch is available at the website ***www.familysearch.org/paf*** that will enable Companion to work with PAF 4.0. The new PAF 4.0 prints many of the same reports that Companion printed for other versions, however, Companion will print reports that PAF 4.0 will not. These include:

- Fan Charts
- Descendancy lists not indented
- Kinship Reports

How to Use PAF 4.0 Within the Companion Software.

You must change the default settings as follows:

1. Start the Companion.
2. Select **File** menu, select **Open**.
3. Click on **Scan Disk**.
4. The Companion will find and display other versions of PAF already in residence on your computer.

How to Protect the Privacy of Living People.

It is important that as you share information with others you respect the privacy of living individuals. DO NOT share information about living individuals that may embarrass or harm those individuals. Especially important are Social Security Numbers and mothers' maiden names.

Hint: You can create a GEDCOM file that excludes information regarding any living individual. You can get help by pressing F1. This will allow you to search topics such as:

- Export information for GEDCOM 5.5
- Export information for GEDCOM 4.0
- Export information for TempleReady
- Export information for the Pedigree Resource File
- Export information for Ancestral File
- Split a database

Hint: Press F1 to view **Tell me more about**.

What's New?

Besides the change to a Windows operation system, PAF 4.0 includes the following features:

- **Pedigree View Screen** - You can navigate through family lines, edit and search and add notes and sources to any individual. (This was the Large Pedigree in earlier versions of PAF.)

- Printing capabilities have been greatly enhanced for printing books, scrapbooks, and calendars.

- Note printing options have been expanded. As with previous versions of PAF, you can elect to print all notes or only notes marked with an exclamation point (!). In the **print all notes** option you can now exclude notes you want to keep confidential by marking them with a tilde (~).

- Marriage List and Descendancy List search capabilities are new.

- You can now add your own events to individual and marriage records.

- Create your own Web page. The Web page creator can help create a Web page to store your family history. This will allow you to share your family information with others who have Internet access.

- New multimedia capabilities allow you to include photos, documents, and video and audio clips in your own multimedia presentation. Photographs and documents can be attached to Family Group Records and Pedigree Charts as well as Scrapbooks, etc.

- You can now open more than one database at a time using the Windows options. This will allow you to switch back and forth between databases.

- Share Notes. Use the Edit feature to cut, copy, or paste your notes from one individual to another.

- In addition to the relationship calculator, there is a optional relationship indicator which allows you to continuously view the relationship of anyone in the database to the selected root person.

- PAF can keep a log that tracks all changes that are made to your database. The log contains the date, time and a code that indicates what changed. See Appendix D for detailed information.

Hint: press F1 to view **Tell me more about.**

How Do I Switch Between the Pedigree View and the Family View Screen?

From the **View** option on the toolbar, select **Family** or **Pedigree**, or
Press CTRL+S.

Hint: F1 to view **Tell me more about** or **How do I?**

Using the Keyboard

Although all of the menu commands can be accessed by pointing and clicking, sometimes you may find you want to use the PAF features without your mouse. (Many of the die-hard DOS users find the mouse cumbersome and slow.)

- Several features have shortcut keys you can access through F1 help or use a pull-down menus on your toolbar. See **What are Shortcut Keys?** below.
- Each option on a screen has an underlined letter, as in File. Press ALT plus the letter to access that function.
- On the screens that have tabs, such as **Preferences** and **Reports**, press CTRL+Tab to go to the next tabbed section.
- Press ESC to close most windows.
- On the pull-down or drop-down menus, press SHIFT+F4 to view all of the options.
- Press the arrow keys, Page Up, Page Down, Home, and End to move around the **Family** and **Pedigree View** windows.

Hint: press F1 to view **Tell me more about** ➛ **Shortcut Keys**

What Are Shortcut Keys?

Many people find it faster to use the keyboard rather than a mouse. If you prefer, the following shortcut keys are available:

Feature	Shortcut Key
Character Map For Foreign Languages	F7
Open a database	CTRL+O
Close a database	CTRL+F4
Print reports	CTRL+P
Exit PAF	ALT+F4
Edit the highlighted individual	CTRL+I
Edit the highlighted individual's notes	CTRL+N
Edit the highlighted individual's multimedia collection	CTRL+M
Add a new, unlinked individual	CTRL+A
Add the highlighted individual's spouse	CTRL+U
Add the highlighted individual's father (works only for initial father not additional)	CTRL+T
Add the highlighted individual's mother (works only for initial mother not additional)	CTRL+H
Add the highlighted individual's child	CTRL+L
Display a list of individuals in the database	CTRL+F
Display a descendancy list of the highlighted individual	CTRL+D
Find an individual by RIN or MRIN	CTRL+R
Return to the individual with RIN 1	CTRL+Home

Set preferences	SHIFT+CTRL+P
Obtain help	F1
Switch from the Family to the Pedigree screen and back again	CTRL+S
Move the spouse to the primary position	S or right mouse click, primary
Move the father to the primary position	F or right mouse click, primary
Move the mother to the primary position	M or right mouse click, primary
Move a child to the primary position	C or right mouse click, primary

Identifying Buttons on the Individual Screen

Button	*Click this button to:*
S	Add a source for the specified information.
Save	Save the record and return to the previous screen.
Cancel	Return to the previous screen without saving the information.
Options	Add or remove other events and attributes. Edit the parents. Access the notes, multimedia, and contact information. View a list of all sources. Add diacritics and other special characters. (See **Character Map**) Access the Date Calculator.

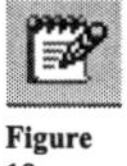
Figure 19

Access the individual's notes.

Figure 20

About the LDS Church

Figure 21

View a list of all of the individual's sources.

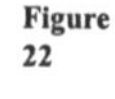

Figure 22

Create WWW Page

Figure 23

Change to Pedigree View

Figure 24

Help

Figure 25

Change to Family View

Figure 26

Open File

Figure 27

Edit Individual

Figure 28

Print

Figure 29

Add Individual

Figure 30

Access the individual's multimedia

Figure 31

Add Parents

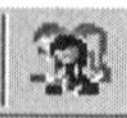

Figure 32

Match/Merge

Figure 33

Edit Notes

Figure 34

Go to Home Person

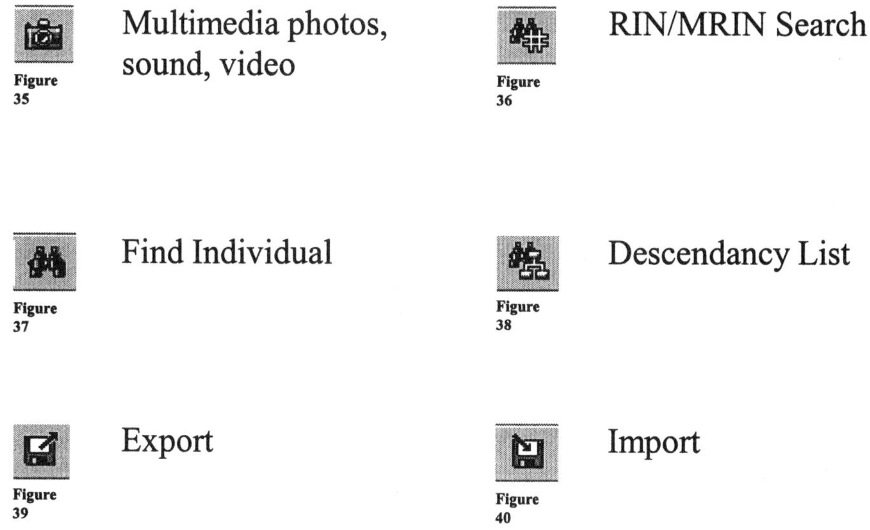

Figure 35 — Multimedia photos, sound, video

Figure 36 — RIN/MRIN Search

Figure 37 — Find Individual

Figure 38 — Descendancy List

Figure 39 — Export

Figure 40 — Import

Identifying Windows

There are two main windows where most work is started. The **Family View** (Fig. 41) and **The Pedigree View** (Fig. 42) are the most commonly used.

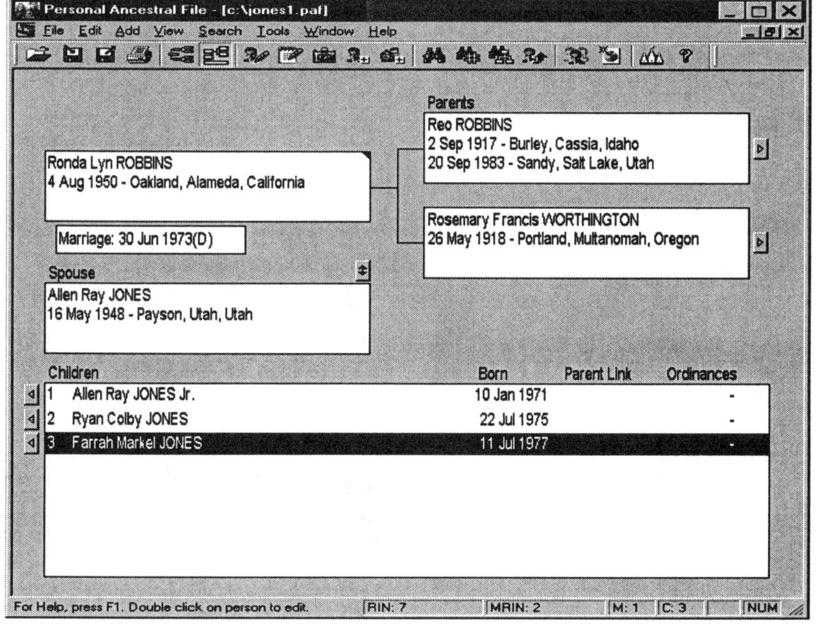

Figure 41

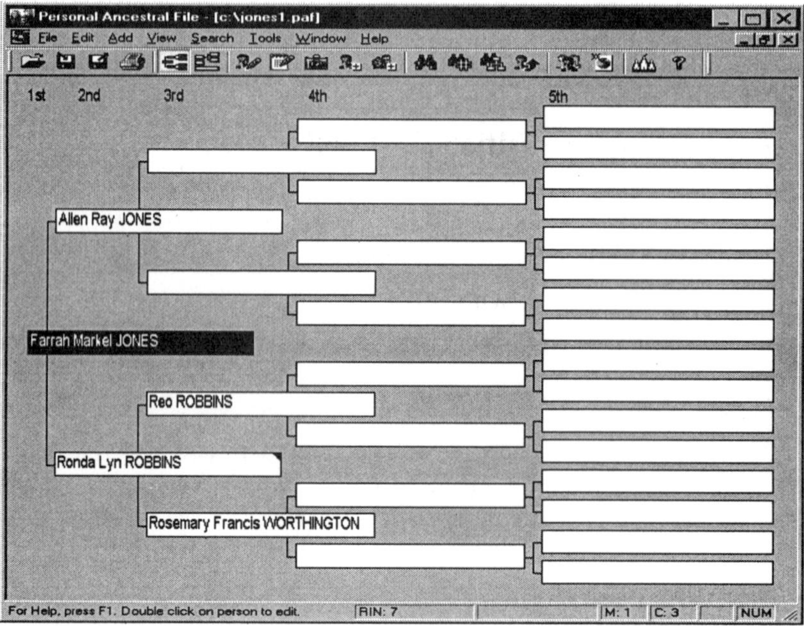

Figure 42

How to Select the Starting Individual

If the individual in primary position is not the individual you want to start with, use the following to locate a different individual.

- From the toolbar, select **Search**; a drop-down menu will offer options to locate the individual. If you know the RIN/MRIN of the individual, enter, and click **OK**. If you do not know the RIN/MRIN, select **Individual List** or **Descendancy List**.
- Once you have located the individual, click **OK**. This action will take you back to your starting window; **Family View** or **Pedigree View** with your chosen individual in **Primary**

position.

How Are the Personal Positions Defined?

Primary Person	The person in the primary position which is in the upper left position in the **Family View** window or the person in the first generation in the **Pedigree View** window.
Home Person	The person displayed, by default, when a database is opened. This is usually the person with RIN 1, but you can specify another RIN in **Tools → Preferences → File**.
Selected Person	The person on the window whose information is highlighted.
Root Person	The person upon whom relationship indicators are based.
Starting Individual	Also the person on the window whose information is highlighted.

Chapter 3

Preferences

This chapter furnishes a complete explanation of the **Preferences** option available under **Tools** on the toolbar.

Setting Preferences

The **Preferences** window allows the user to design the operation of PAF 4.0 to meet certain selected specifications. To open the **Preferences** window:

- From the Toolbar; select **Tools** ➛ **Preferences**.

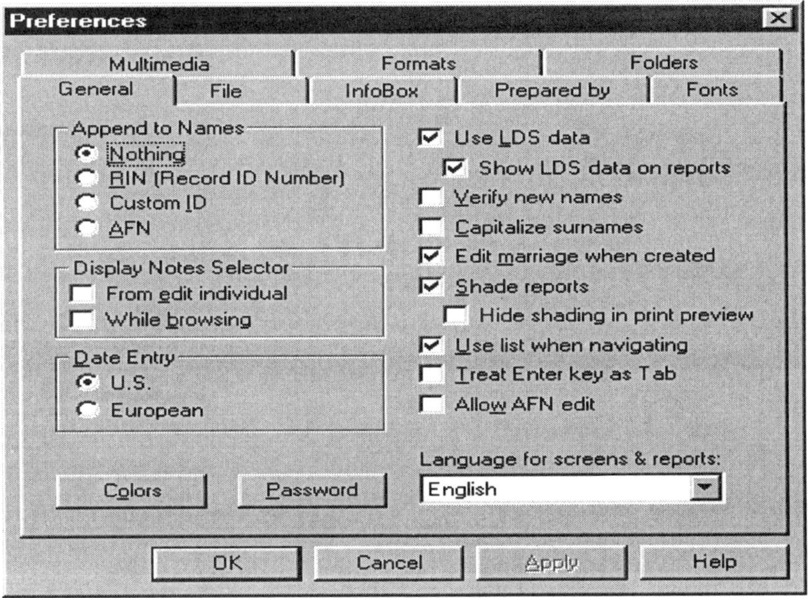

Figure 43

The **Preferences** window has ten categories, eight with tabs and two with buttons. This chapter will discuss each tab and button.

Setting General Preferences

OPTIONS	DESCRIPTION
Allow AFN Edit	Select this option to be able to type and edit Ancestral File Numbers.
Language for screens and reports	Select the language to use for screens and reports. You must restart PAF.
Append-to-Names	You can select which identifying numbers, if any, you want next to an individual's name within your database. • Select **Nothing** if you don't want identifying numbers next to the name. • Select **RIN** to have RIN's appear. • Select **Custom ID** to have custom IDs (input these on the Individual screen) appear next to the name. • Select **AFN** to have Ancestral File numbers appear next to the name.
Use LDS data	Select this option to see fields where you can add ordinance information and make use of other options relating to LDS temple work. By default, the **LDS data** option is turned on.
Show LDS data on reports	Select this option to print ordinance information on reports. This is only available if you selected **LDS data**.
Verify new names	Select this option if you want to verify each new name that is entered into the database. This can eliminate spelling errors.
Capitalize surnames	Select this option if you want PAF to automatically capitalize surnames, regardless of whether you press the SHIFT key.

Edit marriage when created	Select this option if you want the **Marriage** window to appear automatically when you add a spouse, child, or parents.
Shade reports	Select this option to turn shading on or off on printed reports.
Hide shading in print preview	If you chose to shade your printed reports, select this option to hide in print preview window.
Use list when Navigating	The **Pedigree View** or **Family View** windows display a left arrow next to the Primary Person if there are descendants listed. If you select the left arrow, the **Descendants List** appears whenever that individual has more than one child.
Notes selector	The **Notes Selector** lists the tags that you may use in your notes and allows you to see all notes or only those with a particular tag. • Select **From edit individual** if you want the **Notes Selector** to appear when you access notes from the Individual screen. • Select **While browsing** if you want the **Notes Selector** to appear when you access notes from the **Family** or **Pedigree View** window. The **Notes Selector** will **NOT** appear for marriage notes.
Date Entry	Select the way that you want PAF to interpret the dates that are entered as all numbers. • Select **U.S.** if you want 8.3.1997 to be interpreted as 3 Aug 1997. • Select **European** if you want 8.3.1997 to be interpreted as 8 Mar 1997.

Colors

Select **Colors** to change the colors used on the **Family** and **Pedigree View** windows. The bottom half of this window (Fig. 44) displays the **Windows colors** as they will display if you select **OK**.

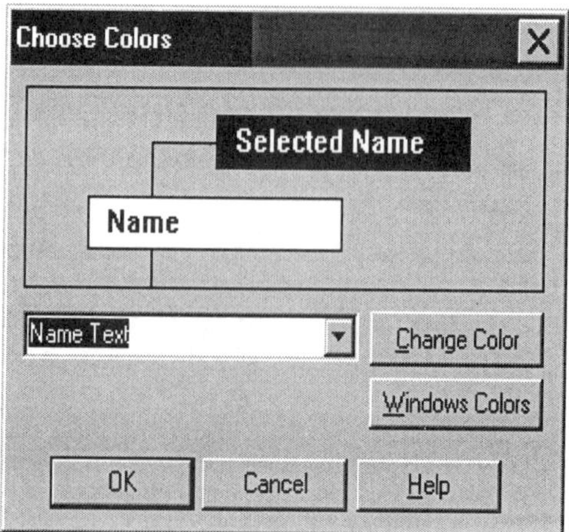

Figure 44

The top half of the window allows you to customize your color options. Select **Change Color** and a screen will appear with a palette of colors. (Fig. 44)

Next, select the title of the element for which you want to change the color, from the drop-down list. If you select **Define Custom Colors** the window will be enlarged on the right side by a rainbow of colors. (Fig. 45) You then can select or create the colors of your choice. If you decide you will return to the default colors, select **Windows Colors**. (Fig. 44)

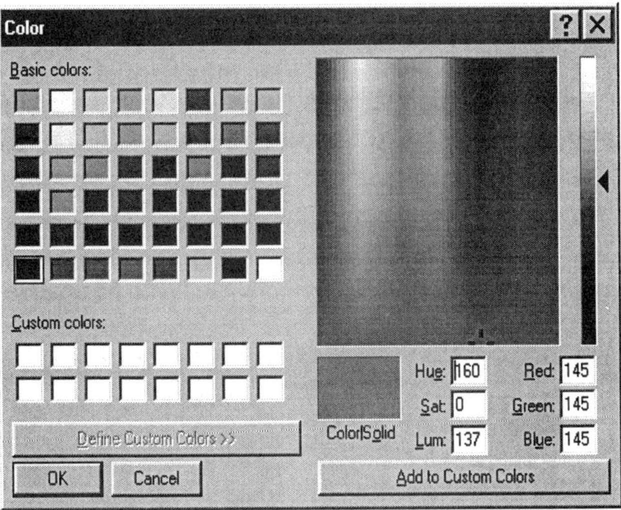

Figure 45

Password	Click **Password** if you want to password protect your database against inadvertent changes. In PAF, the password is intended to prevent another user from unintentionally changing your data. When you set a password, you must then exit PAF and re-enter to activate. The password applies to all databases not just to the open database and is case sensitive. If you wish to remove the password, enter your password and then delete. To change or delete your password, you must know your current password. If you forget your password, you will need to use the Windows Registry and find the key "HKEY_CURRENT_USER\Software\ LDSChurch\FamilySearch\PersonalAncestralFile\ Options" and delete the value named "Pwd."

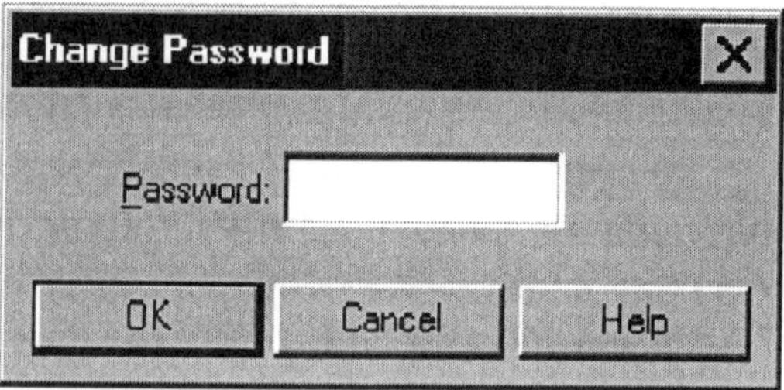

Figure 46

Treat the Enter key as Tab	Click here if you want to use the ENTER key to navigate through each field on the **Individual** and **Marriage** windows.

Setting File Preferences

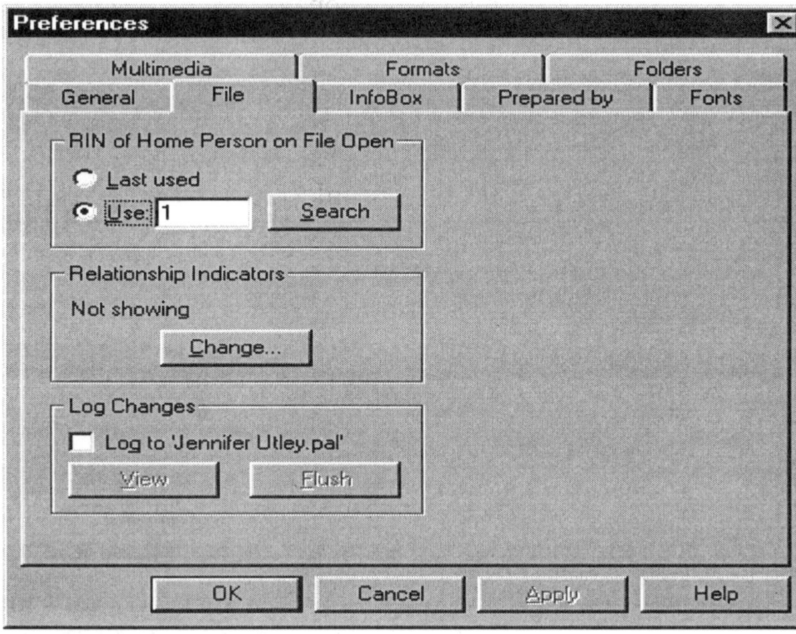

Figure 47

OPTION	DESCRIPTION
RIN of Primary Person on File Open	Specify the individual that you want to appear as the Primary person when you first open a file: • Select **Last Used** if you want the same individual that appeared in the primary position when the database was last closed to be in the primary position when you next open your database.

	Select **Use** if you want to specify RIN number the individual you want to be in the primary position. Type the RIN number in the **Use** field. If you don't know the RIN, Select **Search**.
Relationship Indicators	Relationship indicators show the relationship of everyone in the database to a root person in the database. The indicators can be seen on the status bar in the lower left corner of the **Family** and **Pedigree View** windows. To turn relationship indicators on or off, select **Change**.
Log Changes	If you want PAF to document all the changes made to your database, click here. The changes will be recorded to the file you specify. • Select **View** to view the log in Notepad. • Select **Flush** to empty the log. See Appendix D for more detail. **Hint:** Press F1 to view **How do I** and **Tell me more about**.

Setting InfoBox Preferences

An InfoBox is a box that will appear in the **Pedigree** window to provide additional information about a person and to allow you to view the spouses and children of that person.

To edit, select the **InfoBox** tab at the **Preferences** window. Use the **InfoBox** options to determine how much information that will be displayed in the **Pedigree** window.

The **Pedigree View** window will display in two ways:

OPTIONS	DESCRIPTION
Floating	InfoBoxes that are floating will appear when you pause your cursor over the name of any individual. You can determine what information will display in the InfoBox. • Select **None** if you don't want floating boxes. • Select **Dates only** if you want the InfoBox to display the dates, places, and completed ordinance codes for the marriage, birth and death events. • Select **Dates and Family Information** if you want the event information as well as the spouses and children to appear.
Locked	InfoBoxes that are locked appear when you click an individual or highlight an individual and press the Space bar. You can choose the information that appears in the InfoBox:

- Select **None** if you don't want locked InfoBoxes
- Select **Dates only** if you want the InfoBox to display the dates, places, and completed ordinance codes for the marriage, birth, and death events.
- Select **Dates and Family information** if you want the event information as well as the spouses and children to appear.

Hint: If you select **Dates and Family information**, you will be able to move the person shown in the InfoBox to the primary position of the **Pedigree** window. Highlight the individual and click the right mouse button; then select **move to Primary** from the pull-down menu.

Setting Prepared by Preferences

The information entered into this window is used when PAF exports a GEDCOM file, prints a report, and creates a Web Page.

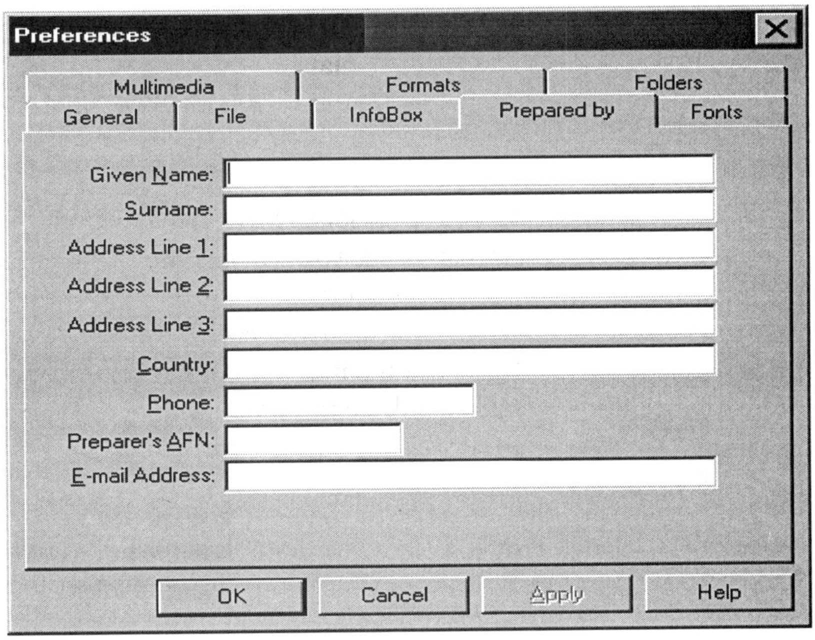

Figure 48

Hint: Use the TAB key to move through each field.

Setting Font Preferences

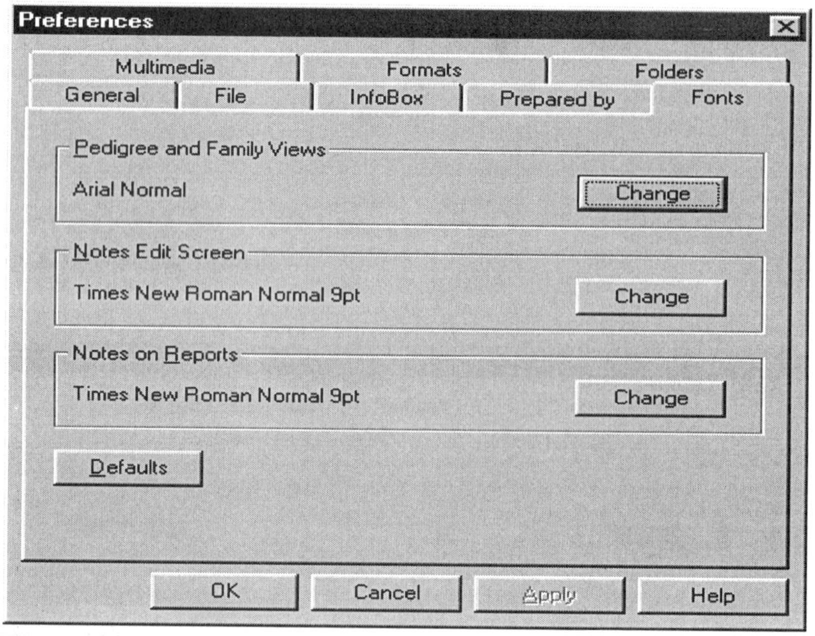

Figure 49

PAF allows you determine which font will be used in three different scenarios: **Pedigree** and **Family View** windows, **Notes Edit** window, and **Notes on Reports**.

OPTIONS	DESCRIPTION
Pedigree and Family View Windows	Select **Change** to select a different font for the text in these windows.
Notes Edit Screen	Select **Change** to select a different font for the **Notes Screen**. This is for display only.
Notes of Reports	Select **Change** to select a different font for the reports you print.
Default	Select **Defaults** to revert to system default.

Hint: Click F1; **How do I**.

Setting Multimedia Preferences

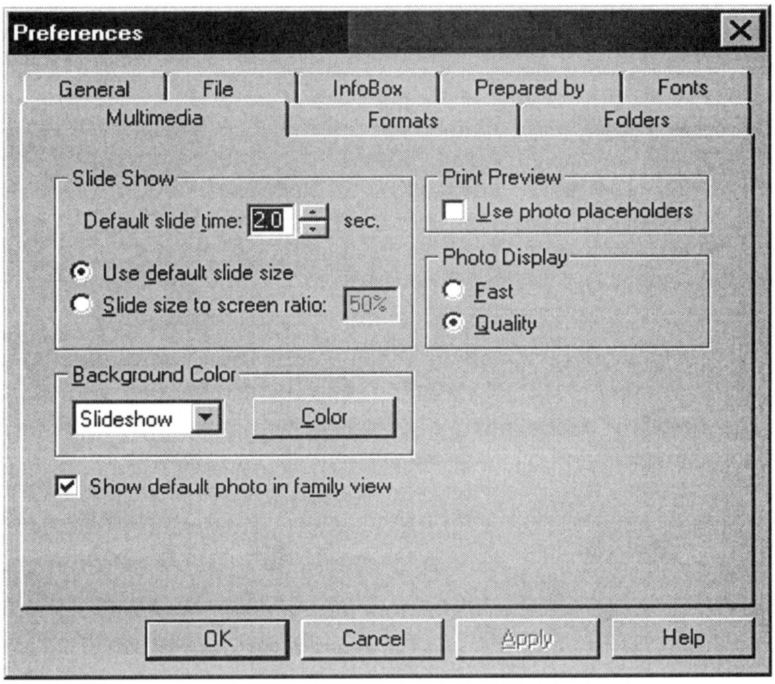

Figure 50

You can add digitized pictures, sound clips, and video clips to each individual record and its sources in your database. You can see these pictures in scrapbooks and in the slide show as well as on reports. However, you can't add multimedia to marriages.

PAF does not store the multimedia files in the database. It only stores the path to the location of the file. The implications are these:

1. When you make a backup copy of your database, only the links (paths) to the multimedia files will be included. You will need to use Windows to backup multimedia files.

2. When you import or export a GEDCOM file, multimedia events are not included. To share a database which contains multimedia files, you will also need to share a .BAK file or a .PAF file.

3. Multimedia files should be stored on your hard disk or a drive where you can store all multimedia files together because:

    - If you store multimedia files in more than one place, such as on floppy disks, you will have to switch disks in order to view your scrapbooks and slide shows or print reports with multimedia pictures.

    - Digital cameras and companies that put pictures on disks use generic file names. This means that different photos on different disks will have the same file name. If you do not give them unique names, PAF has no way to distinguish one photo from another. PAF would default to the disk in the drive at the time.

Most multimedia features usually deal with a specific object, however there are a few common options from which you may choose:

OPTION	DESCRIPTION
Slide show	There are two elements that can influence this setting.: • Use the **Default slide time** to indicate how long each photo or scanned object should stay on the screen during a slide show. **Hint:** If the next picture takes longer to load from the disk than the current slide is intended to show, the current slide will remain until the next slide is loaded and ready to be viewed. • Select **Default slide size** to use the default slide size. Select **Slide size to screen ratio** to show each slide at a certain percentage of the screen's size. Enter that ratio.

Background Color	You can choose the background color for viewing the slide show and scrapbook photos. Use the drop-down list to select the **Slide show or Scrapbook**. Select **Color** to change the color of the background of the slide show or scrapbook. Black is the default for the slide show and white is default for the scrapbook.
Print Preview	Select **Use Photo Placeholder** if you don't want to view the actual photos in the print preview option. This will help the speed for print preview, as PAF won't be required to present the multimedia objects. Instead of an object you will see a gray "place card" that shows the size and placement of the photo.
Photo Display	Any time a photo has to be adjusted, it must be scaled. This takes additional time. PAF gives you the choice of taking the time to do this and getting a better picture or speeding up the process but sacrificing quality. • Select **Fast** if you prefer speed over quality. • Select **Quality** if you prefer quality. **Hint:** The speed will be noticeable when loading a scrapbook page with several photos, or when resizing a photo of an individual.
Show default photo in Family	Select here to see the default photo of the Primary person on the **Family View** window.

Hint: Press F1 to view **How do I** and **Tell me more about.**

Setting Formats Preferences

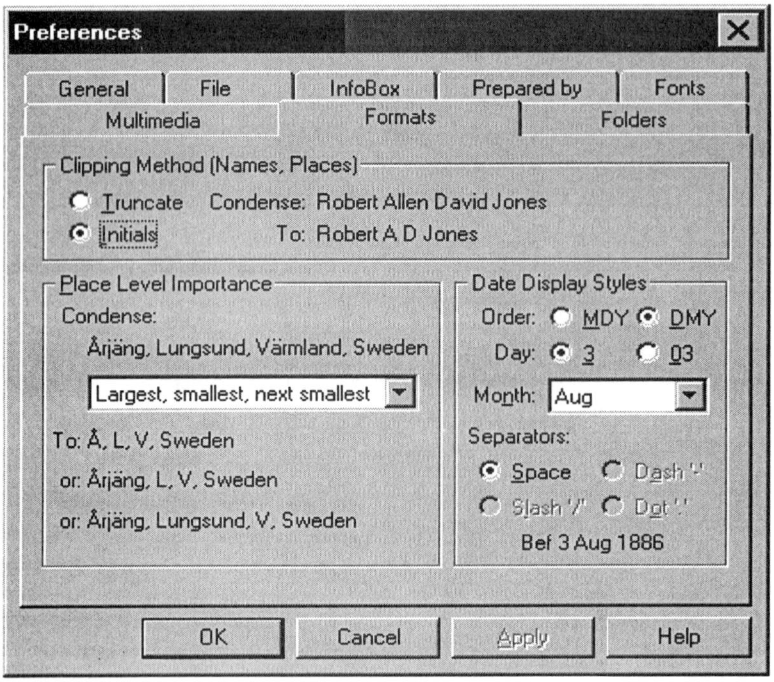

Figure 51

Many users prefer to adjust the way names, places, and dates are displayed on the screen and on the printed reports.

You are allowed to change the following options:

OPTION	DESCRIPTION
Clipping Method (Names, Places)	Many times, names and places are too long to fit the allocated space in reports and on the screen. You can decide what method to use in the clipping methods: • Select **Truncate** to show as much as possible but clipping a portion that does not fit. • Select **Initials** if you would prefer to use initials abbreviation.

Place Level Importance	When the name of place doesn't fit in an allotted space on the window or in reports you can adjust the clipping method (above) and also which level of the place should be "clipped." You are provided six options; select different options until you are satisfied with your choice. As you make your selection you will see the results of your choice.
Date Display Styles	The **Date** entry was selected in **General Preferences**, here you will choose how the dates are displayed. • Select the order in which dates are displayed. • Select how months are displayed. • Select how to separate the day, month, and year if you selected a numeric format for the month. **Hint:** We recommend you leave the format as DD MMM YYYY (11 Jan 1997). It is the preferred genealogical output.

Setting Folders Preferences

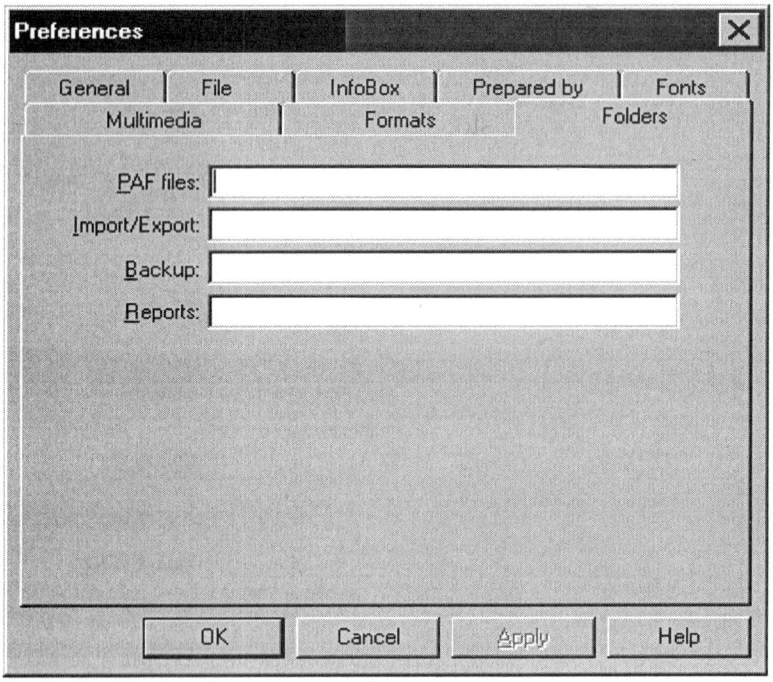

Figure 52

When you save your family information, you save it in a specific location or folder. Just as you fill a file folder with information and then label it, you also create a file folder for your database and it must be named. The name you provide should be something that is specific about what is contained in the file.

The following folders require names:

OPTION	DESCRIPTION
PAF files	Type the path of the folder where you will store your databases.
Import/Export	Type the path of the folder where you will store your GEDCOM files. • When you use **Export**, the folder you name will be the default directory where the files will be saved. If needed, you can change the directory during the export process. • When you use **Import**, the folder you name will be the directory where PAF will first look for GEDCOM files to import.
Backup	Type the path of the folder where you will store your backup files.
Reports	Type the path of the folder where you will store reports which you save as files to print later.

Chapter 4

Start Personal Ancestral File 4.0

If you are going to use an existing database you begin with one of two options:

- If you know the name(s) of your database(s), you begin by selecting **File**.
  or
- Click on the **Open File** icon. 

Figure 53

A pop-up screen will prompt you to **Open, Cancel,** or **Search**. To **Open**, use your mouse to highlight the database you want to open and select **Open**. Your highlighted database will open and you can begin your work.

If you select **Search**, PAF 4.0 will search your computer for all .PAF files. You will be offered the choice of files to open.

To create a new database:

- From the toolbar, select **File** ➛ **New.** A pop-up screen titled **Create New Family File** will ask you to name the new file. (Fig. 54)

Give your file a name and **Save.**

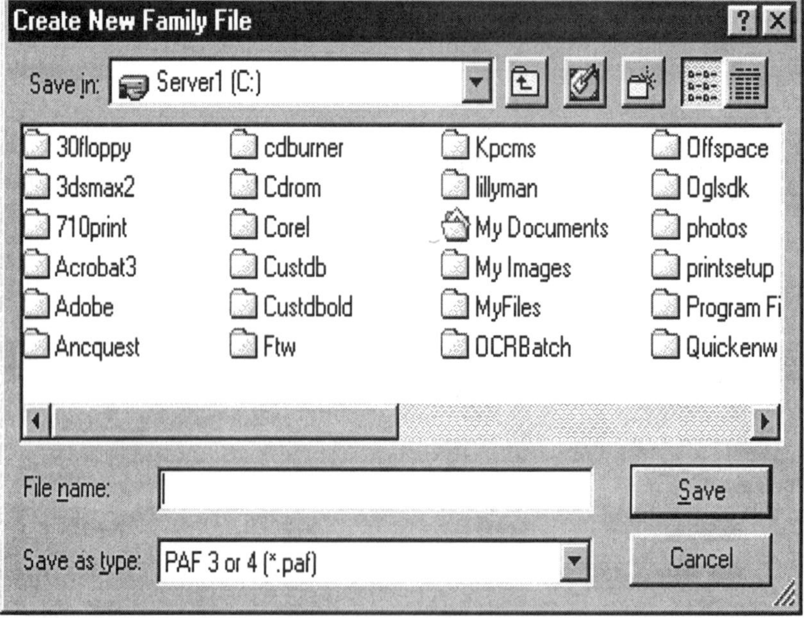

Figure 54

Another pop-up screen titled **Preferences; Prepared by** (Fig. 55) will open. Fill in your personal information as the person preparing this family file. Click on each button to choose the options you want to use on your family file.

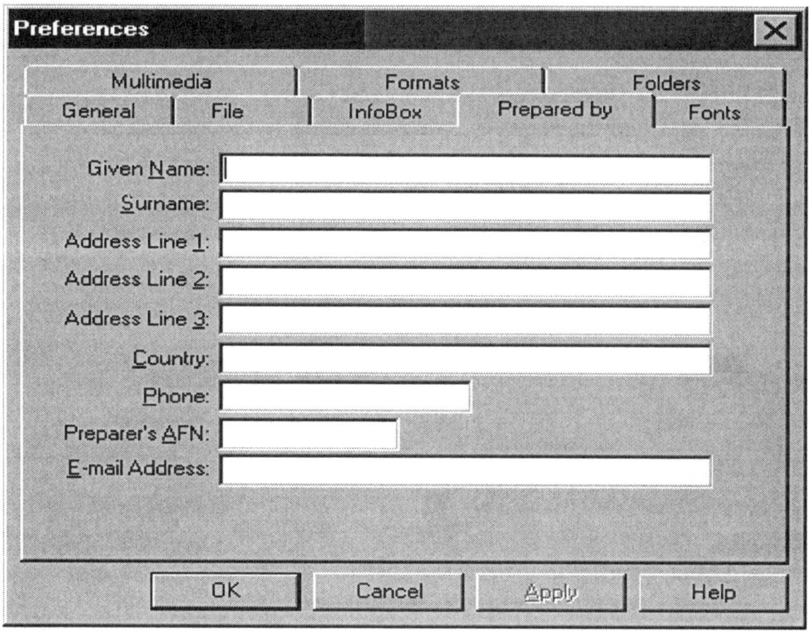

Figure 55

NOTE: THIS WINDOW CAN ALSO BE ACCESSED FROM THE **ADD OR EDIT INDIVIDUAL** WINDOW USING ALT+A

Navigating Family Lines on the Family View Screen

The **Family View** window displays a three generation family: Primary Person, Children, and Parents.
As you look at the **Family View** you will see these items: (See Fig. 56)

- The Title Bar - Shows you the name of the database you are currently using.
- The Main Menu - Provides access to each PAF function
- Toolbar - Uses buttons to access to the most commonly used features. If you are unsure of the buttons to use, place your cursor over the button and the button title will appear.
- Family Display - Shows three generations of family and the buttons used for viewing, adding, and editing each one.
- Status Bar - Provides certain information about individuals in your database. The information displayed will be the result of your selection from several options.

Hint: The **Status Bar** provides the number of marriages and children for the Primary person. For example: A C4 is four children; M2 is two marriages.

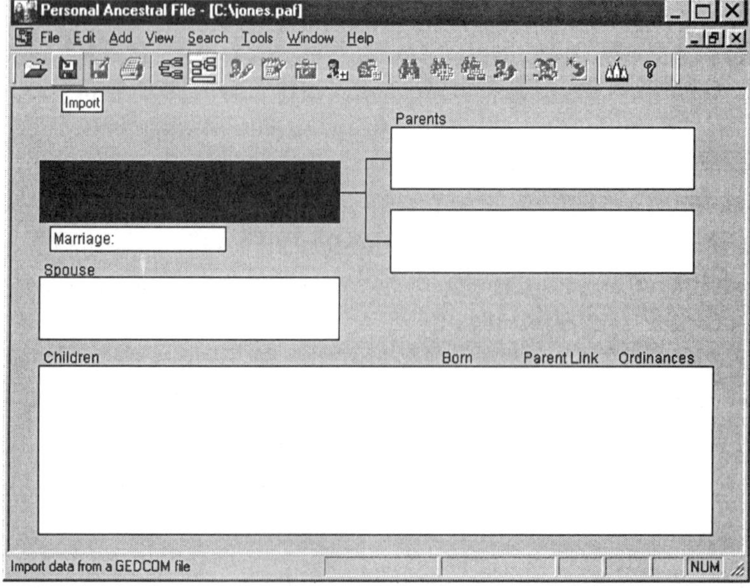

Figure 56

Adding and Editing Individuals in the Family View

To enter a new individual, click on the highlighted name box in the primary position or use CTRL+A, or click on right mouse button and select **Add Individual**. Begin with yourself as the first individual, then add your spouse, parents, and your siblings. (The order that you enter your family isn't important) You can then begin to work back in time through all your families.

Each individual is assigned a **Record Identification Number (RIN)**. This number is assigned automatically by PAF to keep track of individual information and does not determine the order in a family or in your ancestry.

Hint: Because RIN numbers are assigned automatically you will not be able to match any other numbering system you might have in place.

The **Add Individual** window will open with the cursor flashing in the **Given Name** field. If you later edit this person, the same window then is titled **Edit Individual**.

Begin by typing the individual surname, pressing TAB after each field to move to the next field, and entering all the information you have. Fields and buttons are described below.

Under **Tools ➛ Preferences; General**, you may choose to verify names as they are entered. Each time you enter a new name or place, a pop-up window will prompt; **is this name correct?** Choose **Yes** or **No**. A yes answer will store the name and you will not need to verify this spelling again. Names of people and places are stored only once and re-used as needed. If the spelling is incorrect, select **No** and re-type. To delete an incorrect field, highlight the field and press **Delete**.

Hint: Do not press ENTER to move through fields. Use TAB only. In most cases ENTER is the same as SAVE and will exit the window. If you erroneously press the ENTER key, you will then need to press **Edit** on the toolbar. Select **Individual** to finish entering the information.

Hint: ESC is usually the same as CANCEL, do not press ESC unless you plan to cancel. You can change the ENTER key to act as TAB. From the toolbar select **Tools ➛ Preferences; General**.

NOTE: YOU MAY FIND THAT YOU CAN SPEED UP DATA ENTRY BY USING ENTER AND ESC KEYS TO SAVE OR CANCEL.

NOTE: IF YOU INTEND TO PROVIDE THE LDS ORDINANCE DATES AND PLACES, AND THE FIELDS ARE NOT SHOWING, YOU WILL NEED TO SELECT FROM THE TOOLBAR: **TOOLS ➛ PREFERENCES; GENERAL**.

NOTE: ALL DATE FIELDS ACCEPT ANY TEXT. STANDARD DATE MODIFIERS OF ABOUT (ABT), AFTER (AFT), AND BEFORE (BEF) ALONG WITH CIRCA, (CA), AND BETWEEN (BTW) CAN BE USED. ALL DIGITS OF THE YEAR ARE REQUIRED.

Enter duel years to indicate a span of years. For example; 1813-17.

Choose the U.S. or European type of date. From the toolbar, select **Tools ➛ Preference; General**. You can also change the display format in the same area. The accepted standard for genealogy is dd mmm yyyy. It is strongly recommended that you **not** change this format.

Adding or Editing Individual Window

Personal

- **Given Names**. Enter all given names received at birth. Do Not enter nicknames in this field. There is a **Nickname** field under **other** at the bottom of this window.

- **Surname**. Enter the individual's last name given at his/her birth. For female individuals this would be her maiden name. If you do not have this information leave the field blank. For name changes and aliases, another field is discussed later.

- **Title (prefix)**. Enter the individual's title. This is prefix title only. For example: Dr., Capt., Lt., etc.

- **Title (suffix)**. Enter the individual's title. This is suffix title only. For example: Jr. Sr., King Henry III, etc.

- **S**. Select the **S** button to enter a source(s) for the data you just entered. If you have already entered or linked sources you will be provided a list of sources from which you might choose. Detailed instructions for Adding Sources can be found in Chapter 6.

- **Sex.** Select the gender of the individual by selecting the appropriate box. If Unknown is chosen you will not be able to link to another individual until Gender is changed to Male or Female.

NOTE: NAMES, DATES, AND PLACES THAT ARE TYPED IN WILL BE ADDED TO A LIST CREATED BY PAF 4.0. YOU CAN ACCESS THIS LIST BY PLACING YOUR CURSOR IN THE PLACE FIELD, SELECT THE DOWN ARROW OR PRESS F4. THIS WILL PROVIDE THE MOST RECENT NAMES FOR YOU. YOU THEN PICK ONE FROM THE LIST. YOU ARE NOT ALLOWED TO DELETE NAMES FROM THIS LIST, HOWEVER, AS YOU ADD NEW NAMES THE OLD NAMES DROP OFF.

LDS Ordinances

If you selected the LDS data found in **Tools** ➛ **Preferences; General** tab, you can enter the LDS dates and place information at the **New Individual** window or the **Edit Individual** window.

Events

PAF 4.0 has a list of other events besides the predefined events. To access this list select **Options; New Event/Attribute**. Scroll through the list to find the event and click **Select**. (Fig. 57)

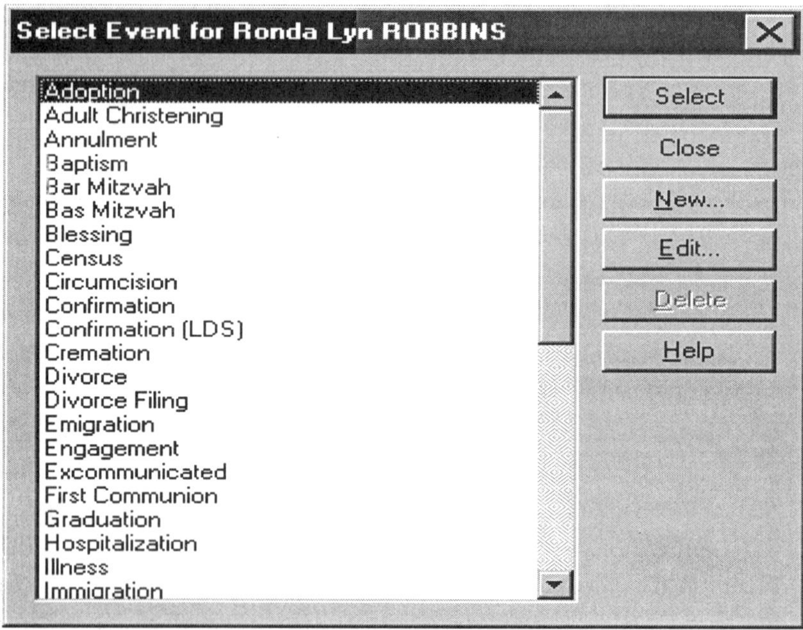

Figure 57

You will then be returned to the **Add Individual** or **Edit Individual** window. The selected event will appear under **Other Events**. You will be prompted to complete the date and place and whether this information should remain confidential. If you do not want this information included on reports or in a GEDCOM file, select **N**. You may enter sources for this information by selecting **S**. This process is the same in the individual as well as marriage record. To **Edit** or **Delete**, select the appropriate button to complete the task. You can repeat this procedure as many times as you have events.

Other

- **Married Name**. Enter a woman's married surname, or a man's married surname if it is different from his birth surname. This option is for printing **Calendars** or **Contact Reports**.

- **Also Known As (A.K.A.)**. This field is used to record any name change that has occurred in an individuals lifetime. This could include immigrant name changes, stage names, etc., but not a married surname. You can print these names on the **Individual Summary** report.

- **Nickname**. Nicknames are entered in this field and will print on the **Individual Summary** report.

- **Cause of Death**. You should enter a very generic cause of death. For example, cancer. Not the type of cancer but just cancer. From this field you can print a filtered report that lists people that have the same cause of death. The cause of death must be entered exactly the same in every case or the filtered search will not be fruitful. (See Chapter 9 **Advanced Focus/Filter**)

- **Physical Description**. The physical description you enter in this field will print on the **Individual Summary Report**. The Physical Description can also be used in a filtered search and report to find those ancestors with the same physical appearance. Again, the exact descriptive adjectives would need to be used to filter correctly.

- **Custom ID**. If you have assigned your own numbering system to your ancestors, type it here. You can use both numbers and letters.

Hint: Using Social Security numbers or other confidential information as Custom ID numbers are not recommended.

Options

Click on **Options**. A pop-up window will display a list of options to further document your ancestors.

- **New Event/Attribute**. See **Add an Event to the Select Event/Attribute List**.

- **Edit Parents**. You can change the parent/child relationship with this option.

- **Notes**. You can add, edit, or view your notes for an individual. Choose **Notes** from the **Options** window or click the **Notebook** icon to access the Notes window. Notes entered here should be biographical notes about the individual, research notes, or confidential information. If notes already exist for this individual an (*) will appear on the **Notes** button.

- **Sources**. To view all sources for an individual or the events for the individual click on the **Book** icon. Marriage sources and custom events are not included here. If you have already entered sources for this individual an (*) will appear on the **S** button.

- **Address**. Click to access the **Contact Information** window where the name, address, phone number, e-mail address, and home page URL are entered. This contact information is used for **Family Reunion** lists.

- **Multimedia**. Click on the **Camera** icon to add, edit, or remove a photo, sound clip, or video clip for the individual, or to create or view a slide show and/or scrapbook for this person. You have the option of making or clearing the default selection here. The default photo will appear in Family View if you chose this option in Preferences under the Multimedia tab. (see Chapter 7 **Adding Multimedia to Individuals and Sources**)

- **Character Map**. The Character Map allows you to use diacritic characters that change the sound a letter makes in different languages. For example the special character Ö changes the way a vowel sounds. You can use two methods to input the diacritics. You can use the **Character Map** under **Options** on the **Individual** or **Marriage** window or you can press F7 or you can hold down the ALT key and type the decimal equivalent on the 10-key pad. (See Appendix G) **This last option is the ONLY way to enter diacritics into a source record.**

Hint: If you can't find the character you are looking for, change the font. Some fonts do not have all the diacritic characters. The font Times New Roman has the most.

- **Date Calculator**. With the **Date Calculator** you can calculate the time elapsed between any two dates within the Gregorian calender or calculate a date based on a date and an elapsed amount of time.

Hint: Press F1 to view **How do I** and **Tell me more about**.

Adding an Event to the Select Event/Attribute List.

1. From the **Edit Individual** window, select **Options; New Event/Attribute; New**. The **Define Custom Event** window will open. (Fig. 58)

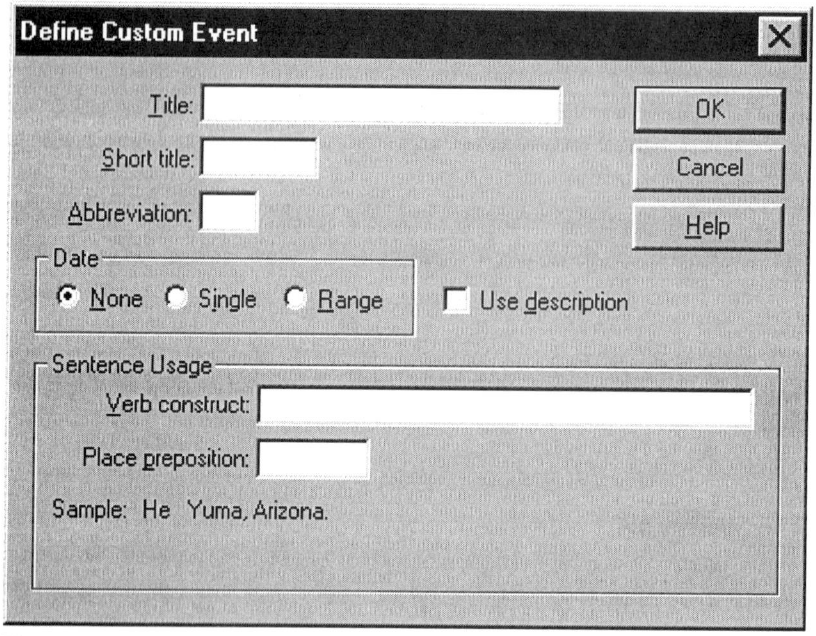

Define Custom Event

Title:

Short title:

Abbreviation:

Date

None Single Range

Use description

OK

Cancel

Help

Sentence Usage

Verb construct:

Place preposition:

Sample: He Yuma, Arizona.

Figure 58

2. Enter the information and select the options that should appear in the data entry window for this event.
   - **Title**. Enter the name of the Event/Attribute; this will then appear on the list of **Events/Attributes** and will print on some reports.
   - **Short Title**. Enter an abbreviation for the title, most reports will use this abbreviated version.
   - **Abbreviation**. Enter a two character abbreviation for the new Event/Attribute. It will be used in reports where space is limited.
   - **Dates**. Select:

     a. **None**, if the event doesn't have a specific date.

     b. **Single**, if the event has a specific date. For example retirement.

c. **Range**. If the event has a range of times during which it occurred, such as education.

- **Description**. Select this if the **Event/Attribute** needs to be descriptive for use in a sentence.
- **Sentence Usage**. This data will be used to construct sentences when printing a book report.

  a. **Verb Construct**. Enter a form of verb that applies to the Event/Attribute that you are adding. For example, if the event is graduation , you would type in *graduated*; the sentence would then would read "She graduated..." If the event describes what a person does the **Use Description** box needs to be checked. Then the report would print "was a..." Watch how the sentence is constructed in the **Verb Construct** box, and do not leave extra spaces after the verb.

  b. **Place Preposition**. Enter the preposition that applies to this event; for example: in, to, etc.

Editing an Event/Attribute on the Select Event List

In the **Select Event/Attribute** window, select **Edit**. The **Define Custom Event** window will open. Edit any information as required. In the case of a permanent type of Event/Attribute, you can not delete or edit the title. When changes are complete click **OK**.

Deleting a Custom Event/Attribute for an Individual

In the **Add** or **Edit Individual** window, highlight the event you wish to remove. Select **Options** (Fig. 54); then **Remove Event/Attribute**. A pop-up window will ask if you are sure you want to delete the Event/Attribute. Select **Yes**.

Editing Individual Information

To edit an individual, highlight the individual:

- From the toolbar, select **Edit**

or

- Press CTRL+I

or

- Click the right mouse button and select **Edit**.

Editing or Viewing Notes

To view or edit notes for an individual:

- Double click on the individual box, select **Options; Notes**

or

- Click the **Notes** icon 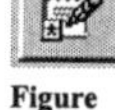

Figure 59

or

- Click the right mouse button to drop down a menu of options pertaining to the individual you highlighted.

Editing Media Collection, Display Photo in the Family View

To display the photo or edit the Multimedia collection of an individual:

- Double click on the individual, select **Options; Multimedia**

or

- Click the right mouse button to access a drop down menu of options pertaining to the individual you highlighted.

Adding Family Members to the Primary Person

You can add a person to a family in several ways.

- From the toolbar; select **Add; Add Individual, Child, Spouse or Parents**

or

- Highlight the individual and click the right mouse button to access a drop down menu of options opens.

NOTE: YOU CAN ADD MULTIPLE PARENTS TO AN INDIVIDUAL.

When you add an individual, spouse, child, or parents, a pop-up window opens from which you must select either:

- **Add a new individual**.
- **Select an existing individual**.

If the person you are adding already exists in your database, **DO NOT add him/her again**. Select **Select Existing Individual** or **Search for Existing Parents** to locate the person and then **Save** the record. This function will then link the existing individual to the selected individual in the desired relationship. If a new marriage is needed to connect two individuals it will be created.

Adding Spouses

To add the primary person's first spouse:

- Click on the **Spouse** box, a pop-up window will open prompting you to choose either:
  a. **Add** a new individual.
  b. **Select** an existing individual.

or

- Highlight the **Spouse** box and click on your right mouse button.

or

- Select **Add** in the toolbar.

An unlimited number of spouses may be entered for any individual. If an individual has more than one marriage an **Other Marriages** box will appear under the individual. Select **Other Marriages** to view all other spouses for the individual.

- **Unknown Spouse**. If you don't know the name of the spouse of the primary person, and the primary person has a child, add the child. This will create a family. If you later learn the spouse's name or other vital information you can select **Add; Spouse**. Add the individual. If you don't learn the name of the spouse and the primary person marries a second time, select **Add; Spouse**. After you enter the spouse's name a pop-up window will ask **Add this spouse to the current marriage?** If you select **Yes**, the spouse becomes the parent of the child in the first marriage. If you select **No**, the spouse becomes the second marriage for the Primary person.

- **Add Spouse from the Children box**. If a child is highlighted and you select **Add** from toolbar or click on right mouse button, you can add a spouse to the primary person or to the currently highlighted child. This feature expedites adding all individuals from a family group record.

After you enter the spouse the marriage window will automatically open if you selected **Edit Marriage when Created** in **Preferences; General**. If you did not check this option you can open by one of the following methods

- Click the right mouse button

or

- From the toolbar, **Edit**

or

- Double click the highlighted marriage box.

PAF 4.0 will automatically assign a Marriage Record Identification Number (MRIN) as soon as you create the marriage.

Entering or Editing Marriage Information

Marriage information can be entered or edited in the main window for the primary person, the parents of the primary person or a child. After a spouse has been entered a marriage box will appear (this is only the case for the primary person and parents). To access the marriage box for a child you must first move that child to the primary position by clicking on the arrow button to the left of the child. Or highlight the individual and click the right mouse button.

- **Date**. Enter the date the marriage took place. If a legal marriage did not take place **Not Married** is a valid date.

- **Place**. Enter the place where the marriage took place.

- **S.** Select this button to add the source for the date and place of the marriage. If one or more sources exist for the marriage, an (*) will appear on the button.

- **Other Events.** You can record any marriage related events. For example, bans, annulment, license, etc. To add another event select **Options** at the **Add Individual** or **Edit Individual** window. Choose from the existing list or create a new event/attribute.

- **LDS Data.** If you checked LDS Data in **Preferences; General**, you can enter the LDS ordinance date and place information in this window.

- **Notes**. Select **Options; Notes** or click the right mouse button for the highlighted marriage to enter notes about this marriage, the status of the marriage or relationship. If notes already exist, an (*) will appear on the button. The notes you create for a marriage are stored separate from notes for the individual.

- **Delete.** To delete a marriage you can select **Edit; Marriage** from the toolbar. A new window, **Marriage** appears. Select **Delete** to remove this marriage from your records.

Adding Children in the Add or Edit Individual Window

If the primary person has had more than one spouse, link the child to the correct parents. The **Other Marriages** button will appear when more than one spouse has been added. Make sure you are adding the children to the correct parent(s). To add a child to the primary individual:

- Click the right mouse button

or

- Select **Add** on the toolbar

or

- Click on the place the child should appear.

The response will be **Add New Individual** or **Select existing individual**.

An (*) next to the birth date of the child indicates an alternate date used to document the birth of the child. This date is displayed only when no date is entered into the birth date field. See **Alternate Birth Field** below.

Child Order

The children you entered are listed in the order you entered them. To change the order of a child:

1. From the toolbar select **Edit; Child Order**

PAF will display the **Child Order** window. (Fig. 60)

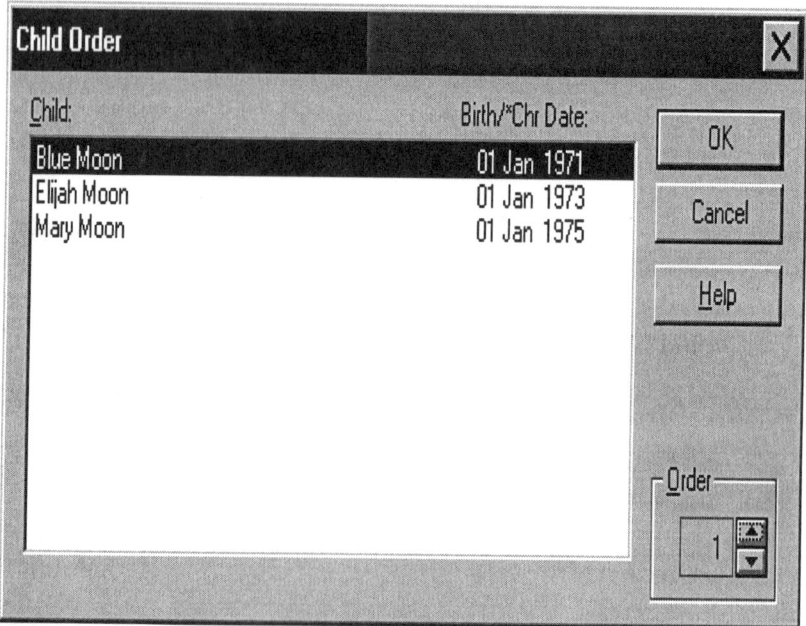

Figure 60

2. Select the child to move.
3. Click an arrow key next to the number in the lower right hand corner. This will move the child to the number you indicate.
4. Repeat steps 2 and 3 as needed to correctly place children in chronological order. When finished select **OK**.

Hint: In the lower right corner of the screen, the number of children of the primary person will be indicated. For example, C:1, indicates 1 child. If the parents of the child have not married, type **Not Married** in the date field. This procedure would also apply to entering the parents of any Illegitimate Children.

Adding Parents and Parent Relationships.

To add a parent(s) to the primary person, who is already in your database (Fig. 61), you can do any of the following:

- Double click on either parent name box;
  or
- Use CTRL+T to add the father or the primary person;
  or
- Use CTRL+H to add the mother of the primary person;
  or
- Select **Add** on the toolbar
  or
- Highlight the parent box and click the right mouse button.

An individual can have multiple parents due to adoption, guardianship, step-parent(s), LDS sealing to different parents, or other reasons. To enter additional parents choose one of the following:

- Highlight the individual and click the right mouse button.
  or
- From the toolbar, select **Add; Parents**. PAF will display the **Parents of ....** window. (Fig. 61)

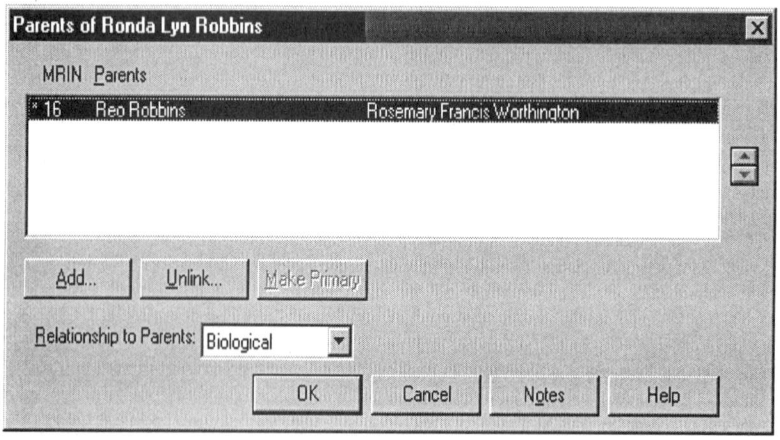

Figure 61

To add a new set of parents, select **Add**. PAF will display the window **Add Parents for…** (Fig. 62)

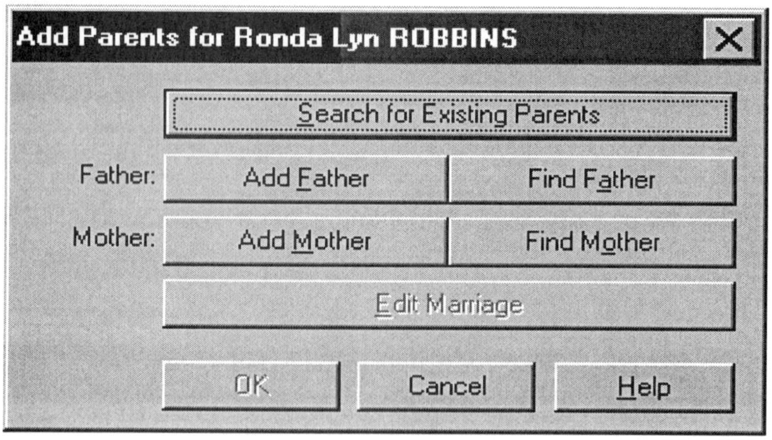

Figure 62

You can either search for existing parents or add a mother and/or father. If you choose to **Search** or **Find**, PAF will ask for a RIN or will allow you to view the **Individual List** or **Descendancy List** to locate your individual. When you have completed adding the parents, select **Relationship to Parents** and choose the relationship that is applicable. If you have the **Sealing to Parents** option available, enter the date the sealing took place and the LDS temple where the ordinance was completed. To enter a source for this event select **S**. If a source is already in place an (*) will appear on the button. To enter notes click on the **Notes** button, if notes already exist an (*) will appear on the button. If you have two or more sets of parents an **Other Parents** button will appear above the father box. To view the other parents click on this box. An (*) will stipulate which parental link is the Primary Parents.

When you are entering the Primary Parents or additional parents and you are not sure if the parents are in your database, from the toolbar select **Add; Individual**. This will prompt a pop-up window which will ask **Add New** or **Find Existing**. (Fig. 63) Click on **Father/Mother** and the window will then allow you to add or find. (Fig. 64) If you are searching for an existing individual you may search by RIN, if you know that number, or look through the **Individual List**. You should then select the correct parent. If your search was unsuccessful, you will then click on **Add** and choose either **Father** or **Mother**. This will facilitate a new window **Add Father/Mother for....** If you selected the option to edit a marriage when it is created, under **Tools ➛ Preferences; General**, the marriage date, place, notes, sources, LDS data or other marriage events are entered. Repeat the procedure again for the next parent.

When you have completed data entry of your Primary Person, Spouse,

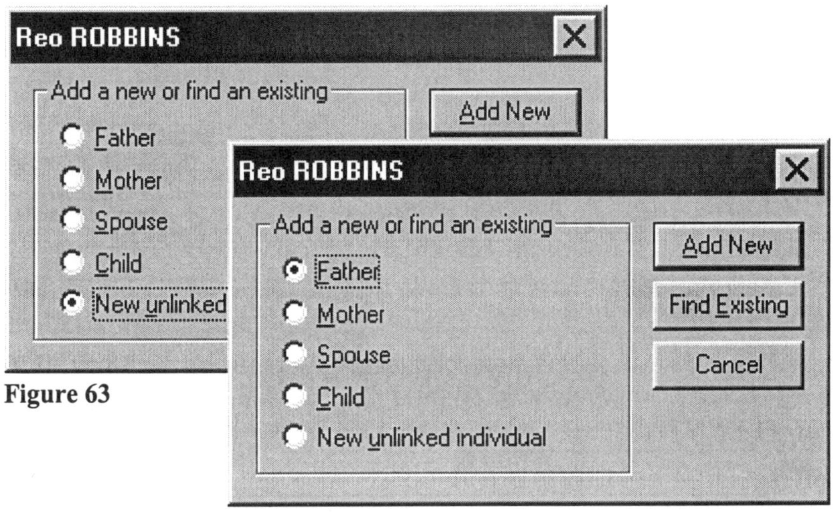

Figure 63

Figure 64

Parents, and Children, your **Family View** record should look similar to Figure 65.

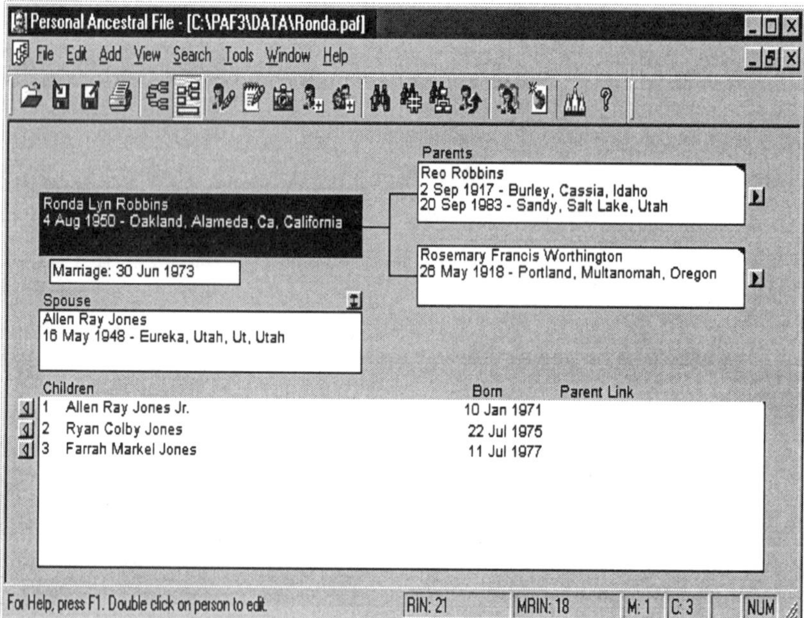

Figure 65

Changing the Primary Parents

Click on the **Other Marriages** button. The window has the name of the Primary Person. There is an (*) by the Primary Parents. To change this you must highlight the parents you wish to change to Primary, select the **Mark Primary** button, which is only visible with two or more sets of parents. The Primary Parents are shown on screens and reports. To show or print the other parents you must first make them Primary parents.

NOTE: NOTES ENTERED INTO THE PARENT FILE WILL ALSO BE ENTERED INTO THE INDIVIDUAL NOTES FILE.

Linking and Unlinking Family Members

Linking Individuals and Families

The individual record includes all the information entered for an individual. Each individual record can point to more than one parent marriage record. Marriage records store only marriage information. Each marriage record can point to one husband, wife, and an unlimited number of children. These pointers are established when you create a link from one individual to another to form a family unit.

The **Family View** window displays the Primary Person, children, and parents. These three people are linked through the parent's marriage record which stores the marriage event for the parents and points to the Primary Person as their child. If the Primary Person is married, then the spouse and children are all linked through the marriage record for the primary couple.

Unlinking removes an individual from a relationship, it does not delete him/her from the database. Similarly, un-linking a marriage does not delete the participants from the database.

Unlinking a Spouse, Child, or Parent

To remove an individual from a relationship but not from your database:

1. Put the person you want to unlink in either the parent, spouse, or child position.
2. Highlight the person you want to unlink from the Primary Person.
3. Select from toolbar **Edit; Unlink** or click on right mouse button and choose **Unlink**.
4. You will get a warning message asking if you are sure you want to unlink this individual from the relationship; select **OK**.

Unlinking a Set of Parents

You can unlink the Primary Person from both parents at one time. To unlink from more than one set of parents, you need to repeat the procedure.

1. Highlight the child you want to unlink.
2. Click right mouse button, **Unlink**.
3. A warning message will pop-up. **This will unlink this child from the family. Do you want to continue?** Select **Yes**.

   or

1. Put the child in Primary position. From the toolbar, select **Edit ➛ Parents; Unlink**. You will get a warning message asking if you are sure. Select **Yes**.

This will unlink the child and parents but will not delete them from the database. The individuals and marriage remain intact.

Deleting

Deleting an Individual

Deleting an individual will remove the individual from your database. You have the option of re-using the RIN assigned to the deleted individual. The next person you enter or import would use the vacant RIN.

1. Locate and select the individual you wish to delete. Any name

displayed in the **Family View** window may be selected: Primary person, spouse, parents, and children.

2. Highlight the selected individual; click the right mouse button, select **Delete**. A warning message will be displayed for the person you are about to delete.
3. Select **OK** to delete or **Cancel** to quit without deleting. The warning message will also list any links to the person you are about to delete. (Fig. 66)

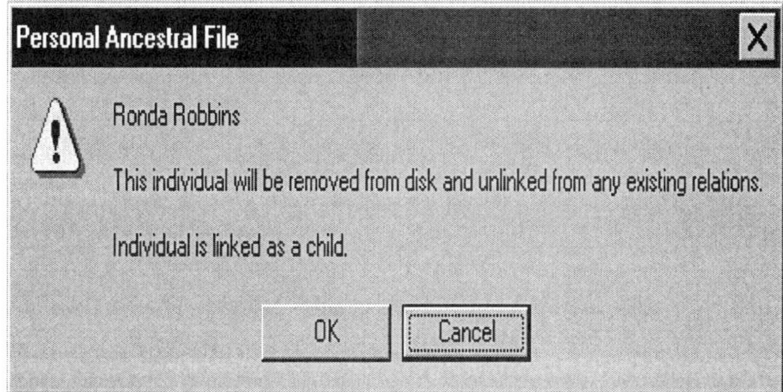

Figure 66

Deleting a Marriage

When you delete a marriage it removes the record from the database. You have the option of re-using MRIN for the next marriage you enter or import. It will not, however, delete the individuals in the marriage. They remain in your database as unconnected individuals.

1. Move the individual to the Primary Person box and double click on **Marriage** or highlight the person you wish to delete from a marriage and select **Edit ➛ Marriage**. The **Marriage** window will open.
2. Select **Delete**. You will get a warning message.
3. Select **OK** to remove the marriage from your records, or select **Cancel** to leave the marriage intact.

Chapter 5

Maintaining Your Database

This chapter provides the information you will need to create, open, split, and repair your databases. You will also learn how to import and export GEDCOM files, backup and restore commands, share your multimedia files, and convert from previous versions of PAF.

Creating a New Database

You will want to create a new database to:

- Record information about a family in PAF for the first time.
- Split an existing database into two or more separate databases.
- Add a GEDCOM file to a temporary file. This allows you to look at the information and correct any errors before adding it to your permanent database.

To begin:

1. From the toolbar; select **File** ➛ **New**.
2. The **Create New Family File** window will appear. (Fig. 67)

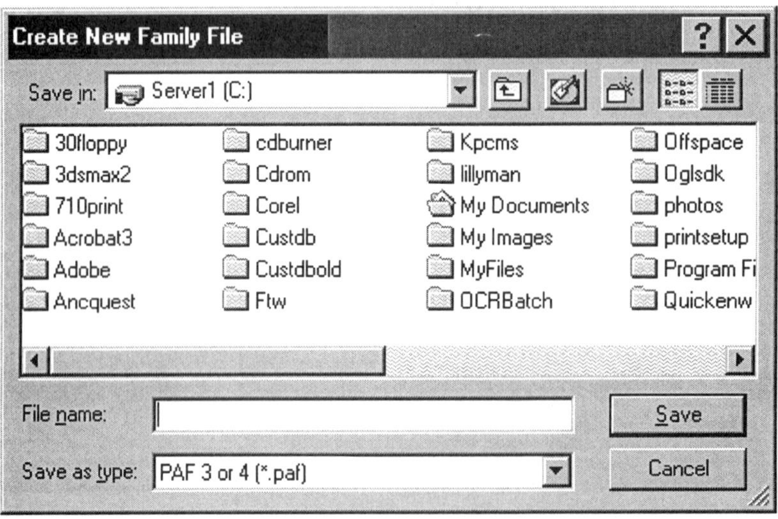

Figure 67

3. In the **File Name** field, type the name of your file (up to eight characters). This name along with **Family**, will appear on the PAF title bar each time you open the file.

NOTE: YOU SHOULD NEVER SAVE DATA IN A PROGRAM DIRECTORY.

4. Select **Save**. PAF will display the **Preferences; Prepared by** window.
5. Enter the information, moving through the fields using the TAB key.
6. When you have entered the information select **OK**.

Hint: Press F1 to view **How do I** and **Tell me more about**.

Opening an Existing Database

To open a database previously created you can:

1. From the toolbar, select **File** ➛ **Open**.

or

2. CTRL+O

or

3. Click on the File Folder Icon.

Figure 68

Choose any one of the above options. PAF will display **Open Family File**. (Fig. 69)

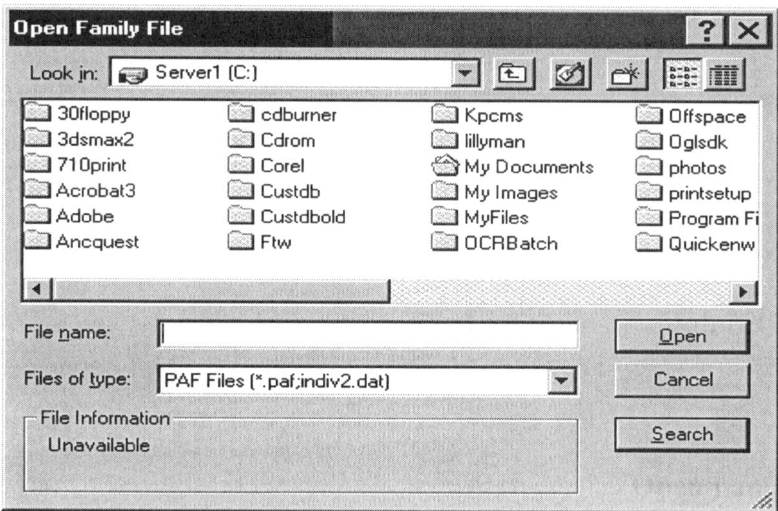

Figure 69

From this window you will open your database. Find your database and double click on the file name. The file will open into the **Family View** or **Pedigree View** window. You are ready to begin your work.

If you have a file from PAF 3.0 or higher, you do not need to convert it. However, if you have a file from PAF 2.0 to 2.31, you must first convert your database before you can use it in PAF 4.0. To convert your database, find the INDIV2.DAT file and open into PAF 4.0. (See Appendix D for a more detailed instruction.) The PAF 2.x File Conversion window will present three options that allow you to complete a customized conversion.

OPTION	**DESCRIPTION**
Wrap note lines into paragraphs	Before version 3.0, notes in PAF did not wrap. This meant that you had to press ENTER after each line. There were 79 characters per line. To separate paragraphs you pressed ENTER twice. Click this option to remove those line breaks in notes. The conversion process will still recognize the paragraph breaks. If you don't choose this option your notes will print across about 2/3 of the width of your page.
Preserve old RINs	Click this option if you want to maintain the numbering system already intact.

Convert old source notes into the new source records	If you used the Silicon Valley PAF Users Group source guidelines or used the sources and notes format discussed in the manual from PAF 2.31 to enter your sources, you can convert those notes into this version of PAF. Every time conversion finds such a source, it will pause and show you how it will be converted. You can then decide to convert or not. All the notes that are not sources will be converted into the notes file. **Hint:** If you didn't use or are not sure if you used these guidelines, click on the option to view the results. This will be faster than converting your notes manually. If you don't like how it is translated don't convert the note.

The software assumes you are familiar with the Silicon Valley PAF Users Group source guidelines or have used the sources and notes format discussed in the manual from PAF 2.31 and that you followed these procedures:

- It identified source notes as those notes that have an exclamation point (!) as the first character.
- It used a semicolon (;) to determine when one fact in the source ended and when the next began.
- It used tags to determine what information to transfer into which fields in a source. The tags are not converted.
- The title is placed in **Source Title** field.
- The author is placed in **Author** field.
- The years covered are placed in the **Comments** filed.

- The series, volume and publisher information are placed in **Publication Information** field.

- The page number in the **Film/Volume/Page** field are placed in the citation detail.

- Any repositories it finds are added to the **Repository List**. In addition, the repository is placed into the source record.

- The text and comments it finds are placed in the **Comments** field.

Hint: If the information isn't transferred as you would like, use the **Edit** feature on the toolbar. You can use the Windows cut, copy, and paste option, found under **Edit** on your toolbar, to move the information around in PAF 4.0.

Hint: Press F1 to view **How do I** and **Tell me more about**.

Backing Up A Database

You should **always keep a backup copy of the most recent update of your database.** A backup copy can prevent you from losing your work should your computer have a problem. It can save you from losing days, months, and even years of work.

> **NOTE: If your backup is on a floppy disk, DO NOT REMOVE THIS DISK FROM YOUR COMPUTER UNTIL YOU HAVE CLOSED YOUR FILE. You should clearly label your backup and keep it separate from where you store your working database.**

To backup your database(s):

1. From the toolbar select **File** ➛ **Backup**.

2. Select the drive and location where your backup will reside.
3. Type in a name for your file.
4. Select **Backup**.
5. A message will confirm completion of the backup process. Select **OK** to continue.

The backup function will backup only the data files. It does not include multimedia objects although it does include the links to the multimedia objects. You will need to use another backup utility to complete a backup on your multimedia objects.

Restoring a Database

From the toolbar;

1. Select **File** ➛ **Restore**.
2. At the **Restore File From** window, double-click on the file name or highlight the name of the backup and select **Restore**. If the database you highlighted is already open, PAF will ask for confirmation to restore. Select **Yes** to continue. If you don't remember the name of your backup, have your computer search for all files with the .BAK extension. Highlight your database and select **Restore**, or double click on the name of the backup file.

Import and Export

There may be times when you will want to share information with other users, move data to different computers, or transfer information to other programs. The best way to handle this exchange of information is to create a GEDCOM file. GEDCOM is the acronym for "GEnealogical Data COMmunications." The format was created by The Church of Jesus Christ of Latter-Day Saints for storing and moving genealogical information between computers. It has become the standard among genealogy software developers. Sharing genealogical information is a constructive way to obtain more information and to enable others to use your research.

Hint: Creating and using a GEDCOM file to share information will allow you to filter the living individuals in your database and ensure their privacy. You can share information using .PAF files, however this will share ALL files, living and dead individuals. Exporting a GEDCOM will allow **you** to decide which files you wish to share.

Before generating a GEDCOM file to share with someone, you should verify which version of PAF they are using. This will determine which version of GEDCOM backup you will create.

To Export Information into a GEDCOM 4.0 File

1. From the toolbar, select **File** ➛ **Export**.
2. Select **GEDCOM 4.0.**
3. Select **All** to select all of the individuals in your database; or select **Partial; Select**. You can use relationship and field filters to select specific names that you want to export. (See Chapter 9 for more information on filters.)
4. From the **GEDCOM Export** window, select from **Include** options.
5. Select **Export**.
6. Select the drive and file where your file is to be saved.
7. Type in a file name and select **Export**.
8. You will see a message upon completion of the GEDCOM export that will provide a count of names exported. Select **OK**.

NOTE: IF YOU SELECT **PARTIAL** FROM THE FILTER, YOU WILL NEED TO GO THROUGH THE SELECTION PROCESS IN THE **SELECT SET OF INDIVIDUALS** WINDOW.

Including Options on the Export Screen

OPTIONS	DESCRIPTION
Notes	Select **Notes** to include all notes. **Hint:** Using the **Notes** option will exclude notes marked with the tilde (~). To include those notes you must select both **Notes** and **Confidential Data**.
Sources	Select **Sources** to include all your source and repository data attached to the records.
Contact Information	Select **Contact Information** to include your name, address, and other information you entered in the **Preferences; General** tab.
Confidential Data	Select **Confidential Data** to include events marked confidential from your notes.
Full information on living	Select **Full information on living** to include full information for all people born less than 110 years ago, and who don't have death or burial information included in the record. **Hint:** If you don't select ***Full Information on Living*** or **Names on living**, the exported individual record will contain the word **Living** in the **Given Name** field, all other fields will be empty except the **Gender** field.
Names on living	You may include the names of living individuals by selecting **Names of Living**. All other fields will be empty except the gender field.

Submitter	Select **Submitter** to include your name and address.
Multimedia (5.5 only)	Select this option to include the links to your multimedia files. This only exports links to where your media is found.
LDS Data	To include LDS ordinances and/or other LDS information select **LDS Data**. **Hint:** If you did not choose to show LDS data in the **Preferences** setting, this option will not appear.

Hint: Press F1 to view **How do I** and **Tell me more about**.

Exporting Information for GEDCOM 5.5

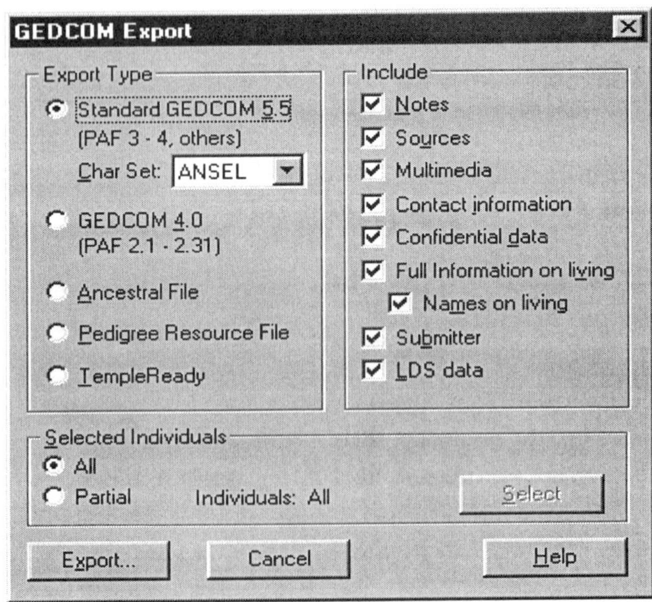

Figure 70

The process to export 5.5 is different only in that you must choose a character set. Select either: **ANSEL** or **ANSI**. Select **ANSI** only if you know the person receiving this information uses a genealogy software program that uses only **ANSI**.

NOTE: MOST GENEALOGY SOFTWARE THAT IS COMPATIBLE WITH THE GEDCOM FORMAT WILL USE ANSEL.

Exporting Information for Ancestral File

1. From the toolbar, select **File** ➛ **Export**.
2. Select **Ancestral File**.
3. To select all individuals, select **All** or, to export specific individuals, select **Partial; Select**. Use the relationship and field filters to select the names you want to include. (See Chapter 9 for additional information on this topic.)
4. Select **Include** to choose the options you want.
5. Select **Export**.
6. Select the drive and directory where you will save this file.
7. When the export is complete, you will see a window verifying the number of individuals included in this export. Select **OK**.

Hint: Press F1 to view **How do I** and **Tell me more about**.

Exporting Information for the Pedigree Resource File (See Appendix E)

1. From the toolbar, select **File** ➛ **Export**.
2. Select **Pedigree Resource File**.
3. To select all individuals, select **All** or, to export specific individuals, select **Partial; Select**. Use the relationship and field filters to select the names you want to include. (See Chapter 9 for additional information on this topic.)
4. From the **GEDCOM Export** window, select from **Include** options.
5. Select **Export**.

6. Read the new window and select **Continue**.
7. Read the requirement for submitting the data. If you agree with the requirements, select **Continue** or, if you don't agree, select **Cancel**.
8. Select the drive and directory where you will save this submission.
9. Type a name for your file and select **Export**.
10. When the export is complete a window will appear providing the number of individuals included in the export. Select **OK**.
11. Read the instructions for Pedigree Resource File Submission; select **OK**.

Hint: Press F1 to view **How do I** and **Tell me more about**.

To Export Information for TempleReady™

1. From the toolbar select **File** ➛ **Export**.
2. Select **TempleReady**.
3. To select all individuals, select **All** or, to export specific individuals, select **Partial; Select**. Use the relationship and field filters to select the names you want to include. (See Chapter 9 for additional information on this topic.)
4. From the **GEDCOM Export** window, select from **Include** options
5. Select **Export**.
6. Read the window **Temple Names Submission**, select **OK**.
7. From the window **Temple Names Submission Options** select those options you want to include in your export.
8. Select the drive and directory where you will save this submission.
9. Type a name for your file, select **Export**.
10. When the export is complete a window will appear providing the number of individuals included in the export. Select **OK**.
11. Carefully read the TempleReady Instructions screen, select **OK** to continue.

Hint: If you choose to print the Submission Report, PAF will display that report in NotePad. You can read, print, or edit the report in NotePad. To close the report, exit the application, or from the toolbar, **File** ➛ **Exit**.

Hint: Press F1 to view **How do I** and **Tell me more about**.

NOTE: AFTER QUALIFIED INDIVIDUALS AND MARRIAGES HAVE BEEN SAVED TO A TEMPLE READY DISK, FINAL PROCESSING FOR SUBMISSION CAN BE COMPLETED AT A FAMILY HISTORY CENTER OR THE FAMILY HISTORY LIBRARY LOCATED IN SALT LAKE CITY, UTAH.

Importing GEDCOM Files

The most efficient way to add information into your database, is by using a GEDCOM that contains the data that you need. You may be able to obtain this file from another family member, an acquaintance researching the same lines, a Surname users group, from Ancestral File, etc.

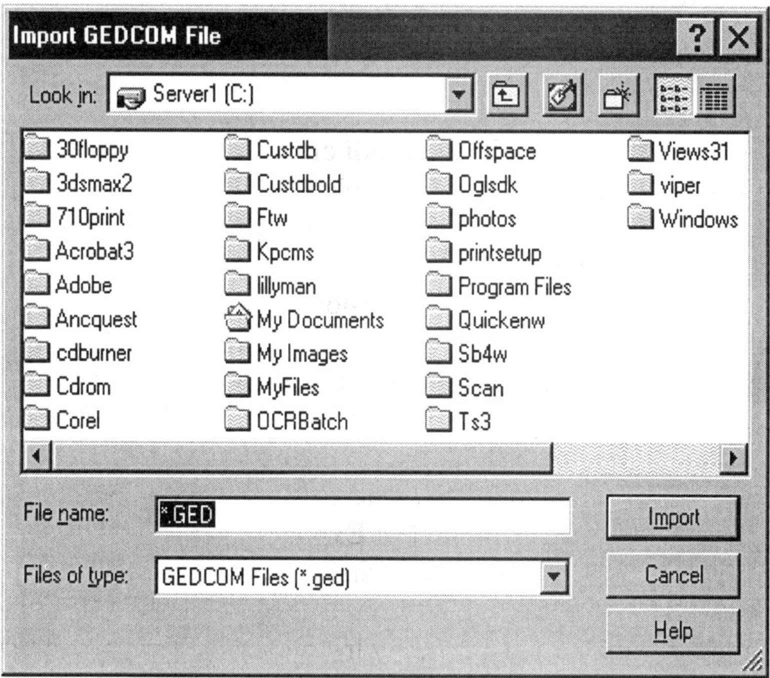

Figure 71

To import a GEDCOM file:

- From the toolbar, select **File** ➛ **Import**.

- You will see on your monitor the **Import GEDCOM File** window. (Fig. 71)
- Select the drive and folder where your file is located.
- Highlight the file.
- Select **Import**.
- Choose from the **Import options** list the items you wish to import. (See list below)
- To begin Import, select **OK**.
- If PAF finds any errors or problems in the file, it opens **NotePad** to display the import log. This report can be printed.
- You will see a box that provides the number of individuals that were imported, select **OK** to continue.
- PAF will ask if you want to view instructions on linking imported data. Select **Yes** or **No**.

Hint: If you select Yes, the help system will automatically open the topic **Working with imported information**.

Selecting Import Options

OPTIONS	DESCRIPTION
Import Notes	To include the notes in the GEDCOM file, select this option.

Include listing file data in notes	Select this option to have messages about errors or problems encountered during the data transfer included in the notes of the appropriate individuals. These messages are normally sent to a list file.
Re-use deleted records	Select this option to re-use RINs that are vacant due to previous deletions. This will integrate them into your database. Don't select this option if you want the imported individuals to be added at the end of your database providing new RINs that are higher than those previously used by your database. **Hint:** Should you later decide to prune imported data from your database, it is easier to do so if you do not use this option.

Hint: Press F1 to view **How do I** and **Tell me more about**.

Working With the Imported Information

Remember the following guidelines:

- The first individual you will see is the person who has the lowest RIN in the imported database.
- If you can't see arrows indicating your ancestors or descendants or if you can't see the individuals that you imported, use **Individual List** accessible from the toolbar choose **Search ➛ Individual List**.
- The imported data will not automatically be linked to your data. You must add them to each family to which they belong. For example, you don't have your Great Grandfather's parents in your database. Someone sends you a GEDCOM file with that information. You must now link your Great Grandfather to his parents. Move your Great Grandfather to the Primary position. From the toolbar, select **Add ➛ Parents ➛ Select existing individual** and search for his parents.

- When importing information, you will frequently have duplicate individuals. Use the match/merge function to combine them. (See Chapter 10 **Merging Duplicate Records**)

Hint: Press F1 to view **How do I** and **Tell me more about**.

NOTE: MULTIMEDIA OBJECTS WILL NOT BE INCLUDED IN THE GEDCOM FILE. TO SHARE THAT DATA, YOU WILL NEED TO PROVIDE A COPY OF ALL APPLICABLE MULTIMEDIA OBJECTS. SEE CHAPTER 7 FOR ADDITIONAL INFORMATION IN REFERENCE TO MULTIMEDIA OBJECTS.

Databases

Repairing Databases

Occasionally your databases will develop errors or problems generally caused by one of the following:

- Turning off your computer before completely exiting PAF.
- Operating system quirks.
- Power failures or fluctuations while using the PAF software.

To repair or check your software, you can use the **Check/Repair** option to scan your databases for problems. If errors are found, the program can fix them. To maintain your databases in good working order, run the **Check/Repair** feature periodically. During the **Check/Repair**, errors will be displayed on NotePad. However, if there are too many errors, NotePad will not be able to display them. You will need to use any word processor to open the report created during the **Check/Repair** option.

NOTE: IT IS ALWAYS GOOD PRACTICE TO FREQUENTLY BACK UP YOUR DATABASE.

PAF allows you to complete a **Check only** or a **Check/Repair**. You will need to choose the option you want to employ with your databases.

Problems with databases are usually caused by one of the following:

- Problem: The individual or marriage records points to an invalid name. Remedy: PAF will provide you with the RIN or MRIN; you will have to verify the validity of this number to see if you need to re-link.

- Problem: A marriage record points to a deleted marriage, or a record that is out of range for possible marriages. Remedy: You will need to check MRIN to check validity of the record and possibly re-link the record.

- Problem: A RIN is invalid. Remedy: Check the individual record to verify validity and possibly re-link.

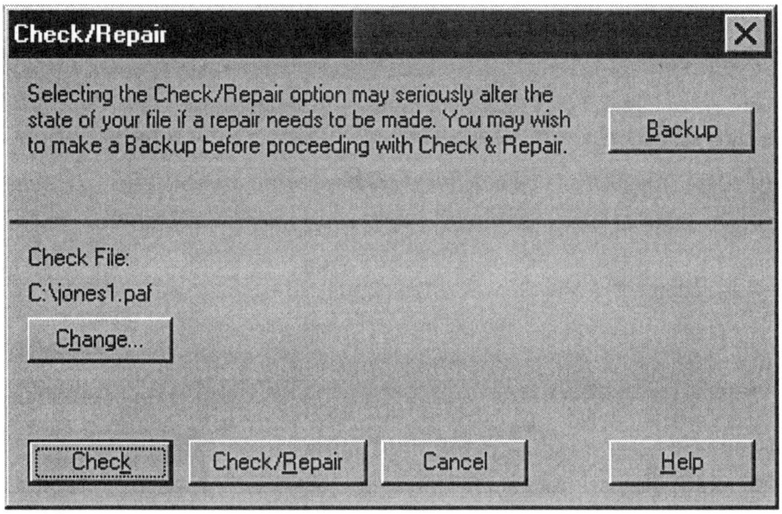

Check/Repair

Selecting the Check/Repair option may seriously alter the state of your file if a repair needs to be made. You may wish to make a Backup before proceeding with Check & Repair.

Backup

Check File:

C:\jones1.paf

Change...

Check | Check/Repair | Cancel | Help

Figure 72

Reading a Database's File Properties

The file properties of a database can show you at a glance the following information about your database:

1. The file name, location, size and the last date updated.
2. The number of individuals, marriages, citations, sources, multimedia objects, notes, repositories, and user events. You will also see a list of deleted items.
3. The available disk space where your file is located.

Viewing the File Properties of a Database

- From the toolbar, select **File ➛ Information**.
- Review the information displayed.
- Click **OK**.

Hint: Press F1 to view **How do I** and **Tell me more about**.

Splitting a Database

Many people feel it is much easier to maintain many smaller databases, instead of a larger, consolidated one. If you should decide to use this option, follow the instructions below to ensure you don't lose any information stored in your database.

1. **Make a backup copy of all databases.** This will ensure that you will not lose any valuable information if you make any errors during this procedure.
2. Determine which ancestral lines you will re-locate to a new database.
3. To create A GEDCOM file; from the toolbar select **File ➛ Export**.
4. Create the new database.
5. Use the **Import** feature to transfer the information into the newly created database.
6. Verify that all imported information is correct.
7. Delete the redundant records.

Hint: Press F1 to view **How do I** and **Tell me more about**.

Chapter 6

Sources and Notes

Using Sources

A critical step for any researcher is documenting the sources of information. It ensures to any researcher critiquing your work, that you have verified and documented your assertions. Good documentation will support your work if it is ever challenged. Sources will benefit any researcher following your work in that he/she will be able to avoid duplicating the examination of records used in your research. All events can have an unlimited number of sources attached.

Hint: More is best, you can never provide too much detail when documenting your sources.

Guidelines for Citing Sources

- Write down all source citation before leaving the library or other repository. (See Research Form in Appendix F).
- To ensure that you don't forget your sources, enter the sources during the same work session in which you enter the individual and marriage data.
- Cite the source actually used. For example, abstracts and indexes may contain errors as they are not the actual record, hence, the source citation would be the abstract, not the original document.
- Document contributions from other researchers.
- Record all sources, including those that did not contain information applicable to the individual or marriage. This will reduce the chance that work will be duplicated.

Hint: Press F1 to view **How do I** and **Tell me more about**.

How Sources are Stored

Each source will be entered into the database only once. You can link sources to any event, whether individual or marriage. You can then use that same source over and over again, attaching it to as many individuals and/or marriages as it applies.

A source has three types of information:

1. A **source description** describes the source in totality and is stored as a separate record in your database. Once entered, it is accessed by selecting from the list of sources.

2. The **citation detail** provides the location of the information within the source. For example, page numbers, volume number, line number, etc. The citation is attached to an individual or marriage record. Consequently, you may use the source over and over again, entering citation detail each time you select a source.

3. The **Repository** includes the name, address, and telephone number of the source location. This will allow subsequent researchers to find the source.

Hint: Press F1 to view **How do I** and **Tell me more about**.

Adding Sources

There are two ways to add sources in PAF 4.0:

1. Add sources directly from individual or marriage records while adding or editing data in the database.
   or
2. Complete your entry session and add all the sources at one time, linking them to individual or marriage records as you enter the source. To follow this procedure use the **Edit Source List**. (Fig. 73)

Hint: Press F1 to view **How do I** and **Tell me more about**.

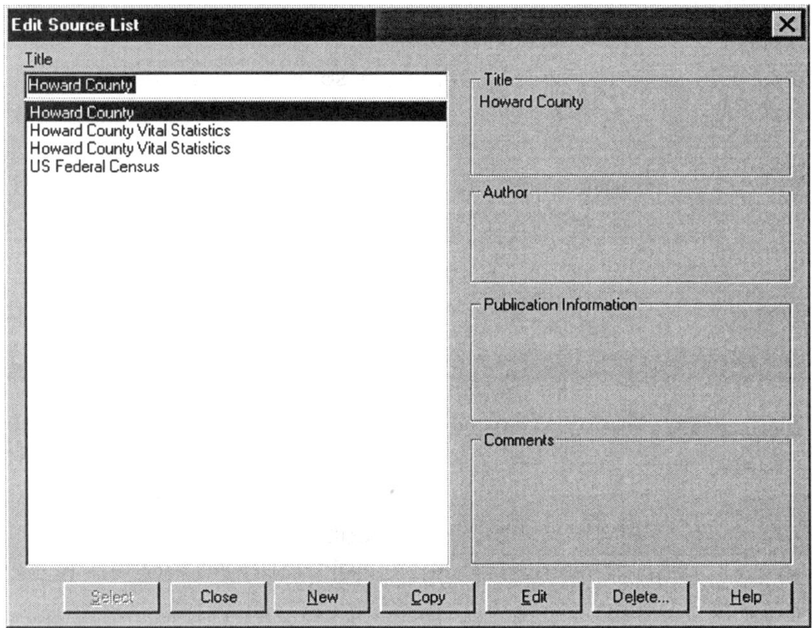

Figure 73

Adding a New Source to an Individual Record

There are two procedures here:

1) Adding a source where there are NO sources present in a new database; and

2) Adding sources to a database that already has sources added.

Add a Source to an Individual Record in a New Database
Display the record for which you want to add a source. At the Individual record, place your cursor over the **S** that is located to the right of the item to which you want to add the source and double-click. The new window displayed is the **Select Source for.....** PAF will display **Select Source for.....** (Fig. 74)

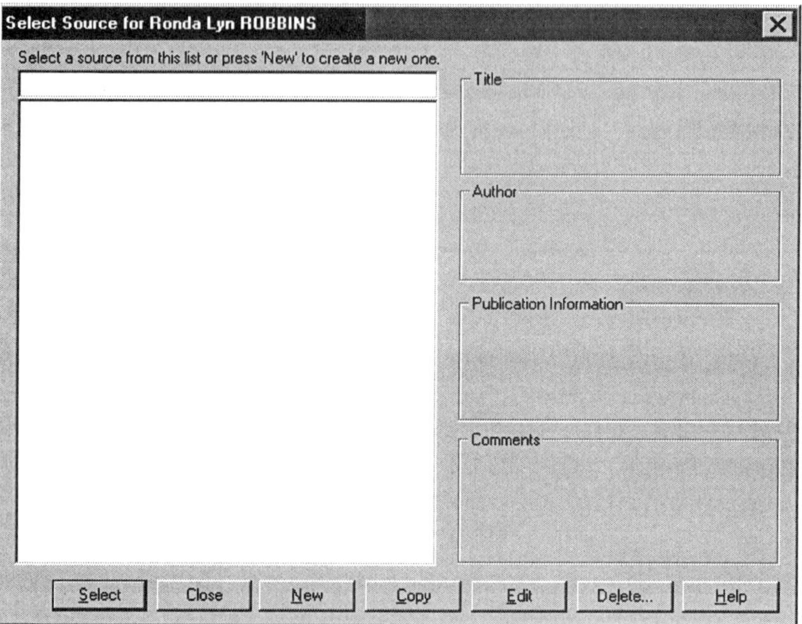

Figure 74

As there are no sources present, select **New** to add a source.

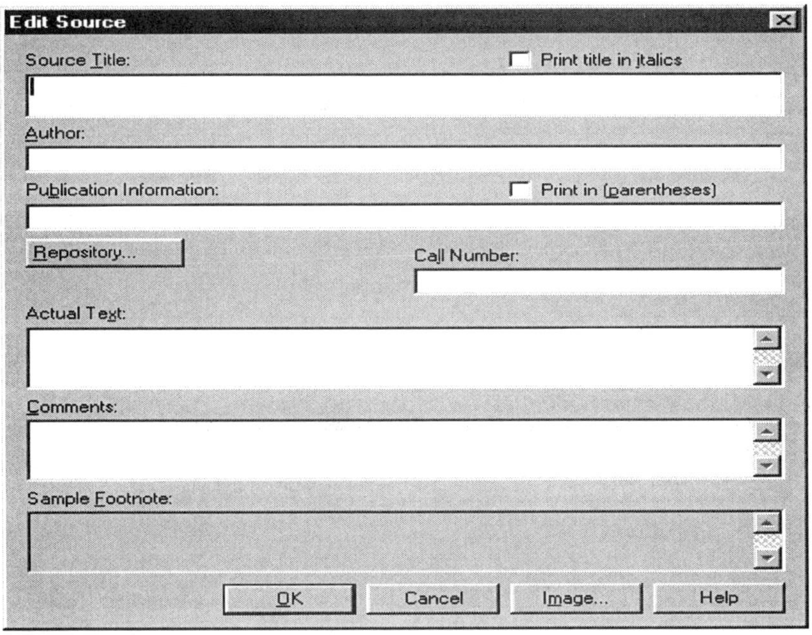

Figure 75

The new window is **Edit Source**. (Fig. 75) Complete each field using the TAB key to move to the next field. Select **Repository** to add the repository where the source may be found. If Repositories have already been entered, a list will appear from which you may choose your Repository or enter a new repository location. (See **Repositories** on page 108 for additional information) To add a multimedia object for the source, select **Image**. (See Chapter 7 **Multimedia Objects**)

When you have finished entering the data in this window, select **OK**. PAF will return to **Select Source for....** (Fig. 76) Highlight the source you have created and click **Select**.

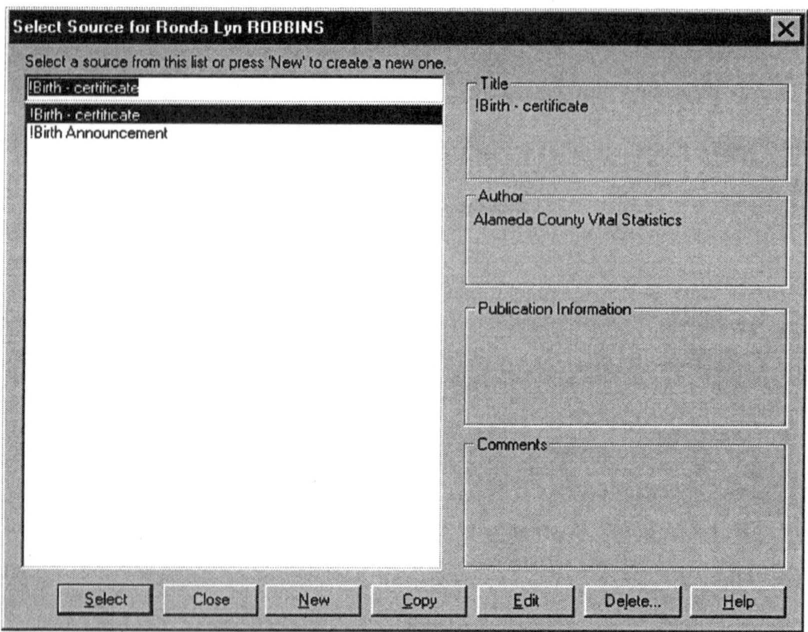

Figure 76

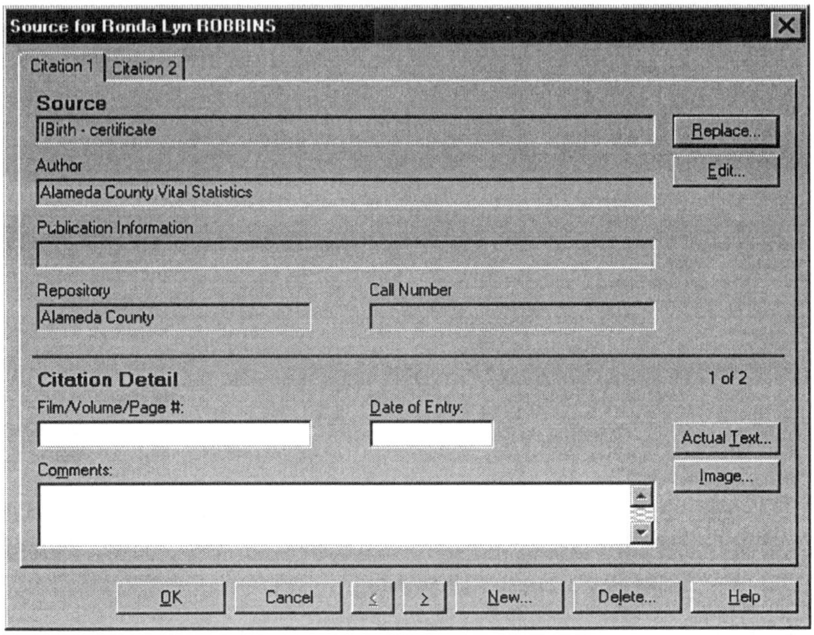

Figure 77

PAF then displays **Source for...** (Fig. 77). Enter the information for the citation detail.

- Film/Volume/Page #. For example, US Film 1045611, pg 10, line 12 or Vol. 3 p7.

- Entry Date. This is the date when the record was created, NOT the date you entered the information. (This date is often unknown)

- When your entry is complete, select **OK**.

NOTE: ONCE YOU HAVE ENTERED MORE THAN ONE SOURCE YOU CAN EASILY MOVE BETWEEN SOURCE CITATIONS FOR AN INDIVIDUAL. AT THE **SOURCE FOR...** WINDOW (FIG. 74) YOU WILL SEE AT THE BOTTOM OF THE WINDOW TWO ARROW BUTTONS. YOU CAN USE THESE ARROW KEYS TO MOVE BETWEEN CITATIONS OR YOU CAN CLICK ON THE TAB.

Adding New Sources to a Record that Already Has Sources Attached

At the **Edit Individual** window (Fig. 78) you will see an (*) located in the **S** box to the right of the name box. The (*) indicates that sources exist for this individual. In addition to sources you have entered, this may result from a conversion, import, GEDCOM file, etc.

Click on **S** at the right hand corner of the Personal box.

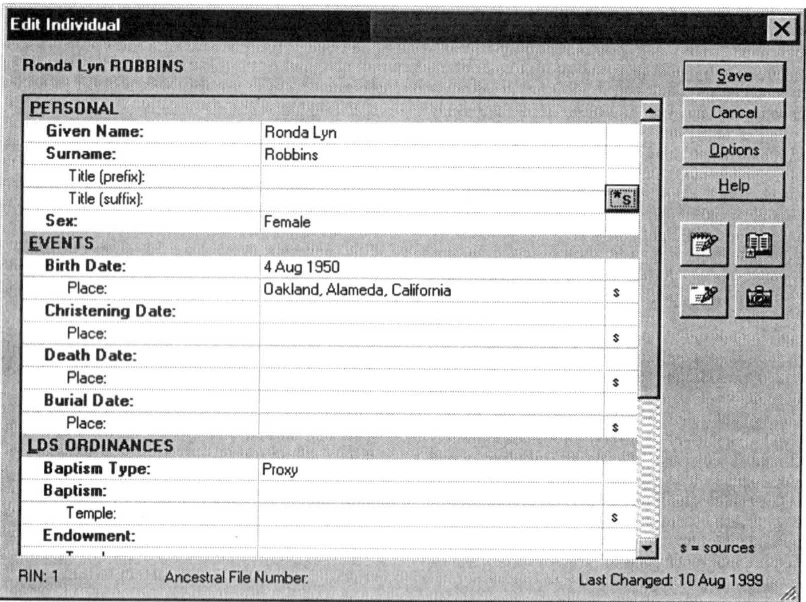

Figure 78

The next window PAF displays is **Source for...** (Fig. 77). This window displays all sources that have been linked to this individual record. To add a new source, select **New**. PAF will then display the **Select Source for....** window. (Fig. 76)

To add a source to this list, choose **New**.

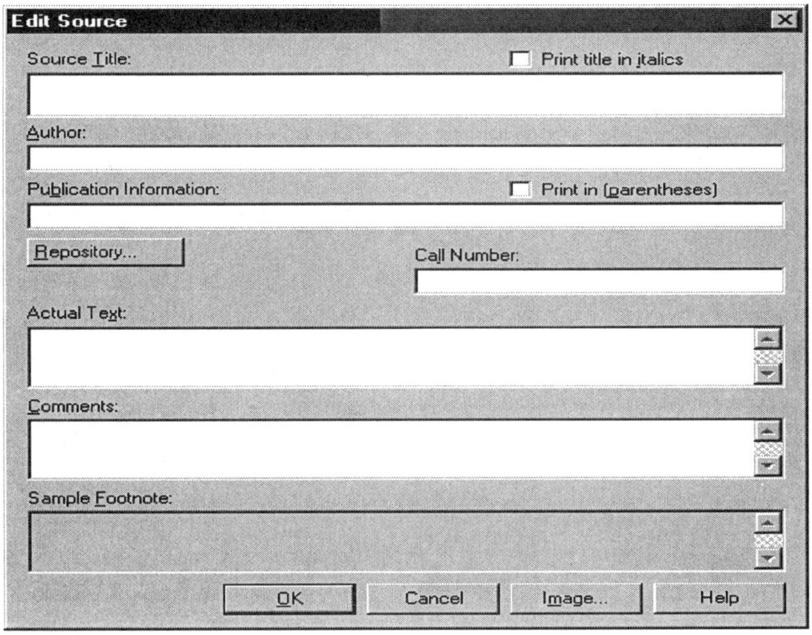

Figure 79

The new window is **Edit Source**. (Fig. 79) Complete each field using the TAB key to move through each field. Select **Repository** to add the repository where the source may be found. If Repositories have already been entered, a list will appear from which you may choose your repository or enter a new repository cite. To add a multimedia object for the source, select **Image**. (See Chapter 7 **Multimedia Objects**)

When your entry is complete, select **OK**. PAF will return you to the Source List. (Fig. 73) . To add the actual text from your source, first select the particular source, then select **Actual Text** in the **Source For...** window. Enter the text exactly as it is recorded in the original source document and save. When you have completed the data entry, click **Save,** then **OK**.

The **Source for...** (Fig. 77) window is displayed. Enter the information for the citation detail.

- Film/Volume/Page #. For example US Film 1045611, pg 10, line 12 or Vol. 3 p7.

- Entry Date. This is the date when the record was created, NOT the date you entered the information. (This date is often unknown)

Click **OK**. PAF now displays the **Edit Individual** window (Fig. 78).

This concludes the topic of adding a source to an individual or marriage record. We have demonstrated how to add a source to a **new individual** and how to add a **new source** to an individual. You can add an unlimited number of sources for each individual in your database, PAF will add each new source to the **Source List** for use with any individual or marriage record.

Hint: Press F1 to view **How do I** and **Tell me more about**.

Adding a Source to a Marriage Record

From the **Marriage** record, select **Source** and follow the same steps as the **Individual** record. Follow instructions found in **Adding a Source to a Individual Record**.

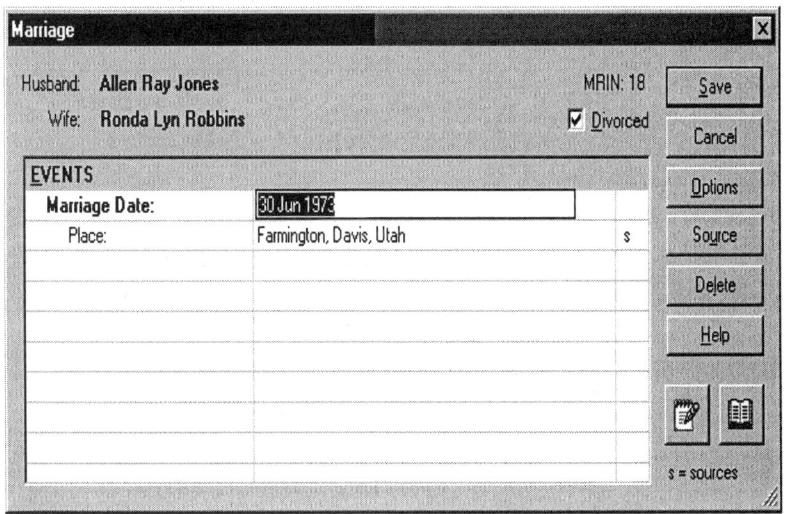

Figure 80

Deleting and Removing Sources

When you no longer need a particular source, you can delete the source from your database. This is an option that should be used with great caution, as you could accidently remove sources that are applicable to your database. (See **Merge Sources** this chapter) The best advice is to NEVER use the Delete/Remove option unless you are absolutely sure there are no records or citations attached.

If you have duplicate sources, merge rather than delete the duplicates. Deleting will not only delete the sources but all citations attached to that source as well.

From the toolbar, select **Edit** ➛ **Source List**. The **Edit Source List** window appears. Highlight the source you wish to delete, click **Delete**. A warning message will appear asking if you are sure you want to **Delete** the source. Select **Yes**.

Or:

If you want to maintain the source to use with other records, you can **Delete** the source from the individual or marriage record. Click **S**. The **Source for…** window appears. Highlight the source you wish to delete. Click **Delete**. A warning message asks if you are sure you want to remove this source. Select **Yes**.

Hint: Press F1 to view **How do I** and **Tell me more about**.

Converting sources stored in notes

If you are converting a database created in an earlier version of PAF and you used source guidelines determined by the Silicon Valley PAF Users Group or followed the directions in the PAF 2.31 manual, to enter your sources, you can choose to convert the sources you have previously entered into the notes field. As the conversion process moves through the database and encounters a source, PAF will pause and show you how the source will be converted into PAF 4.0. You are offered the opportunity to accept or reject the conversion. All your notes that are not sources will be moved into the notes file. To help you understand the process conversion employs please read the following guidelines:

- Those notes that have an exclamation point (!) as the first character will be identified as sources.
- PAF uses semicolons (;) to separate the elements of a source.
- PAF uses tags to determine what information to transfer to which fields in the source record. PAF does not convert the actual tags.
- PAF puts the title in the Source Title Field.
- PAF puts the author in the Author field.
- PAF puts the years covered in the Comments field.
- PAF puts the series, volume, and publisher information in the Publication Information field.

- PAF puts page number in the Film/Volume/Page # field in the citation detail.
- PAF adds the repository name and address to the list of repositories and adds the repository to the source record.
- PAF places text and comments to the Comments field.

Hint: You may edit the transferred data in the Source Record by using the **Edit** option on the toolbar. Use Cut, Copy, and Past to move information from field to field.

Hint: Press F1 to view **How do I** and **Tell me more about**.

The list of all entered sources and repositories can be viewed:

- From the toolbar, select **Edit** ➛ **Source List** or **Repository List**. Either option will produce a new window listing the items you requested.

A list of sources for an Individual can be viewed:

- Click the **Source** icon from the **Add** or **Edit Individual** window.

or

- Select **Sources** from the **Notes** window. If sources have been entered an (*) will be seen on the **S** button.

A list of sources for a marriage record can be viewed:

- Selecting **Sources** at the **Marriage** window.

or

- Selecting **Options** ➛ **Sources**.

or

- Select **Source**.

Repositories

Using the Repository List

The **Repository List** displays the repositories in your database and allows you to add, copy, edit, or delete. Each repository should have one record in your database. That means you enter each repository only once and link to sources as frequently as needed. From the **Edit Individual** window, select the **S** button. PAF displays the **Source for....** window, select **Edit**. PAF displays the **Edit Source** window. (Fig. 81) Select **Repository**.

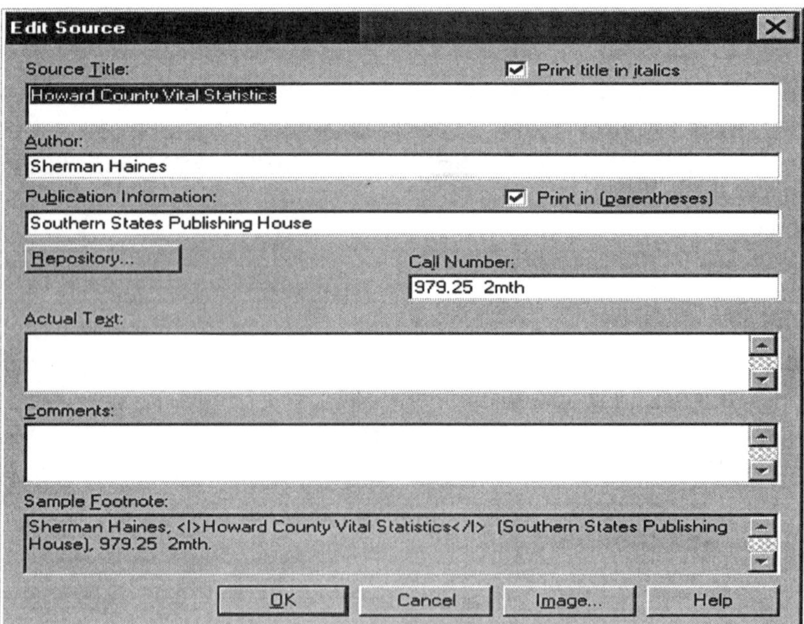

Figure 81

PAF then displays the **Select Repository** window. (Fig. 82)

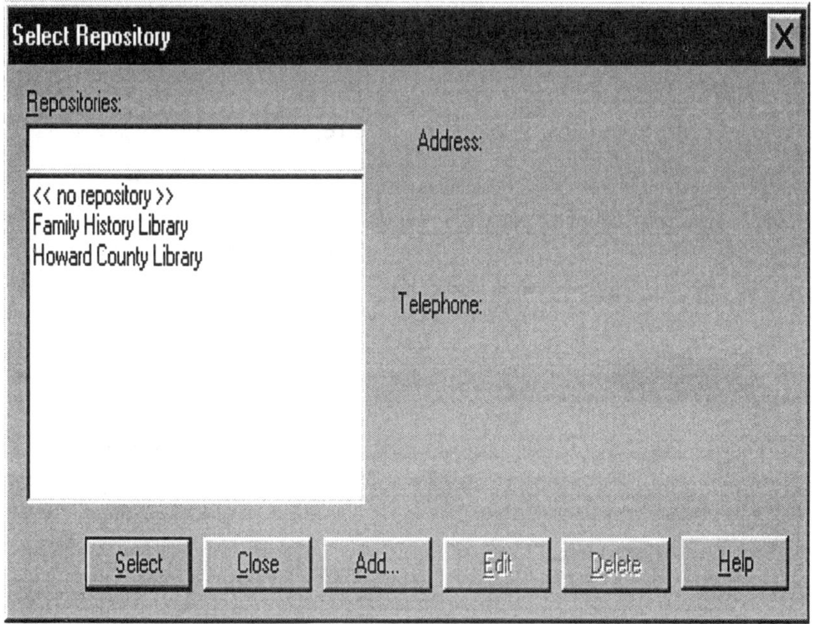

Figure 82

The five options displayed on this window are:

- Select–Click **Select** to link a repository to a source. This option is not available from the toolbar, **Edit ➛ Repository List**.
- Close–Select **Close** to return to the previous screen.
- Add–Select **Add** to add a new repository.
- Edit–Select **Edit** to edit the selected repository.
- Delete–Select **Delete** to delete the selected repository from your database.

Select **Add**. PAF displays the **Repository** window. (Fig. 83)

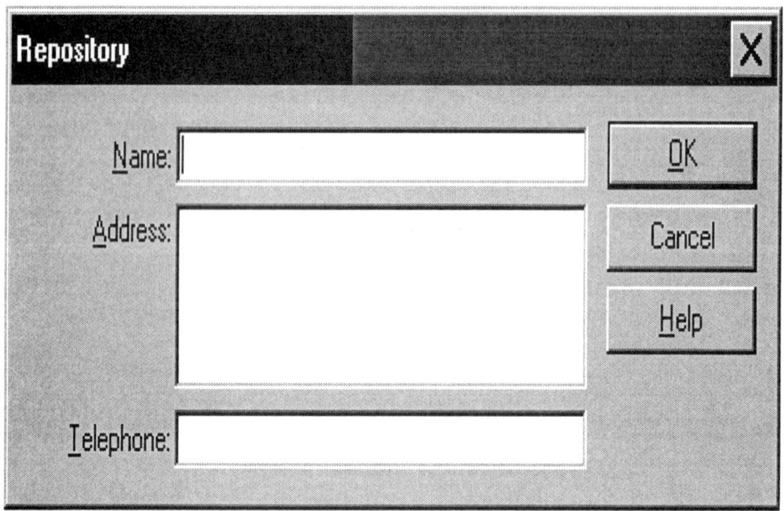

Figure 83

The fields on the **Repository** window are **Name**, **Address, Telephone**.

Adding a Repository

There are two ways you can add a repository.

1. Add a repository while you add or type a source record. (This alternative has been discussed in the sources information in preceding pages.)
   or
2. Use the Repository List.

Adding a New Repository at the Repository List

From the toolbar, select **Edit ➛ Repository List; Add**. Type the information requested for each field using the TAB key to move field to field. When finished select **OK**.

Editing Repositories

Editing can be accomplished in two ways:

1. Edit the repository while adding or editing sources.

or

2. Edit the repository from the Repository List. From the toolbar, select **Edit ➛ Repository List; Edit**. Make your changes and when finished click **OK**

Whichever alternatives you use, the changes made will be universal. The changes will appear in all records where you used the Repository.

Changing a Source's Repository

PAF allows you to change the Repository on the Source Record if, for example, the repository listed moves or closes. You can change the repository associated with a source from:

- toolbar, **Edit ➛ Repository List**.
- Change while adding or editing a source.

Hint: Remember, the change is universal and applies where ever the repository is used.

Removing a Repository

You can remove a repository from any source or from the entire database. However, if you plan on removing the repository from your database you should determine to which sources it is linked. If you remove it and then change your mind, you will have to re-enter and then re-link to all applicable sources.

Removing Repositories from Sources

When you remove a repository from a source, the repository remains in your database and can be linked to other sources. To remove a repository from a source:

- From the **Source** window (Fig. 81), select **Repository; <<no repository>>; Select**.

Removing a Repository from your Database

From the toolbar; select **Edit ➛ Repository List**

- Highlight the Repository; **Delete**.
- When the computer prompts, click **Yes**.

Merging a Duplicate Repository

As your database increases in size it is very possible that you will find duplicates. This process merges duplicate repositories as well as duplicate sources. **The merge process is automatic**. You will not be able to stop it once started. Before you begin the merge process you should review the Source List and Repository List to verify what information can be merged. This process will not eliminate duplicate source citations on the individual or marriage records. Those must be removed manually.

To begin the merge process:

1. From the toolbar; select **Tools ➛ Merge Duplicate Sources**. The next window will display how many sources and repositories were merged. There are no warnings, no prompts, NO SECOND CHANCES. Be very careful with this feature.

Using Notes

PAF 4.0 has note fields where you can enter notes for each individual or marriage in your database. Notes might include interesting circumstances surrounding an event, humorous anecdotes, journal entries–anything that brings life to your ancestor. You might want to include research notes, documenting the research you have completed and the next steps that should be taken in the research process.

Guidelines for Notes

You can enter any information you wish in any format, however, if you intend to print a book from the report option you should consider what notes you will include, how you will spell places–abbreviated or spelled out, the date format, American or European, how you will handle confidential information. These are all items that need careful thought.

PAF will automatically wrap your text so you don't have to press the ENTER key unless you are beginning a new paragraph or you are typing short lines. Do not insert blank lines unless you are using a **Tagged** and/or **Confidential** note. Notes are easy to enter; as the **Notes** window allows you to type in notes much the same as you would within a word processor. Make sure that anyone that reads your notes is able to easily understand what is being said.

Types of Notes

There are two types of notes:

- **Regular Notes** have no special formatting. They are those notes that tell stories, jokes, journal entries, etc.
- **Tagged Notes** contain specific information, begin with a specific word or a unique character. Separate a tagged note from regular notes by blank lines. (See **Tagged notes** for more detail). To make the selection of Tagged Notes easier, a **Note Selector** (See **Note Selector**) window containing a list of frequently used tags can be accessed. From the toolbar, select **Tools** ➛ **Preferences; General**.

Confidential notes can be tagged by creating a new tag, however, it is easier to type the (~) than to create a new tag and pull it from the tags list each time there is a need to mark a note.

Entering and Editing Notes

To add or edit notes about:	You can:	Notes Selector Y/N
An individual	Select **Notes** on an Individual record.	Yes
	At the **Family View** or **Pedigree View** window, highlight the individual. From the toolbar, select **Edit** ➛ **Notes**.	Yes
	or At the **Edit Individual** window, select the **Notes** icon.	Yes
	or At the **Family View** window, highlight the individual and from the toolbar, select the **Notes** icon.	Yes
	or Highlight the individual, click the right button on your mouse, and select **Notes**.	Yes

A marriage	Click the **Notes** button on a marriage record.	No
	or	
	At the **Family View** window, highlight the marriage box; from the toolbar, select **Edit** ➤ **Notes.**	No
	or	
	At the **Family View** window, highlight the individual and on the toolbar, select the **Notes** icon.	No
	or	
	At the **Family View** window, highlight the marriage information, right-click your mouse and select **Notes**.	No

Copying notes

On the Notes screen the Edit menu lists several features that you can use to copy notes from one record to another. From the toolbar, select **Edit ➛ Notes**. PAF will display **Notes Selector for....** Select **Open**. PAF will display **Notes for....** (Fig. 84)

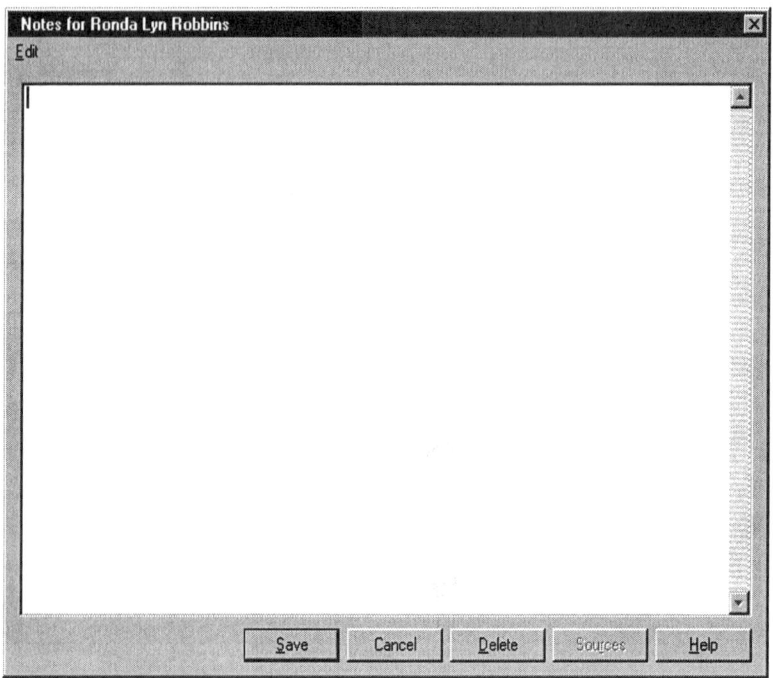

Figure 84

Select **Edit** in the upper left corner; a pull-down list will offer you the following options:

- **Cut, Copy, and Paste**. If you want to copy some of the notes from one record to another, use these features to accomplish this task with ease. To access this option you must highlight the notes you want to cut, copy, or paste. Once highlighted, select **Edit** and make your choice of options.

- **Ditto**. If you want to copy all of your notes, use the ditto options. You can **ditto** notes from the following records:

- Individual's father
- Individual's mother.
- Individual's next oldest sibling.
- Primary individual (that person in the Primary position)
- Last record in which you added or edited notes.

Hint: Press F1 to view **How do I** and **Tell me more about**.

Deleting Notes

To delete all notes for an individual or marriage, select **Delete** at the **Edit** window. A **Warning** window will appear asking if you want to delete all notes for this individual or marriage. Select **OK** or **Cancel**. To avoid this warning, simply highlight the text and select **Delete** on your keyboard.

You can delete a particular note by highlighting that portion you want to remove select **Edit** ➛ **Cut**. The note is gone. It has been copied to a bulletin board. This means the next time you hit **Paste** that particular note will paste unless you copy or cut another note.

You can delete a group of **Tagged** notes at the **Notes Selector** window. Highlight the **Tag** you wish to remove and select **Remove**.

Using Note Selector

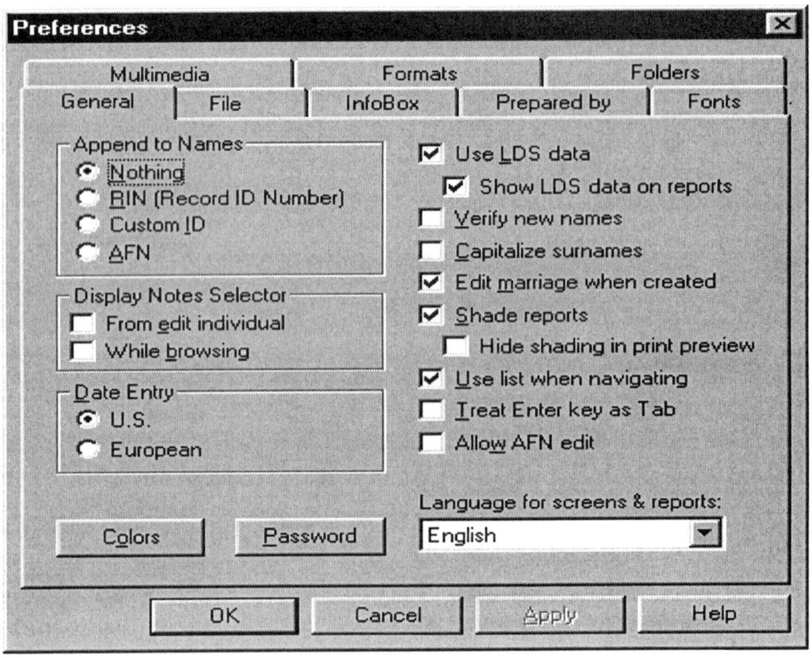

Figure 85

If you use **Tagged Notes**, you may want to use the **Note Selector**. The **Note Selector** allows you to choose whether you want to work with all of your notes at once or work with notes with a particular tag. You can use the **Notes Selector** from the **Edit Individual** window and/or the **Family View** or **Pedigree View** windows. The option to view from these windows can be turned on/off in the Preferences window.

From the toolbar, select **Tools → Preferences; General; Display Notes Selector**. (Fig. 85) The options are :

- **From edit individual**

or

- **While Browsing**.

Hint: You can't use the **Notes Selector** with notes on a Marriage record.

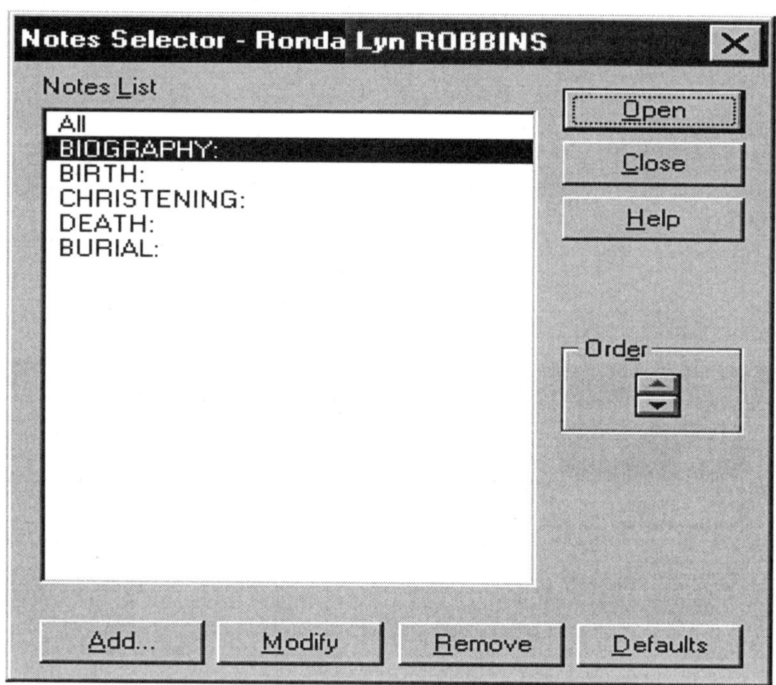

Figure 86

You can use the Notes Selector to:

- Display notes (All notes or those with a particular tag).
  (At the **Notes Selector** window, (Fig. 86) highlight the tag you want to view, select **Open***)*
  or
- Delete Notes (All notes or those with a particular tag).
  From the Notes Selector window, highlight the tag you want to view; select **Open** ➛ **Delete**. (Fig. 86) This will delete all the notes displayed.

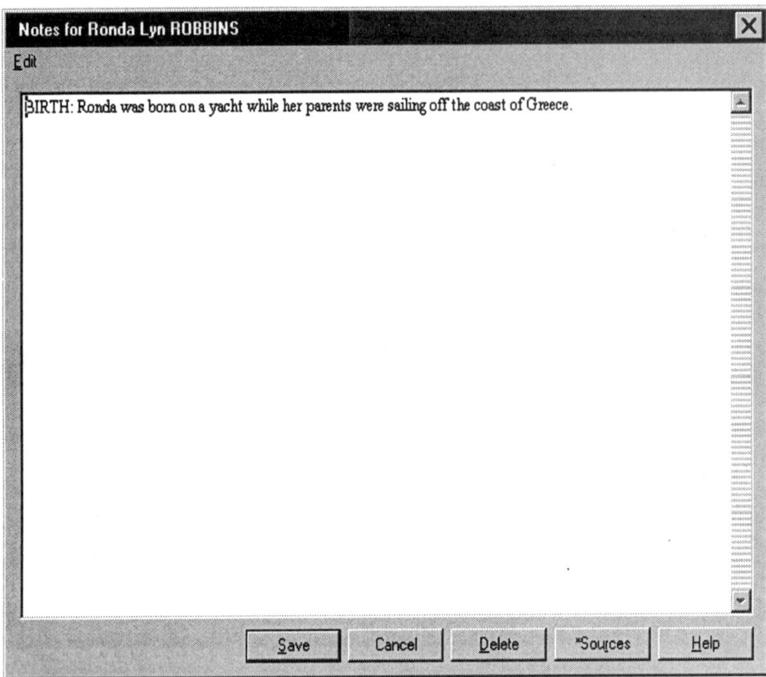

Figure 87

You can add, modify, or remove tags from the **Note Selector** by selecting the appropriate button. You can also change the order of tags by using the up/down arrows.

Tags that have been added to the notes, and are not on the default list, will automatically appear on the list of tags displayed in grey. You can elect to remove the added tags by selecting the **Default** button. You would not usually want to remove the added tags.

An (*) in front of a Tag indicates that there are notes in the record using that tag.

Hint: If you want to print tagged notes when the print option, **Marked (!) only** is selected, you will need to put the exclamation point (!) in front of your tag. (For example, !Birth) (See Chapter 12; **Printing Charts, Reports and Lists**).

Hint: Press F1 to view **How do I** and **Tell me more about**.

Converting Notes

If you have been using PAF 3.0 or higher you need not convert your files. However, if you have PAF 2.0-2.31 you will need to convert your databases. To convert your database, find the INDIV2.DAT file (See Appendix E for a more detailed description) and open it into PAF 4.0 The **PAF 2.x File Conversion** screen has three options that allow you to customize the conversion process. One of those options applies to **Notes**.

OPTION	DESCRIPTION
Wrap note lines into paragraphs	Before version 3.0, the notes in PAF did not wrap. This meant that you had to press ENTER after each line. You pressed ENTER twice to separate paragraphs. Select this option to remove the line breaks within notes. The conversion process will maintain the double line breaks between paragraphs. If you do not select this option, your notes will print only about two-thirds of the way across a page.

Chapter 7

Multimedia Collections

This chapter will explain what multimedia objects are available in PAF 4.0 and how you can use them to enhance your genealogical output. You will learn how to organize your objects to create presentations for your family that will educate and entertain while bringing your ancestors to life. You will learn how to attach photos, documents, video clips and audio clips to your family history database. From these items, you will be able to compile an interactive scrapbook for any individual, choreograph a slide show including background audio–using narration or music–and print the objects in your reports.

When adding a multimedia object keep the following in mind:

- If you add a multimedia image to a source, it will appear every time you use that particular source.

- If you add a multimedia image to the citation detail, it appears only with the citation you attached it to.

- You can add a multimedia object to an individual record and to source records; you **cannot** add a multimedia image to a marriage record.

PAF does not store the multimedia files (photos, sounds, etc.) in the database. It stores only the path where the object is stored. That fact has the following implications:

- When doing a backup copy of your database, only the links to the multimedia objects will be saved. You must back up your multimedia objects separately.

- Use Global Search and Replace in the **Tools** menu to change the references to all of your multimedia files at once. This is useful if you have renamed a multimedia file, you want to use a different file, or if you have moved your multimedia files to a new folder.

- You should store your multimedia objects on your hard drive, not on a floppy disk. Because your objects are not stored in PAF, the software must go find the objects; if they are on floppy disks, you could be changing disks **often** when showing your scrapbooks, slide shows and when printing reports. Another reason to use your hard drive: when using a digital camera, the pictures on the disks are stored with generic names. This means that different photos on different disks could wind up with the same name. The photos should be given unique names and copied to the hard drive. If this procedure isn't used, PAF could end up using the wrong photo.

Acceptable Multimedia Formats

MEDIA TYPE	DESCRIPTION	EXTENSION
Photo	BMP Compuserve PNG Encapsulated PostScript (EPS) JPEG PCX Photo CD (Kodak) Tagged Image File Format (TIFF) Windows Metafile WordPerfect graphics Icons and cursors DICOM Photoshop 3.0 Truvision TARGA SUN Raster Format Macintosh formats LEAD TIFF CCITT and other fax formats	bmp png eps jpg, jff, jtf pcx.dcx pcd, fpx tif* wmf, emf wpg** ioc, cur dic psd tga ras pict, mad, img, msp cmp
Sound	Wave MIDI	wav mid, rmi
Video	Audio/Video	avi

* Several of these photo formats have many sub-types that may not be supported. If PAF is unable to read the file, a **Cannot Read Image File** message displays. Many TIFF, and most GIF, images use LSW compression. This is a proprietary compression that is losing acceptance and may not be supported.

** There are two types of WordPerfect graphic; raster and vector. PAF accepts only raster images, which is another name for bitmaps. However, vector images are more common.

Setting Multimedia Preferences

Before entering multimedia objects into your computer you should set the multimedia preferences. From the toolbar, select **Tools ➛ Preferences ➛ Multimedia**.

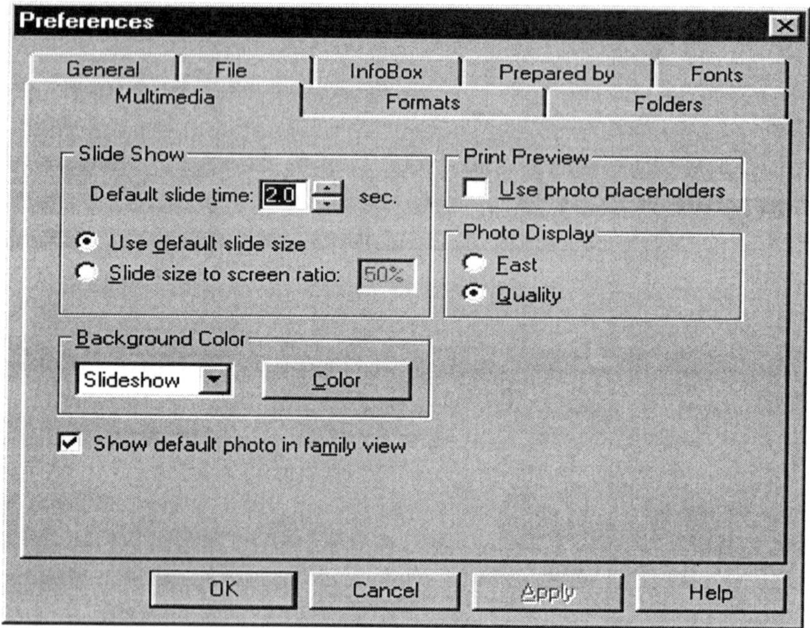

Figure 88

While most multimedia features deal with a specific object, there are a few common options:

OPTION	DESCRIPTION
Slide show	Set the **Default slide time** to indicate how long each photo or object should stay on the screen during your slide show. There are a few components that can influence this setting: • As mentioned, the **Default slide time** determines how long each slide will be displayed. If your next slide takes longer to load than the current slide is meant to show, the current slide will remain on the screen until the next slide is loaded and displayed. • Select **Default slide size** to use the default size. • Select **Slide size to screen ratio** to show and standardize each slide at a certain percentage of the screen size.
Background Color	• The background has colors for two different scenarios while displaying your slides. Use the pull-down menu to select either **Slide Show** or **Scrapbook.** Select **Color** to add the background color for your pictures in the presentation. The default background is black for the slide show and white for the scrapbook.

Print Preview	Select **Use Photo Placeholder** to hide the actual photos or documents while in print preview. This will increase the speed for your preview, as PAF doesn't have to find and load the multimedia objects from your disk. You will see a gray **placeholder** that shows the placement and size of the photo or document.
Photo Display	Any time you change a photo from the default size you will need to **scale** it. This takes additional time. PAF provides you two choices; • Select **Fast** for speed rather than quality. • Select **Quality** if speed isn't a concern.
Show default photo in Family	Select this option to see the default photo of the primary person on the **Family View** window.

Adding multimedia to individuals and sources

1. At the **Family View** (Fig. 89) or **Pedigree View**" window there are four ways to add multimedia. First, highlight the individual that you want to add a multimedia object to, then:

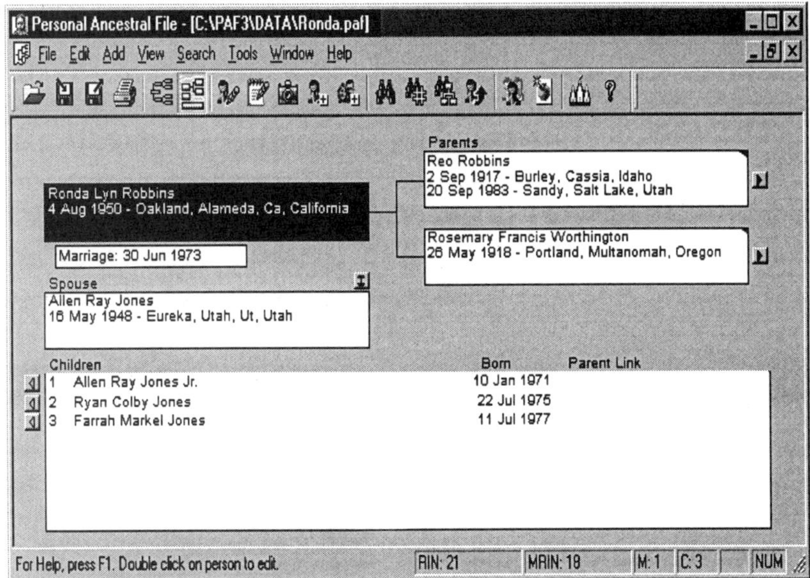

Figure 89

- Right-click your mouse and select **Multimedia**.
  or
- From the toolbar, select **Edit ➛ Multimedia**.
  or
- From the toolbar, select the **Multimedia** icon
  or
- Press CTRL+M.

Figure 90

2. At the Individual window, use one of these options:

- From the toolbar, select the **Multimedia** icon.
  or
- Select the **Options** ➛ **Multimedia**.
  or
- Press CTRL+M.

At the new window **Multimedia Collection…**, select **Add**.

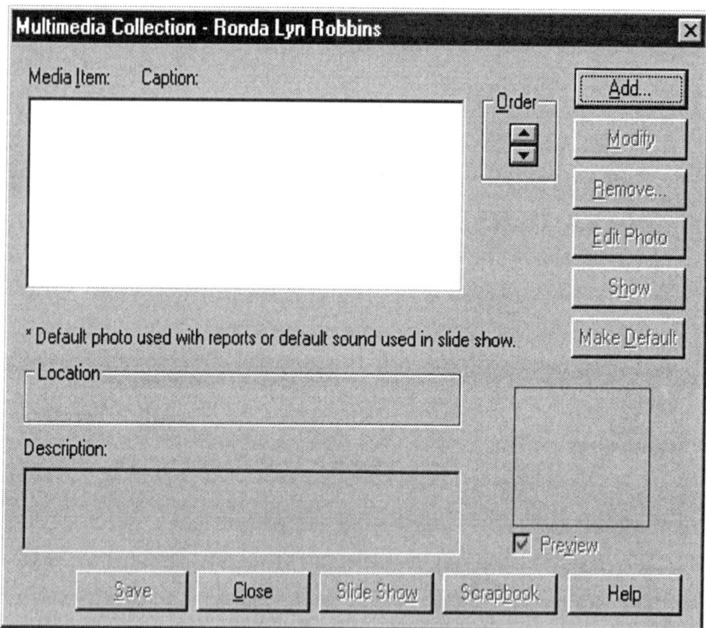

Figure 91

The **Add Multimedia Object for...** window appears.

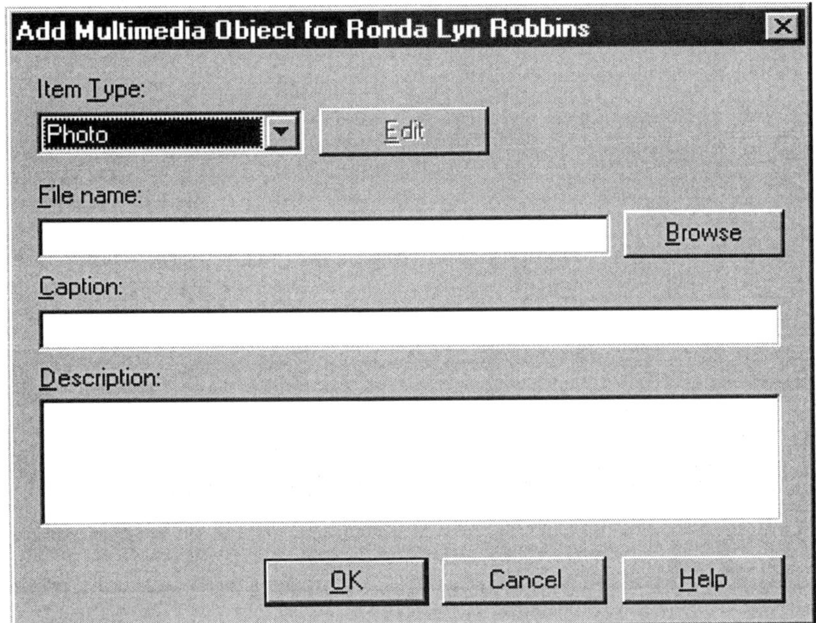

Figure 92

- Select the arrow to the right of the **Item Type** field to choose the type of file you are attaching. You can add a photo, a video clip or audio clip.

- Type in the **File name**. You can select the **Browse** button if your aren't sure of the name. The **Browse** option will allow you to use the standard Windows file box to change drives and directories to locate you file. If you are looking for a photo, select the **Preview** box, this will allow you to see a thumbnail of the currently selected image in your directory.

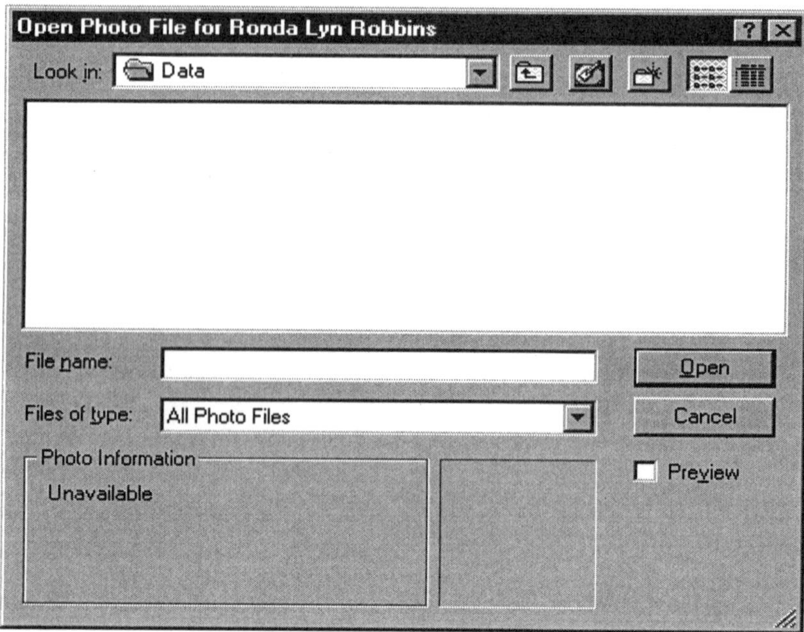

Figure 93

By default, the entire path of the File will be placed in the **Filename** field by the **Browse** option. But if you are putting together a database for sharing with family members, you may want to change these to relative (that is to say, subdirectories) file names. For example, let's say you have your database in a directory call *C:\PAF\data*. You decide to put all media objects in *c:fam_hist\scrapbk*, for consistency with what you are compiling, and could then refer to all objects as *scrapbk\media.ext*, rather than *c:\paf\data\scrapbk\media.ext*. PAF will look for a subdirectory under the current database directory for *media.ext*, and as a result, you can pass this database to relatives who want or need to use a different database location on their computer. As long as their media subdirectory is named the same as yours, and you use relative paths, you will be able to send them your database and media files, and they will be able to enjoy the documentation and presentations you have put together, using their own copy of PAF.

- Add your **Caption** and **Description**. The caption will be displayed in scrapbooks and in the Media Collection window. This identifies who is in the photo, e.g. Caption - Ronda Robbins. The description can contain any information, such as the date the photo was taken, who was present or participated in the sound clip, etc. Be sure to use something that can be understood by anyone viewing this photo or video clip and listening to the audio clip.

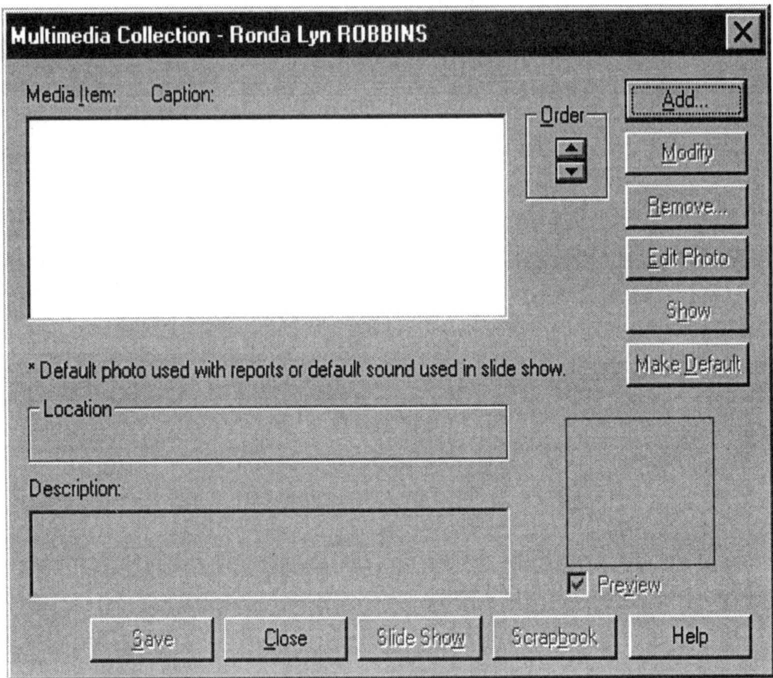

Figure 94

After you have added multimedia items to your file, the **Multimedia Collection** window will have a list of all the media objects you added. From this list, you can assemble the photos, scanned documents, audio and video clips. Other options include:

- assembling a scrapbook for an individual;
- choreographing a slide show including audio clips (narrative or music).

Terms You Should Know

Media item box	The list box, in the upper left corner, allows you to scroll through all media items you have attached to the individual. As you scroll down the list, if you have checked the **Preview** box, each time you highlight a photo the preview box will show the thumbnail of the photo.
Location box	The box shows you the full path where the media item is located. As you scroll through the media item list, the location will change simultaneously.
Description box	This box shows the description of each item as you scroll through the media items.
Order	The up/down arrows to the right of the **Media Item** list allow you to change the order of the items, which determines the order of items in the scrapbook and/or slide show.
Add	Select **Add** to add another media item to the individual or source.
Modify	Select **Modify** to change the item type, path and file name, caption, or description. (See **Modify Item Screen** below)
Remove	Select **Remove** to remove the highlighted item from an individual or source. **This does not delete the item from your database.**
Edit photo	Select **Edit Photo** to crop the photo or to include or remove the photo from the scrapbook and/or slide show.

Make default/clear default	Select this button to set the selected photo as a default photo for the individual or source record. This photo will show on the **Family View** window and print on reports.
Preview	Select **Preview** to display the object on the **Multimedia Collection** window.
Save	Select **Save** to save the Multimedia Collection as it appears and return to the previous screen.
Close	Select **Close** to return to the previous screen without saving your changes.
Slide show	Select **Slide Show** to view the slide show you have created.
Scrapbook	Select **Scrapbook** to view the scrapbook you have created.

Modify Multimedia Item

To modify a multimedia item, follow steps 1 and 2 of **Add a Multimedia Item**. Then:

3. Select **Modify.**
4. Make changes to your item and click **OK**.

Adding Multimedia to Source Description While Adding or Editing a Source from the Multimedia Collection Window

From the **Multimedia Collection** .... window, select **Image** ➛ **Attach**.

- Click on the arrow to the right of the **Item Type** field to choose the type of file you are attaching. You can add a photo, a video clip, or audio clip.

- Type in the **File name**. You can select the **Browse** button if your aren't sure of the name. The **Browse** option will allow you to use the standard Windows file box to change drives and directories to locate you file. If you are looking for a photo, click **Preview** box, this will allow you to see a thumbnail of the currently selected image in your directory. By default, the entire path of the File will be placed in the **Filename** field by the **Browse** option. But if you are putting together a database for sharing with family members, you may want to change these to relative (that is to say, subdirectories) file names. For example, let's say you have your database in a directory call *C:\PAF\data*. You decide to put all media objects in *C:\fam_hist\scrapbk*, for consistency with what you are compiling, and could then refer to all objects as *scrapbk\media.ext*, rather than *C:\paf\data\scrapbk\media.ext*. PAF will look for a subdirectory under the current database directory for *media.ext*, and as a result, you can pass this database to relatives who want or need to use a different database location on their computer. As long as their media subdirectory is named the same as yours, and you use relative paths, you will be able to send them your database and media files, and they will be able to enjoy the documentation and presentations you have put together, using their own copy of PAF.

- Add your **Caption** and **Description**. The caption will be displayed in scrapbooks and in the Media Collection window. This identifies who is in the photo, e.g. Caption - Ronda Lyn Robbins. The description can contain any information, such as the date the photo was taken, who was present or participated in the sound clip, etc. Be sure to use something that can be understood by anyone viewing this photo or video clip and listening to the audio clip.

- When finished, click **OK**.

- To return to the **Source** window, select **Close**. When you have successfully added a multimedia file to a source, the **Image** button will display an (*).

NOTE: EVER TIME YOU USE THIS SOURCE, THE MULTIMEDIA ITEM WILL BE INCLUDED.

Adding Multimedia to Source Description While Adding or Editing a Source from the Source Window

From the **Source** window, select **Image** ➛ **Attach**.

- Click on the arrow to the right of the **Item Type** to choose the type of file you are attaching. You can add a photo, a video clip or audio clip.

- Type in the **File name**. Again, you can select the **Browse** button if your aren't sure of the name. [Remember: The **Browse** option will allow you to use the standard Windows file box to change drives and directories to locate you file. If you are looking for a photo, click the **Preview** box, this will allow you to see a thumbnail of the currently selected image in your directory. By default, the entire path of the File will be placed in the **Filename** field by the **Browse** option. But if you are putting together a database for sharing with family members, you may want to change these to relative (recognizable) file names.]

- Add your **Caption** and **Description**, The caption will be displayed in scrapbooks and in the Media Collection window. This identifies who is in the photo, e.g. Caption - Ronda Lyn Robbins. The description can contain any information, such as the date the photo was taken, who was present or participated in the sound clip, etc. Be sure to use something that can be understood by anyone viewing this photo or video clip and listening to the audio clip.

- When finished, click **OK**.

- To return to the **Source** window, select **Close**. When you have successfully added a multimedia file to a source, the **Image** button will display an (*).

NOTE: EVER TIME YOU USE THIS SOURCE, THE MULTIMEDIA ITEM WILL BE INCLUDED.

Add Multimedia to Citation Detail

From the **Individual** or **Marriage** record:

1. Locate the citation detail to which you want to add a multimedia object.
2. Select **Image ➛ Attach**.
3. Select the **Item Type**
4. Select the **File**.
5. Enter a **Caption** or **Description**.
6. Click **OK**.

NOTE: WHEN A MULTIMEDIA ITEM HAS BEEN ADDED TO THE CITATION DETAIL, AN (*) WILL APPEAR ON THE IMAGE BUTTON.

Using Edit Photo

To edit a photo, select **Edit Photo** at the **Multimedia Collection** window.

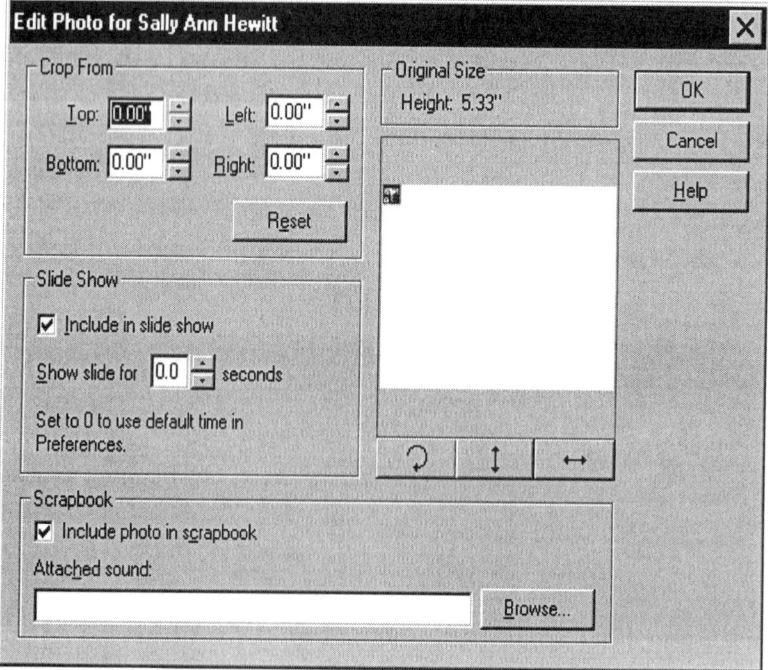

Figure 95

NOTE: A PHOTO THAT IS EDITED IS CHANGED ONLY IN PAF, NOT ON YOUR DISK. USE THE FOLLOWING GUIDELINES TO EDIT YOUR PHOTO.

SCREEN ITEM	DESCRIPTION
Top, Bottom, Left, Right	Use these options to crop the photograph. **Hint:** The fastest method to crop a photo is use your mouse. Click the mouse where you want the upper left corner of the photo to be. While holding the mouse button down, drag the mouse to where you want place the lower right corner of the photo. Release the mouse. To make small changes use the items in the **Crop From** box. To return the photo to its original size, select **Reset**.
Include in Slide Show	Select this option include this photo in the slide show.
Show slide for	Determine how many seconds you want to display your photo and enter that number in this box. Use 0 to default to the **Preferences** time setting.
Include photo in scrapbook	Select to include this photo in your slide show.
Attached sound	If you want to add sound to this photo, type the path and file name. If you don't know this information select **Browse** to find the file.
↺	Select this button to rotate the photo 90° to the left.

Select this button to flip the photo vertically.

Select this button to flip the photo horizontally.

OK — Click **OK** to save the photo as it appears on the screen.

Cancel — Select **Cancel** if you don't want to save your changes.

Creating a Scrapbook

From the **Media Collection**... window select **Scrapbook**. The **Scrapbook for...** window will appear. (Fig. 96) The window will display six items at a time, and interact with the screen using the audio buttons, if you have attached audio selections. You can scroll through descriptions using the up and down arrows and through the scrapbook collection using the right and left arrow at the bottom of the window.

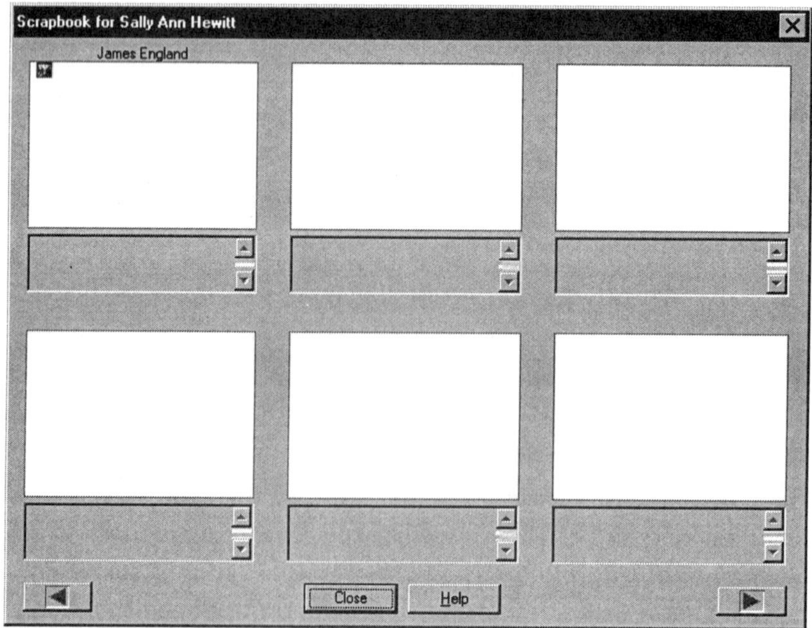

Figure 96

Selecting Scrapbook Options

When you have completed entry of your photos or images, you are ready to select your printing options. From the toolbar, select **File ➤ Print Reports**. The **Reports and Charts** window appears.

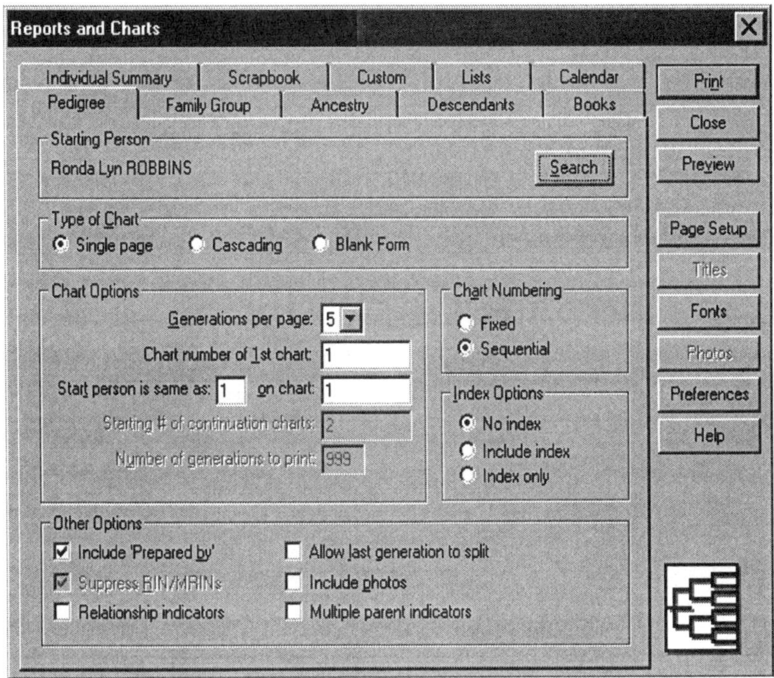

Figure 97

Select **Scrapbook** and make your print choices using the following guidelines.

OPTION	DESCRIPTION
Include Caption	Select **Include Caption** to include the information that you typed for the photo. You can place the caption below or above the photo.

Include Filename	Select **Include Filename** to include the name of the file and the path where it is stored.
Include Description	Select **Include description** to include the description you previously typed for the description of the photo.
Suppress RINs	Select **Suppress RINS** if you don't want RINs to print.
Print boxes	Select **Print Boxes** if you want each photo to be printed in a box. Select **Box Styles** to determine how the box will look.
Items per Page	You determine the number of items on each page. The more items on a page the smaller the image. Type in the number or use the arrow keys to display the number you want.
Use Photo Size	Select **Exact Size** to print the size you specify or Select **Minimum Size** to print the photo as large as possible, staying within the preset margins.

Printing Scrapbook Pages

The Scrapbook report will allow you to print out all or part of the photos and/or scanned documents that have been scanned for your multimedia collection. You may choose which items to print. Go to the **Edit Photo** (Fig. 95) window, under the heading **Scrapbook** select this box to print the image.

NOTE: IF YOU EXCLUDE AN IMAGE FROM PRINTING ON A REPORT, YOU HAVE EXCLUDED THAT IMAGE FROM APPEARING IN THE **ON-SCREEN** SCRAPBOOK. UTILIZE THE **USE LIST** TO DETERMINE WHETHER THE REPORT SHOULD INCLUDE ONE INDIVIDUAL OR A LIST OF INDIVIDUALS.

Assemble a Slide Show

You can create a professional quality slide show for private viewing, for a large gathering as a family reunion or for other types of presentations, by attaching the appropriate projection and sound equipment to your computer.

Your first step is gathering your photos as you did for the **Scrapbook**. You can scan them yourself, or use the services of any photo finishing service to place your photos on a floppy disk or CD-ROM.

Next, use the same procedure you did with **Scrapbook** to attach your photos. Use the **Order** arrows to place your images in the correct chronological order.

If you intend to use a background audio, you can choose a selection that is already properly digitized, or you can record it yourself. Most newer computers come with sound cards and the software needed to record. You may have to buy a microphone and study the users manual to learn to use the sound system on your computer.

To view your slide show, use one of the following options.

From the **Individual** window:

- Select the **Multimedia** button.
  or
- Select **Options** ➛ **Multimedia**.
  or
- Press ALT+M.

From the **Family View** or **Pedigree View** window:

- From the toolbar, select **Edit** ➛ **Multimedia**.
  or
- From the toolbar, select the **Camera** icon (**Multimedia photos, sound video button**.)
  or
- Press CTRL+M

You might find, as you watch your slide show, that some photos or images need to stay on the screen for a longer period of time, you might want to change the size of the images, or you might decide that the image doesn't work for your slide show. Use the **Multimedia Collection** window to change colors, time of display, sizes, etc.

With your photos scanned in, attached, sized, in chronological order, and your background music attached, you are now ready to test run your slide show. Select the desired audio and set as default, thus creating a sound track for your show. With a few test runs, you should be able to have a polished slide show ready to present.

NOTE: IF YOU ARE GOING TO SHARE THIS SLIDE SHOW WITH ANOTHER INDIVIDUAL, YOU WILL NEED TO EXPORT OR SAVE THE MULTIMEDIA IN ADDITION TO YOUR DATABASE.

Chapter 8

Searching and Navigating

PAF 4.0 provides unsurpassed tools for searching and locating individuals in your database and for navigating through your family tree. You can quickly and easily locate any individual using a RIN, name, relationship or by using a more sophisticated complex filtering system. (See Chapter 9 **Advanced Focus/Filter**)

Searching for a Record

PAF provides five ways to find any individual. You can use any of the following to narrow your search.

- RIN
- MRIN
- Individual List
- Marriage List
- Descendancy List

You can access the **Find Individual** window from almost anywhere in PAF. From the **Family View** or **Pedigree View** window:

- From the toolbar click **Search**

  or
- Select the Search icon

  Figure 98

  or
- Press CTRL+F

On the top left corner of the **Find Individual** (Fig. 99) window, a text field and a scrollable list box are displayed. To sort the individuals within the scrollable list box, Press **Sort**, then choose **RIN** or **Alphabetic**.

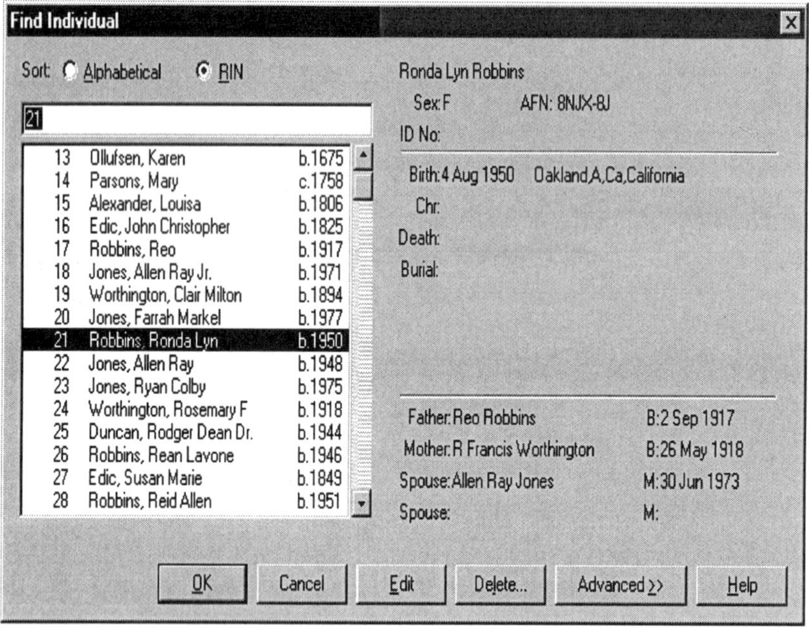

Figure 99

In the text field, type the surname of the individual for whom you are searching, or scroll through the list until you locate the individual you are looking for.

Clicking the **Advanced** button adds an advanced/focus filtering function. The **Advanced** button is a toggle switch. You click to add the filter and click to remove the filter. Select **Clear** in the Field and Relationship filters to ensure that Advanced filtering does not appear. (See Chapter 9 **Advanced Focus/Filtering**)

To Find an Individual Using the Marriage List

From the toolbar, select **Search** ➛ **Marriage**. A new window **Find Marriage** appears. Scroll through the list to locate the individual. Highlight the couple and double click, this will take you to the **Family View** and display the couple you highlighted putting the husband in Primary position.

To Find an Individual Using the Descendancy List

You can search for any individual by navigating through the database using the Descendancy List. From the **Family View** or **Pedigree View** window:

- Press CTRL+D
  or
- Click the **Descendancy List** Button 

  Figure 100

  or
- From the toolbar, select **Search** ➛ **Descendancy List**

Hint: This will display three generations for the selected individual. You can use the **Descendancy List** to:

- Move a person to the primary position.
- View a person's descendants.

When (<) appears next to an individual's name, it means that the individual has descendants. Click on the individual to view them in the list. Click once on an individual to move that person to Primary position and display his or her three generations. Double click to select and subsequently display the individual as Primary person at the **Family View** window.

Navigating your databases

PAF provides three methods to navigate through your database:

1. **Family View** window. Use this to view an individual, his/her parents, spouse and children. The **Family View** window displays event dates, places, ordinances, and links for an individual. **Family View** provides about the same navigational capacity as the **Descendancy List**, but provides more detail on the Primary Person. This chart explains how to use the buttons and the keyboard for navigation:

BUTTON OR KEY	DESCRIPTION
	1. Select this button to move the father or mother to primary position. 2. When a child is selected, press the left arrow to move the child to the primary position. 3. When the primary person, marriage information, or spouse is selected, press the left arrow to select the first child. **Hint:** When the arrow is darkened, it means that the father/mother are linked to parents. Likewise, when light there is no link.

1. Select this button to move a child to primary position.
2. When the primary person, spouse or marriage information is highlighted, press the right arrow to highlight the father.
3. When the father or mother is selected, press the right arrow to move the parent to the primary position.

Hint: When the arrow is darkened the child is linked to a spouse and child(ren). When light there is no link.

Select this button to move the spouse to the primary position.

F	Press **(F)** to move the father to the primary position.
M	Press **(M)** to move the mother to the primary position.
S	Press(**S)** to move the spouse to the primary position.
C	Press **(C)** to move the child to the primary position.
Home	Press **Home** to select the primary person.
End	Press **End** to select the last child.
Page Up	When a child is selected, press **Page Up** to select the first child.
Page Down	When a child is selected, press **Page Down** to select the last child.

Hint: To move a specific individual to Primary position, you can also click the right mouse button on the individual, click Primary; or press the CTRL key and double-click on an individual.

2. **Pedigree View** window. This window displays up to five generations of an individual's ancestry, but displays less information for an individual than in the **Family View**. The **Pedigree View** window provides an expanded display of your database. You can use it to quickly move through long ancestral lines. This tool is probably the best tool for quickly locating a direct ancestor. This chart explains how to use buttons and the keyboard to navigate the Pedigree.

BUTTON OR KEY	**DESCRIPTION**
	This button appears when a person in the fifth generation is linked to parents. Click to see the next generation of that line.
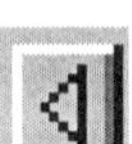	This button appears when a person in the first generation is linked to children. Click to move a child to the Primary position. **Hint:** To move a specific child to the Primary position, you can either open the InfoBox and click on the child or go to the **Family View**, select that child, and then return to the **Pedigree View**.
Arrow Keys	Press the arrow keys to select different individuals.
Page Up	Press this to move through the **paternal** line.
Page Down	Press this to move through the **maternal** line.

F	Press **(F)** to select the father.
M	Press **(M)** to select the mother.
C	Press **(C)** to select the child.
Home	Press **Home** to select the primary person.
End	Press **End** to select the last individual (the one on the lower right corner).

Hint: To move a specific individual to Primary position, you can also right-click on the individual, click Primary; or press the CTRL key and double-click on an individual.

3. **Descendancy List**. Use this list to find siblings and cousins of any individual. The **Descendancy List** is the best of these options for moving onto side branches of your tree. Each time you Click on an individual in the list, that person becomes the new Primary Person. For example, you are trying to locate a cousin, use this list, click on the parent, then on the sibling of your parent. A list of cousins in that family are now displayed and you can select the cousin of choice.

Chapter 9

Advanced Focus/Filter

PAF 4.0 will search for a group of records that contain similar information or that are linked to relationships. In previous versions of PAF this feature was known as a focus list.

In the **Advanced Focus/Filter** feature, you will use two type of filters:

1. **Relationship Filters** allow you to create a new database with only the individuals, families, descendancy lines or ancestors based on their relationship to a specific individual. You can use each relationship filter more than once and combine them in any way you want. You can also combine selecting and deselecting to fine-tune your list. For example, select everyone in your file and then deselecting a particular person's ancestors or descendants.

2. **Field Filters** allow you to refine the list of selected individuals. With a field filter, you can limit the list to include only those with similar information in particular fields in the individual record, marriage record, notes or sources. PAF searches for records that contain the information you specified in field filters in the order in which they appear on the **Current Filter** list. If you create a particularly complex filter, you can save it for use later.

Hint: You can edit individual records from the **Advanced Focus/Filter** feature.

This means you can use field to filters to find incorrectly spelled names and places. You **cannot** edit marriage records using the **Advanced Focus/Filter** option. You then combine these filters in any number of ways to meet your criteria. A selected individual will be indicated with (»). The total number of individuals, selected with each type of filter appears at the bottom of your screen.

Access the Advanced Focus/Filter Option

- From the toolbar; select **Search** ➛ **Advanced Focus/Filter**
  or
- From the toolbar, click

Figure 106

PAF displays the **Find Individual** window. (Fig. 107)

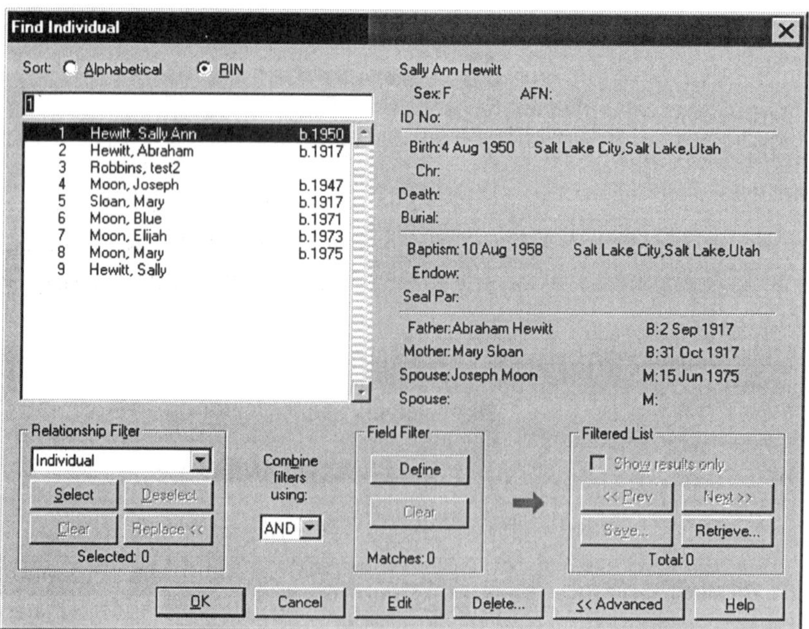

Figure 107

Hint: You can access the **Advanced Focus/Filter** feature when exporting and printing information. From these screens, click **Select**. The Advanced button is not present because it isn't needed.

Using Relationship Filters

1. From the Toolbar, select **Search** ➛ **Advanced Focus/Filter**. (Fig. 107)
2. Select the **Relationship Filter** you want to use.
3. Click **Select**. A (») will appear next to each name you select.
4. Repeat steps 1 and 2 until you have selected all the individuals you want to use.
5. If you want field filters, select AND, OR, or NOT to combine the filters. (See **Using AND, OR, or NOT** below)
6. Define the **Field Filters** you want to use. (See Fig. 107)
7. When you have finished, click **OK**

Choosing a Relationship Filter

Using **Relationship Filters** is the simplest way to select individuals you wish to export. PAF has nine **Relationship Filters**. You can use them as many times as needed and in any combination you desire. The **Relationship Filters** available are:

RELATIONSHIP FILTER	USE THIS FILTER TO SELECT:
Individual	Only the highlighted Individual.
Couple	The highlighted Individual and spouse. If the Individual is linked to more than one spouse, you can select which to include.

Family	The highlighted Individual, spouse and children, as well as his/her parents and siblings. If the Individual is linked to more than one family, you can select which to include.
All	All individuals in the list. **HINT:** This filter is useful if you want to select everyone in your file **except** for a certain line or family. Select everyone and then use another filter to deselect the ones you don't want.
All Related	The highlighted Individual and all ancestors and descendants. This is usually everyone in the file. **HINT:** Use this option to identify the Individuals not linked to any other individual in the file.
Ancestors	The highlighted Individual and ancestors. You select the number of generations to include and whether to include his/her spouses. From the **Find Individual** window select **Ancestor**. Select one of three options:

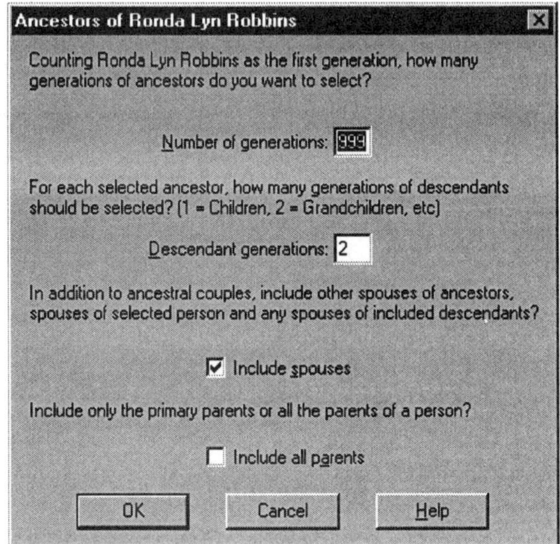

Figure 108

1. Number of generations of ancestors, from 1-999, where 1 will select only the Individual.
2. Number of generations of descendants for each selected ancestor. Choose 0 to select only direct line ancestors, 1 to include their children, etc.
3. Which spouse to include in addition to direct line spouses: other spouses of ancestors, spouses of a selected person, all spouses of descendants.

All Ancestors Related	The highlighted Individual and everyone related to the Individuals ancestors. This **does not** include any of the Individual's children, his/her spouse or the spouse's ancestors. This option will select an entire branch of your family tree. **HINT:** If two or more lines have intermarried, this filter will give you the same results as **All Related**. In this case, you might need to temporarily unlink one or more marriages, then perform the desired operations on the group and relink the marriages.
Descendants	The highlighted Individual and descendants. You decide how many generations to include and whether to include spouses.
All Descendants Related	The highlighted Individual, all descendants of the Individual, and everyone related to any of the descendants. You will get spouse, siblings, ancestors, etc. **HINT:** If two or more have intermarried. This filter will give you the same results as **All Related**.

Using Field Filters

In the **Field Filtering** window, you will define a set of criteria for filtering based on data in the individuals' records. There are 65 fields and data types on the list, including # of Children, # of spouses, End of Line (Ancestors), Multimedia, Cause of Death, Notes, Sources, Date last changed, and many others.

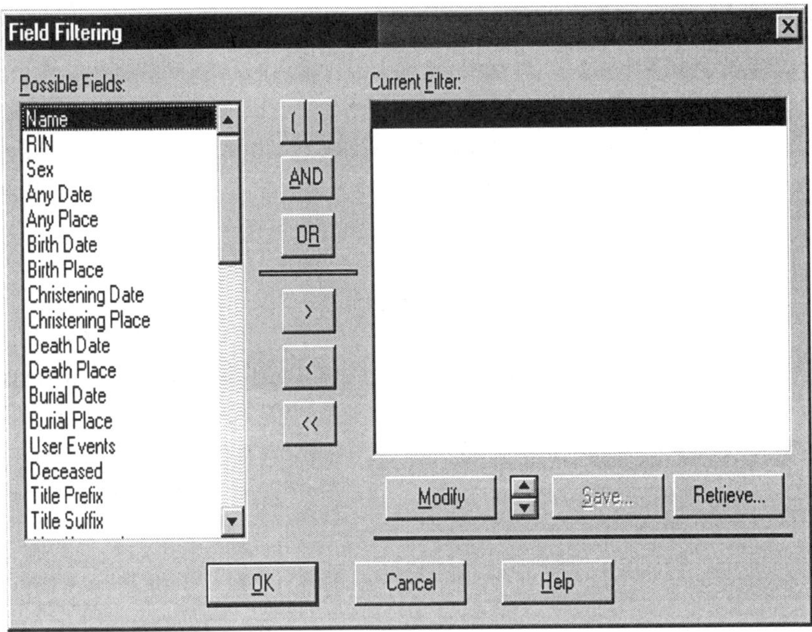

Figure 109

If you want to filter individuals who meet one criteria, select a field on the **Possible Fields** (Fig. 109) list by double-clicking it or clicking the (>) button. A dialog box will ask for the specific information you want to filter on, such as the name of the city, certain text in the notes, or an author's name. Filtering options for each field or data type vary, but include choices such as matches, does not match, equals, greater than, less than, exists, does not exist, contains, does not contain. You can use wild cards in some situations. In the Name, Place, ID or Title fields you can use an '*' when performing a text match. "New*" means any text that starts with "New". "*ville" means any text that ends with "ville". Click **OK**. The criteria you have selected will appear under Current Filter, click on **OK** to perform the filtering, return to the Search for Individual screen, and see the filter individuals.

OPTIONS	DESCRIPTIONS
>	Selects the highlighted field under **Possible Fields**.
<	Clears the highlighted criteria under **Current Filter**.

<<	Clears all the criteria under **Current filter**.
Modify	The **Modify** button allows you to change the highlighted criteria. The **Up & Down** arrows allow you to change the order of the criteria in the Current Filter box.
Save	The **Save...** button will store the filter criteria for use later.
Retrieve	The **Retrieve**... button will list the saved files containing set filter criteria; it can later be opened or deleted.

1. From the **Field Filter** box on the **Advanced Focus/Filter** window (Fig. 107), select **Define**. (See Fig. 107) The **Define** button brings up the **Field Filtering** window. The Field Filter definition screen allows you to choose individuals based on information contained in the individuals' records. The **Clear** button resets the Field Filtering criteria and the people selected in that list.
2. In the **Possible Fields** box, click on the field that you want to include in your filter.
3. Click >.
4. Fill out the information needed for the filter.
5. If you want to add another field to the filter, use **AND, OR, NOT** and **( )** to combine the filters.
6. Repeat Steps 2-5 for all the other filters you want to use.

Hint: If you created a complex field filter, you should save it for later use. Select **Save** and type in a name for the filter.

7. When you are finished, click **OK**.

Hint: To select individuals, you need to use a relationship filter and then use **AND, OR,** or **NOT** to combine the relationship filter with the field filter. For example: To select everyone in your database who matches the criteria you specified in the field filter, use the relationship filter to select all individuals, and combine the filters and AND.

Combining the Lists

If you are only using one of the two lists, that list acts as the active list and the Filtered List count will mirror the count of the list you are using. However, if you are using BOTH lists, then the active list is a COMBINED list. You can choose how the two lists work together by selecting an option in the **Combine lists using** drop-down.

Using the List

There are a variety of uses for the **Focus** list your created:

- You can print them on reports. For example, select all of your grandchildren to use on the **Birthday/Anniversary Calendar**. Or, select all your mother's ancestors born in France between 1820 and 1862 and create a custom report using only those people.
- You can export them using a GEDCOM file. This is useful when you want to share only a common line of ancestors with a relative.

Hint: If you are exporting a TempleReady file, the window will show you which ordinances the individuals qualify for or why they would not qualify. You can edit the marriage information as well as the individual information.

- You can edit the records. This would be very helpful in correcting similar errors, such as a spelling error.

Manipulating the Filtered List

In the **Filtered List** field in the lower right corner of the **Find Individual** window there are buttons that will help you manage and view the filtered list. The **Retrieve** button is **always** available regardless of the results of your filtered list. The following **Filtered List** options are available:

BUTTON	**DESCRIPTION**
Show Results Only	Eliminate from view all individuals who are not in the active or filtered list. For example, you have 5,000 people in your database, and you have selected 15 of them using relationship and field filters, select this button to display only the 15 individuals.
Prev., Next	Move the highlight bar to the selected individual who is next or previous on the list.
Save	Save a filtered list of individuals. In the **Save Filter** window, name your filtered list.
Retrieve	Display a list of all previously saved filtered lists. If you didn't save and name your list, you **can't** retrieve any earlier attempts at filtering. From the list of **Filtered Lists,** select the name of the list you created and select **Open**.

Using AND, OR, or NOT in Relationship and Field Filters

	When to use	Example	Results
AND	Use AND to select individuals who match both the relationship filter and field filter. This search usually finds fewer records than Or.	You select Ancestors as the Relationship Filter. You combine the searches with AND. You define a field filter that specifies that the birthplace is Mexico.	PAF selects only the Individual's ancestors who were born in Mexico.
OR	Use OR to select Individuals that match either the relationship filter or the field filter. This search usually finds more records than AND.	You select Ancestors as the Relationship filter. You combine the searches with OR. You define a field filter that specifies that the birthplace is Mexico.	PAF selects all of the individual's ancestors and anyone who was born in Mexico.
NOT	Use NOT to select all individuals who match the relationship filter except those who match the field filter.	You select Ancestors as the Relationship filter. You combine the searches with NOT. You define a field filter that specifies that the birthplace is Mexico.	PAF selects all of the individual's ancestors except those who were born in Mexico.

Chapter 10

Merging Duplicate Records

Each individual within your database should have only one record. If you think you have duplicates in your database, or have imported databases that may be similar to your own, you may want to merge the individual records. PAF can merge two records into one and allows you to decide what information to save.

You can merge duplicate records in one of two ways:

- You can use the **Match/Merge** feature. If you use this feature, PAF will identify potential matches, allow you to select the information to keep, and merges the records.

- You can manually identify duplicate records, copy the information you want to keep from one record to another, and when done, delete the duplicate. This method takes time but gives you total control over the merge process.

To begin the merge process:

1. From the toolbar, select **Tools** ➛ **Match/Merge**

or

2. Press 

Figure 111

Two windows will be displayed, the **Merge Individuals** and a **Warning** window.

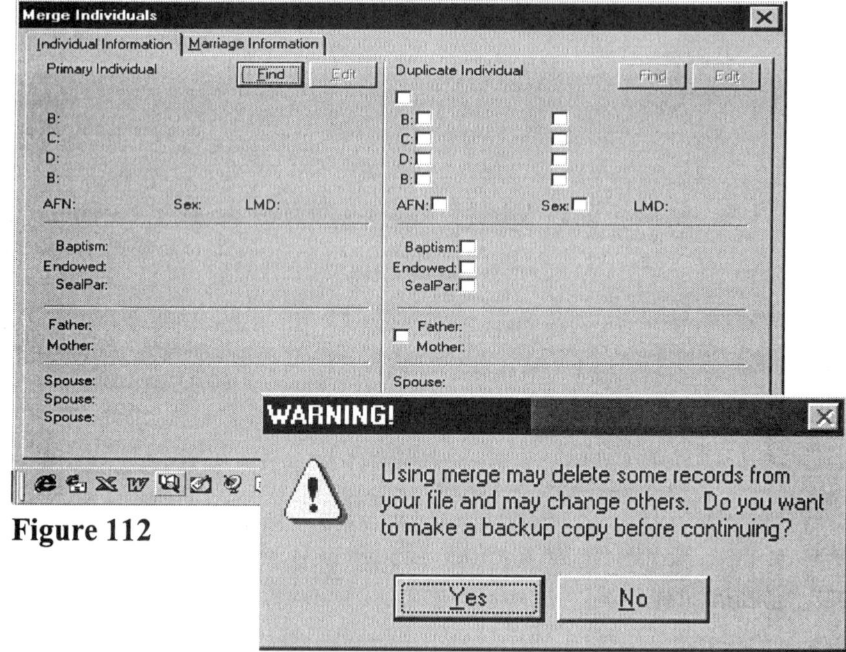

Figure 112

Figure 113

Make a backup of your database before your begin.

NOTE: IT IS ESSENTIAL YOU REALIZE THAT WHEN YOU MERGE RECORDS, ONE RECORD WILL BE DELETED. BE CAUTIOUS IN YOUR MERGE SELECTIONS; IT IS VERY EASY TO DELETE ESSENTIAL INFORMATION CONTAINED IN EACH RECORD. PAF ALLOWS YOU TO DECIDE WHAT INFORMATION TO SAVE.

When you begin the merge process, the **Merge Individual** window will be empty. The left side of the window is where the Primary Individual will be displayed. The Primary Individual will become the record that is saved when two records are merged.

1. To find the record you want to keep, select **Find** for the **Duplicate Individual**
2. Find the duplicate record
3. On the **Duplicate Individual**, select any information that you would like to transfer to the Primary Record. Check boxes will appear next to the information; if you check any of the boxes, that data will replace the data in the same field on the Primary Individual.

Hint: If you would rather keep the record on the right screen, click **Switch**.

4. Click **Merge**
5. To merge other records, repeat steps 1-4.
6. To quit the merge window, click **Close**.

Using the Merge Screen

OPTION	DESCRIPTION
Find	Select **Find** to locate records that you want to merge.
Edit	Select **Edit** to edit the Individual record.
Select All	Click **Select All** to select all of the data in the duplicate record.
Clear All	Select **Clear All** to deselect the selected data in the duplicate record
Merge	Select **Merge** to merge the two records displayed on the screen. If any information on the right window has been selected, it will replace the information on the left window.

Switch	Select **Switch** to have the two records change places.
Next Match	Select **Next Match** to find another duplicate record.
Previous Match	Select **Previous Match** to return to the previous duplicate record.
Options	Select **Options** to change the settings that determine how Match/Merge works.
Marriages	Select **Marriages** to see the marriage records for both individuals.
Close	Select **Close** when you have finished the **Merge** session.

Merge Options

You can add supplemental criteria to narrow the matches by selecting **Options**.

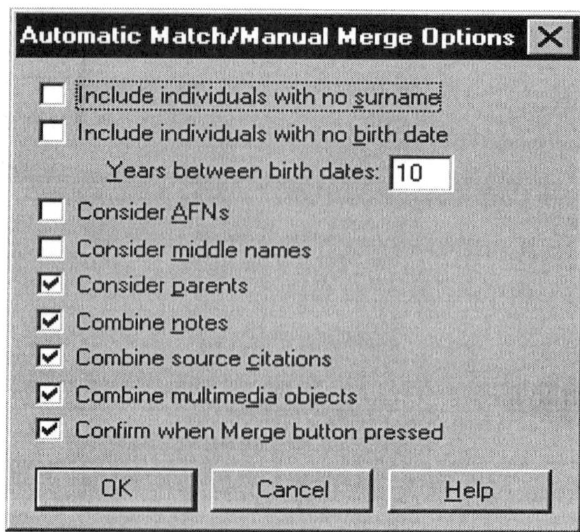

Figure 114

Use the following **Merge Options** to select or deselect options to include when PAF is searching for matches. After you have made your selections, click the **Next Match** button to begin the automatic search.

OPTION	SELECT THIS OPTION TO:
Include Individuals with no Surname	Include records that have no surname as potential duplicates. This option may increase the number of duplicates found.
Include Individuals with no Birth Date	Include records that have no birth date as potential duplicates. This option may increase the number of potential duplicates found.
Years between birth dates	Specify an exact number of years between birth years that could be considered as a duplicate. Using a large number will increase the number of duplicates found.
Consider Ancestral File Numbers	Limit potential duplicates to individuals who have the same AFN. Using this option may decrease the number of potential duplicates found.
Consider middle names	Limit potential duplicates to individuals who have the same middle names or initials. Using this option may decrease the number of potential duplicates found.
Consider parents	Limit potential duplicates to individuals who have the same parents. Using this option will decrease the number of duplicates found.
Combine notes	Combine the notes of both records.
Combine multimedia objects	Combine the multimedia objects associated with both records.
Confirm when Merge button pressed	Require PAF to confirm the merge each time you click the **Merge** button.

Merge Records with matching AFNs

Before you begin this session, you should create a custom report listing only individuals with matching Ancestral File Number. This report will indicate who could be merged and aid in the decision to proceed with the merge.

1. From the toolbar, select **Tools** ➛ **Merge on AFNs**.
2. PAF asks if you want to merge records with the same AFN. Click **Yes**.
3. PAF asks if you want to backup your database. If you don't have a current backup, click **Yes** and make a backup.
4. PAF displays the first two duplicate records. To merge them, go to step 5, or if you don't want to merge, select **Next Match**.
5. To merge the records, click **Merge**.
6. PAF asks if you want to merge, if you want to merge one at a time, select **Yes**.

or

7. If you want PAF to merge all records with matching AFNs automatically, select **Yes to all**.

or

8. From the toolbar, select **Tools** ➛ **Merge on AFNs**.

> **A Note About Considerations**
> If both records have data in the mentioned field, then the data must match for the two records to be considered a match. If either record is missing the data, that criteria will not be included as a consideration when determining a match. When considering parents and middle names, the data entered in the text field must sound alike, not necessarily be spelled identically to constitute a match.

Searching

If you want to find a specific record and display as either the primary or duplicate individual, select **Search** on the appropriate window. The **Find Individual** window will open. Once found, his/her record will appear on the desired side of the window. This is a good way to view and compare two records.

Viewing Marriages

From the **Merge Individual** window, select **Marriages** to open the **Marriage Information** window.

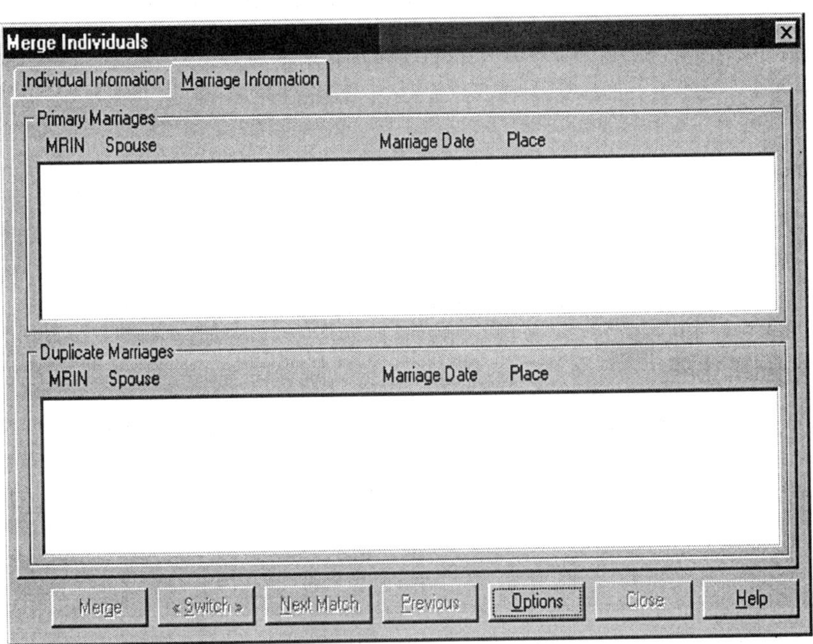

Figure 115

Use this window to select all marriages associated with a duplicate individual record. The **Marriages** button is changed to **Individuals** button in this window, allowing you to move back and forth between this window and the standard **Merge** window.

Editing a Record

To edit the information that has been saved for an individual from within the **Merge** window, select **Edit**, located beneath the individual that you would like to edit. The individual's information window will open, you can then edit and save specific information.

Merge Duplicate Sources and Repositories

This merge is automatic. You can't stop it once it starts. Before you begin, you should display the **Source List** and the **Repository List** to see what information will be merged.

1. From the toolbar, select **Tools** ➛ **Merge Duplicate Sources**.

2. Upon completion of the merge, PAF will show you how many sources and repositories were merged. Click **OK** to continue.

Chapter 11

Calculators

Relationship Calculator

The **Relationship Calculator** can be used to determine the relationship between any two individuals in your database. After locating two individuals, PAF will search back generation by generation until it finds a common ancestor. PAF then determines the relationship. PAF will **not** show the in-law or step family relationships, nor will it show aunt/uncle relationships by marriage.

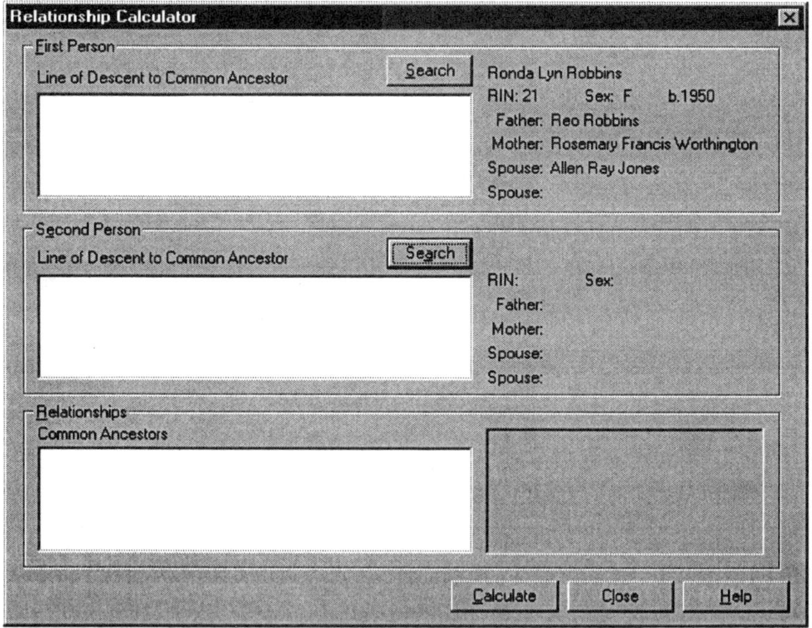

Figure 116

From the toolbar; select **Tools** ➛ **Relationship Calculator**.

- Select **Search** to select the first person.
- Select the second **Search** to select the second person.
- Select **Calculate**.
- The relationship(s) that the individuals share will appear. To calculate another relationship repeat the first three steps.
- When you have completed all individuals, click **Close**.

.

Date Calculator

You can calculate the time elapsed between any two dates within the Gregorian calendar or calculate a date based on one date and an elapsed amount of time. The **Date Calculator** can help you determine the birth or death dates based on other information. If you have a death date and an age at death, you can calculate the birth date. Or if you have the birth date and an age at death you can calculate the death date.

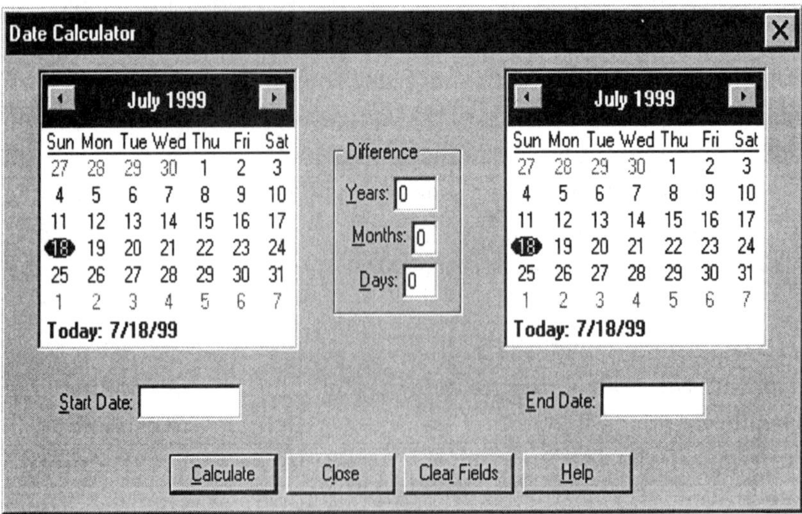

Figure 117

From the **Family** or **Pedigree View** window:

1 Select **Tools ➛ Date Calculator**.
2. Select the starting date on the calendar or enter the date in the **Start Date** field.
3. Select the ending date on the calculator or enter the date in the **End Date** field.
4. Select **Calculate**. The elapsed time will appear in the fields in the middle of the window.
5. To do another date calculation, select **Clear Fields**.
6. When finished, click **Close**.

NOTE: THE DATE CALCULATOR DOES NOT WORK FOR DATES BEFORE OCTOBER 1752. BEFORE THIS DATE, A COUNTRY MAY HAVE USED THE JULIAN CALENDAR. IF THE DATE CALCULATOR TRIED TO CALCULATE A DATE, IT WOULD BE INACCURATE.

To calculate a date based on one date and an elapsed amount of time:

1. From the toolbar, select **Tools ➛ Date Calculator**
2. Select the starting or ending date on the calendar, or type the date in the **Start Date** or **End Date** field.
3. Type the years, months, and dates in the fields in the middle of the screen.
4. Select **Calculate**. The other date will be displayed.
5. If you want to calculate another date, select **Clear Fields**.
6. When finished, click **Close**.

When you perform a calculation, the day of the week of the start and end dates will display.

Soundex Calculator

The **Soundex** is a type of index that groups surnames together that sound similar but aren't spelled exactly the same. Each surname is given a Four digit code that consists of the first letter of the name; the next three consonants are assigned a number. Vowels are ignored as are duplicate letters. The **Soundex** has been used to index the 1880-1920 U.S. censuses and other types of records, such as naturalization and passenger lists.

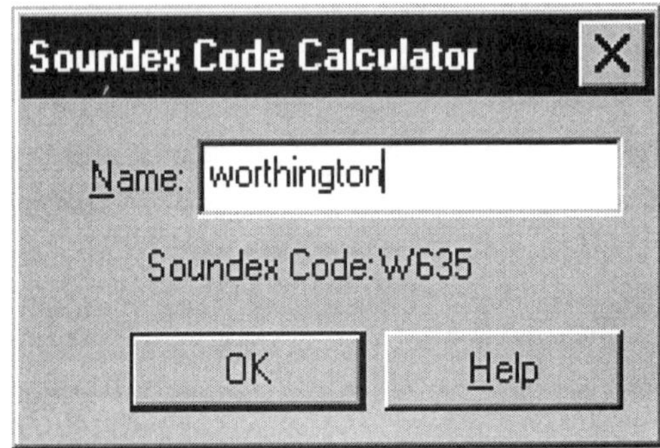

Figure 118

From the toolbar, select **Tools** ➝ **Soundex Calculator**. Type in the surname, the Soundex Code will be displayed in the center of the window.

Chapter 12

Printing Charts, Reports, and Lists

PAF allows you to print many different reports, charts, and lists including:

- Pedigree Charts
- Family Group Records
- Ancestry Charts
- Wall Charts
- Descendancy Charts
- Change Log
- Books
- Individual Summaries
- Scrapbooks
- Custom Reports
- Lists
- Calendars

Report Window

You can begin selecting specific report options from any one of the windows.

- From the toolbar select **File** ➤ **Print Reports**.

or

- Use CTRL+P.

or

- Click. 

Figure 119

or

- Click the right mouse button on the Individual's name and select **Reports**.

From the **Reports and Charts** window, you can easily choose any report type by selecting the tab across the top of the window. The icon in the lower right corner presents a visual representation of the report.

Pedigree Reports

The **Pedigree Report** prints the report very much as it is displayed in the **Pedigree View** window. You choose between 4, 5, or 6 generations on a page. It includes recorded birth dates and places; recorded death dates and places; marriage information; and the spouse for the starting individual. You can also attach photos to the report.

Select **Preferences** on the right side of the **Reports and Charts** window (Fig. 120). PAF will display **Report Preferences**. (Fig. 121) You can adjust your report preferences from this window, including the LDS data option, capitalization, and place card holders. If you select LDS options, some printed reports will contain additional information that reflect the data entered in the LDS fields. For example, the family group record or the individual summary include information and dates regarding the completion of ordinances for the listed individuals.

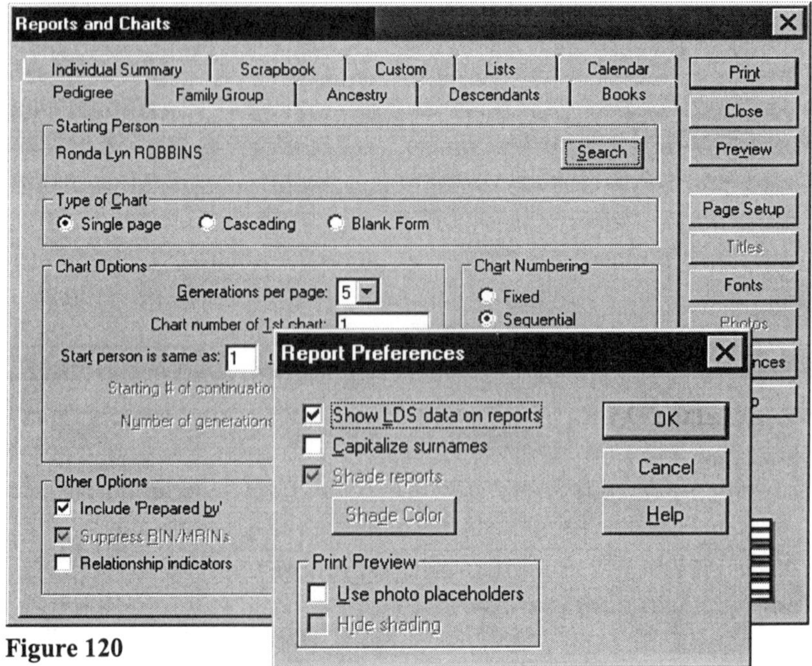

Figure 120

Figure 121

If you would like to review specific ordinance information, use the **Print Reports; List** option. A list will be printed of individuals or marriages that are missing one or more ordinance(s).

You can determine what font is used on your report. By selecting the **Fonts** button, the following window will open. (Fig. 123)

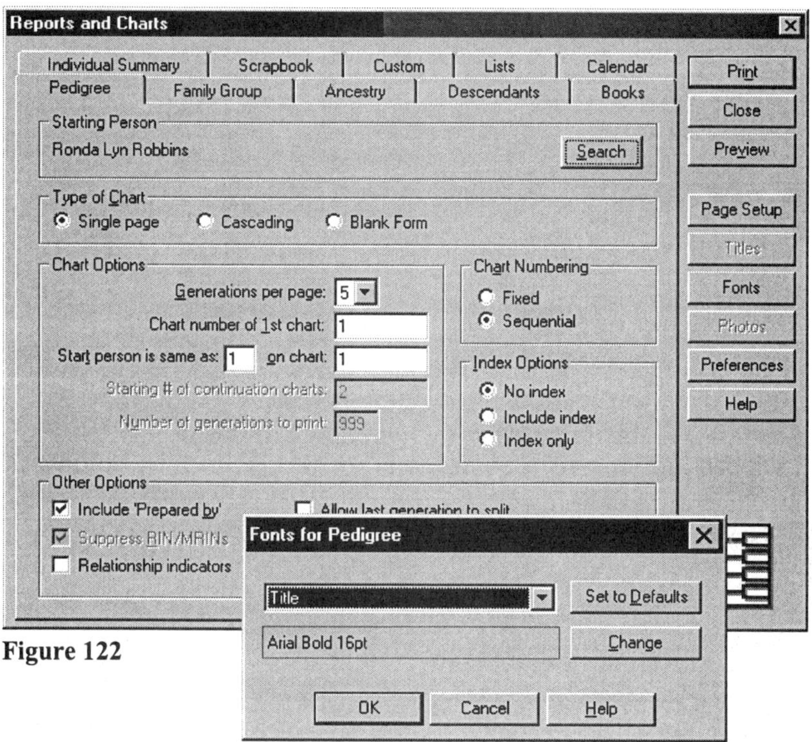

Figure 122

Figure 123

For more detailed information concerning fonts, see **Fonts** later in this chapter.

Chart Type

Use the options listed below to determine the type of chart you wish to print.

OPTION	DESCRIPTION
Single Family	Select **Single family** to print the chart for one family only, listing up to six generations.
Cascading	Select **Cascading** to print Pedigree Charts with up to six generations appearing on each page. The **Cascading** option prints several pages, depending on the number of generations you specify. Each page is numbered to enable you to keep the pages in order.
Blank form	Select **Blank Form** to print a blank Pedigree Chart on a single page that results in a four generation form that you can fill out by hand.

Index Options

An index to a pedigree chart is an alphabetical list of individuals within the pedigree. It contains the following information about each individual:

- RIN
- Birth date or christening date
- Death or burial dates
- Chart position and chart number

When you print an index for a pedigree chart you can choose any of the following options:

OPTION	DESCRIPTION
No Index	Prints the **Pedigree Chart** without an index.
Include Index	Prints an index of all of the individuals who appear on the set of charts as well as the entire set of **Pedigree Charts**.
Index Only	Prints an index, but not a **Pedigree Chart**. Use this option if you already have a set of cascading charts, but do not have an index. If you choose the same options on the **Index Only** as you did on the set of charts, the index will match the charts.

Hint: If the terms **Submitted**, **Sub 12 Jan 1999**, **Cleared** or **Done** have been typed in the ordinance date fields, the ordinance codes are printed in lowercase letters, indicating that the ordinances have been submitted but not completed.

Chart Numbering

Chart numbering determines how **Cascading Chart** numbers are generated. This is useful when you generate cascading charts, and if you need to reprint a single chart from a previously printed set. If later you find continuation information on any lines that were previously missing, you can print the new charts without having to renumber other charts if you choose **Fixed Numbering**. Because chart numbers can grow astronomically with fixed numbering, you are limited to about 32 generations in the series. However, if you used **Condensed Numbering**, chart numbers remain relatively small with no reasonable limit to the number of cascading charts you can generate in a series. (Previous versions of PAF always printed in condensed mode.)

Select the appropriate option to choose how your **Pedigree Chart** will be numbered:

OPTION	DESCRIPTION
Fixed	Each continuation chart is preassigned a specific, fixed number based on its position. For example, if you don't have much information on your father's line, but a lot of information on your mother's line, and you are printing four-generation charts, the first chart is 1, the continuation chart for your mother's paternal grandfather is 6, the continuation for his spouse is 7, etc. Charts 2 through 5 are not used, because they are for your father's four grandparent lines.
Condensed	Each continuation chart is assigned the next available chart number in sequence. For example, if you don't have much information on your father's line, but a lot of information on your mother's line, and you are printing a four-generation chart, the first chart is 1, then the continuation chart for your mother's paternal grandfather is 2, the continuation for his spouse is 3, etc.

Chart Options

Some of these options are available only when certain chart types and index options are selected.

OPTION	DESCRIPTION
Generations per page	Choose four, five, or six. The number you choose determines the number of generations printed on each page of the report.

Chart number of 1st Chart	If you want a number other than the 1 as the chart number, enter the desired number.
Starting person (same as) chart	Specify that the starting person is to be the same as a specific individual on another chart.
Starting # of continuation charts	Available only when printing cascading charts. Specify the starting number for subsequent charts in a cascade.
Number of generations to print	Available only when printing cascading charts. Specify the number of generations to print. This field accepts any number of generations up to 199.

Other Options

The bottom of the window is allocated to **Other Options** and is used to define specifics about your report.

OPTION	DESCRIPTION
Include "Prepared by"	If you want the Submitter information to display on each chart.
Suppress RINs/MRINs	Even though you prefer to see RINs or IDs on the screen, you may not want them to print.
Relationship indicators	The parent relationship that you had selected for each individual can be printed in codes in { }. An explanation of the codes prints at the bottom of the chart.

Allow last generation to split	Depending on the various other options you choose, (generations per page, margin size, font size, page layout, photos, etc.) PAF tries to fit as much information on a page as possible. If you split the last generation so the wife's information prints to the right of the husband rather than below him, more information will fit on the page. If you check this box, PAF will split the last generation when it is calculations show it is advantageous. If you leave this box unchecked, you will get the traditional layout. This usually provides less information for each person in the last generation, but may look better.
Include Photos	If you want to include photos next to each individual. To adjust the size and positioning of the photos, select **Photos**.
Multiple parent indicators	If an individual has more than one set of parents, a (+) will be printed in { }. If there is both a relationship indicator and a multiple Parent indicator, they will be enclosed in a single set of brackets. The explanation of the codes prints at the bottom of the chart.

Family Group Record (FGR)

The **Family Group Record** prints the basic birth, marriage, death, and burial information in the form of a report. The **Alternate Birth Event**, **Custom Individual** and **Marriage** events along with notes and footnoted sources can be included. **Photos** and **LDS** ordinance information can also be included.

Select the **Family Group** tab.

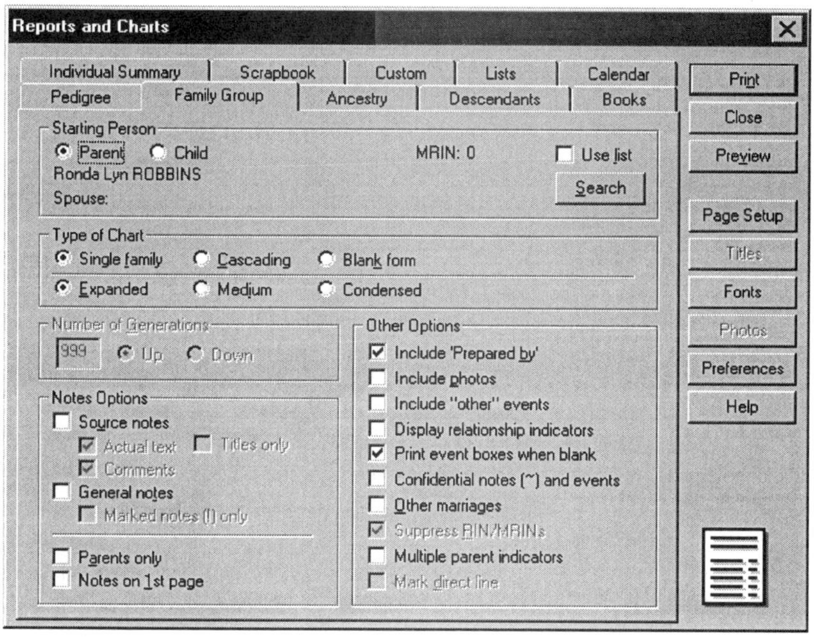

Figure 124

Chart Options

These options are based on a standard 8½" x 11" sized paper, with minimal top/bottom margins. You can select other page layouts using Window's **Page Setup** and **Print Preview**.

OPTION	DESCRIPTION
Single Family	Select **Single Family** to print the chart for one family only.
Cascading	Select **Cascading** to print family group sheets for up to 199 generations of an individual's ancestors. Type the desired number in the **Number of Generations** field.

Blank Form	Select **Blank form** to print three-page blank family group sheets. These blank forms use the **Expanded Layout**, described below.
Expanded	Select **Expanded** to print four children on the first page and six children on subsequent pages. If the option **Include Prepared by** is turned on, the Submitter is included, the first page will have only three children.
Medium	Select **Medium** to print six and eight children per page.
Condensed	Select **Condensed** to print eight and ten children per page.

Hint: These options are based on an 8 ½" x 11" page, with minimal top/bottom margins. Some printers may not provide enough printable room, so you may see less children even with the smaller margins. To select other page layouts use the **Window's Page Setup** and **Print Preview**.

Notes Options

You can choose which type of notes to print on the **Family Group Record** from the list below.

OPTION	DESCRIPTION
Source Notes	Select **Source Notes** to include sources on your Family Group Record. Choose from these options: • Select **Actual Text** to include any information typed in the **Actual Text** field of the source. • Select **Titles Only** to include the source titles only. • Select **Comments** to include any information you typed as comments in your sources.
General Notes	Select **General Notes** to print all general notes on the Family Group Record. Select **Marked (!) Notes only** if you want to print only those notes that have been marked with an exclamation point. If you marked your confidential notes with (~) Select **Confidential Notes (~) and events** in the **Other Options** box to prevent their being printed on the Family Group Record. **NOTE:** THE EXCLAMATION (!) POINT AND THE TILDE (~) CHARACTERS WILL NOT PRINT ON THE REPORTS.

Parents Only	Select **Parents Only** to print notes and other marriage information for only the parents, but not the children. If you are printing Cascading Family Group Records, this option eliminates duplication of notes. CAUTION: If you have any notes for unmarried children, they will not print on the charts.
Notes on 1st page	Select **Notes on 1st page** to begin printing the sources and notes immediately following the last child in the family on the first page. If the family as a whole doesn't fit on a single page the notes and sources are printed immediately following the last child regardless of the page he/she is printed on.

Other Options

OPTION	DESCRIPTION
Include 'Prepared by'	Select **Include Prepared by** to print the **Prepared by** information from **Preferences** at the bottom of the first page of the FGR.
Include photos	Select **Include photos** to include photos on your FGR. If you use this option, space is reserved for photos by each person whether or not there is an actual photo attached. Select the **Photos** button to select where photos are placed on the FGR. The photo size is determined by page layout options.
Include "Other" events	Select **Include other events** to include other events you have added to the individual and marriage records in your database.
Display relationship indicators	Select **Display relationship indicators** to include the parent relationship for each individual on your printed report. The relationship will appear as a code in { }. An explanation of the codes is printed at the bottom of the FGR.
Print event boxes when blank	Select **Print event boxes when blank** to have all boxes, whether filled or not, printed on your FGR.
Confidential notes (~) and events	Select **Confidential notes (~) and events** to print your confidential notes or events on your printed FGR.
Other marriages	Select **Other marriages** to have additional marriages for an individual and print in the notes section of the FGR.

Suppress RINs/MRINs	Select **Suppress RINs/MRINs** if you prefer not to include these numbers on your printed FGR.
Multiple parent indicators	Select **Multiple parent indicators** to print a (+) in brackets next to an individual who is linked to more than one set of parents. **NOTE:** IF A PERSON HAS BOTH A RELATIONSHIP INDICATOR AND A MULTIPLE PARENT INDICATOR, BOTH ITEMS ARE ENCLOSED IN { }BRACKETS, AN EXPLANATION OF THE CODES IS PRINTED AT THE BOTTOM OF THE PAGE.
Mark direct line	Select **Mark direct line** to mark each direct-line ancestor with an X.

Fonts

Figure 125

Select **Fonts** from the **Report and Charts** window. From this window you can choose to change the font used in a specific report. Click on the down-arrow in the drop down box to select the report element whose font you wish to change. You will see the font information, to change this selection, select

Change to access the standard Windows fonts. To re-select the default font, select **Set to Defaults**. This returns you to the original font.

Ancestry

Ancestry Charts are very similar to the pedigree charts. However, in general, they show more generations of an individual's direct-line ancestors with less overall information about each individual. There are two types of Ancestry Charts: the **Standard Chart** and the **Wall Chart**.

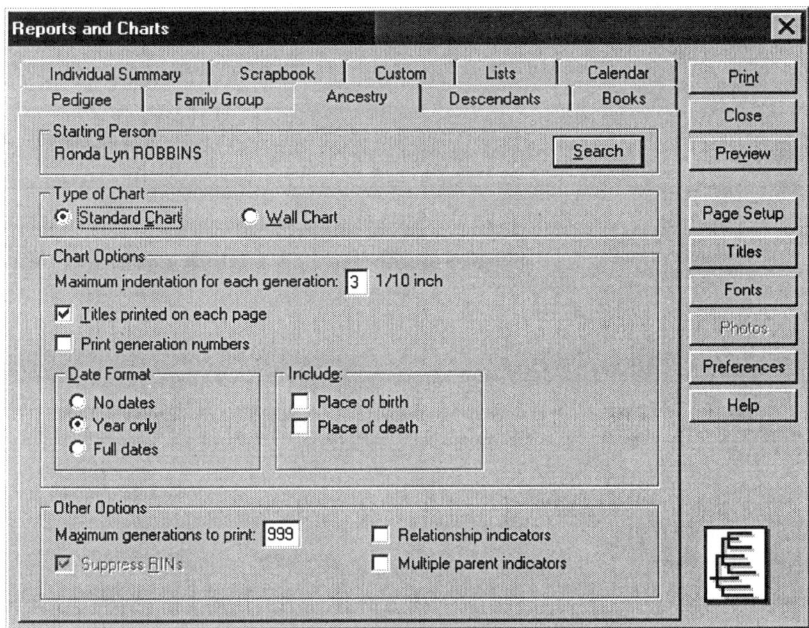

Figure 126

Standard Chart

This chart provides only birth and death date information for each individual. It uses single page width, but continues for as many pages as necessary to include all ancestors.

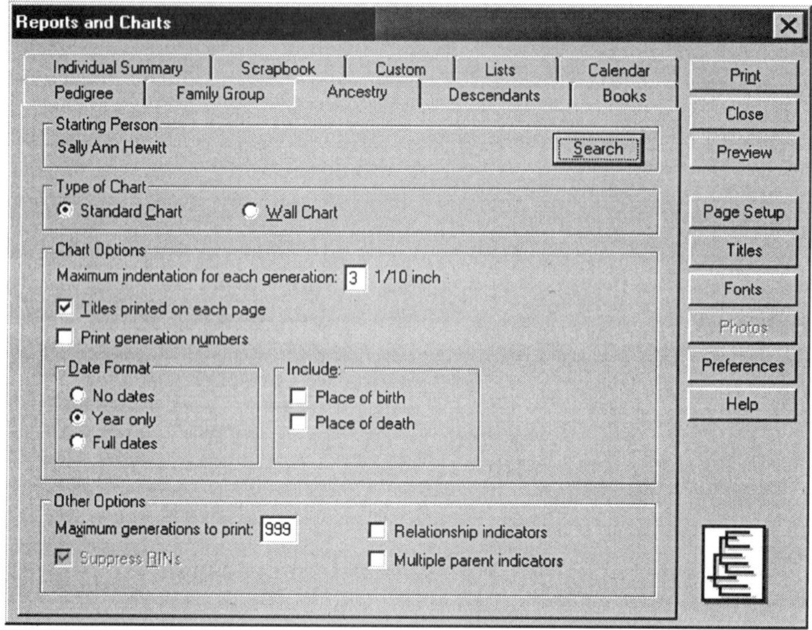

Figure 127

Standard Chart Options

These options are exclusive to the **Standard Ancestry Chart**.

OPTION	DESCRIPTION
Maximum indentation for each generation	Enter in tenths of an inch, the amount of white space you require between generations. If there are too many generations to fit on a standard page, PAF will reduce the value as needed.
Titles printed on each page	Select **Title printed on each page** to have the title appear on every page of the **Standard Chart**.

Print generation numbers	Select **Print generation numbers** to include the generation number in front of each name on the chart.
Date Format	Your **Standard Chart** can include birth, christening, and death (or burial) dates for each individual. Select the date format you wish to utilize. • No Dates • Year Only • Full Dates **Hint**: The more information you require, the more abbreviation will occur.
Include	Your **Standard Chart** can include places of: Birth (or Christening) and Death (or burial) **Hint**: Again, the more information you ask for, the more abbreviation occurs.

Wall Chart

The **Wall Chart** supplies varying degrees of information for each person, uses more than a single page width, and will continue for as many pages as necessary to include all ancestors. Select the **Wall Chart** option. PAF will display an appended window.
(Fig. 128)

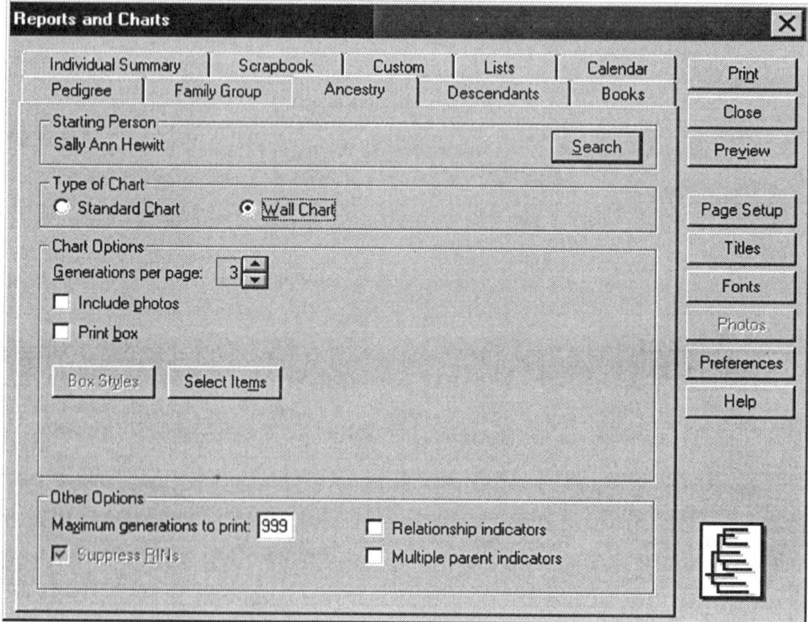

Figure 128

Chart Options

Make your chart selections from the following list:

OPTION	DESCRIPTION
Generations per page	Click the up and down arrow to choose the number of generations to print on each page. Three generations will work best on a standard 8½" x 11" page. Selecting more than three generations will likely cause undesired truncation of information.

Include Photos	Select **Include Photos** to print attached photos on the chart.
Print Box	Select **Print Box** to print a decorative box around each individual's information.
Select Items	Click **Select Items** to display a new window. Choose which items to print for each individual.

Click on **Select Items**. PAF displays **Ancestry Wall Chart Item Selection**. (Fig. 129)

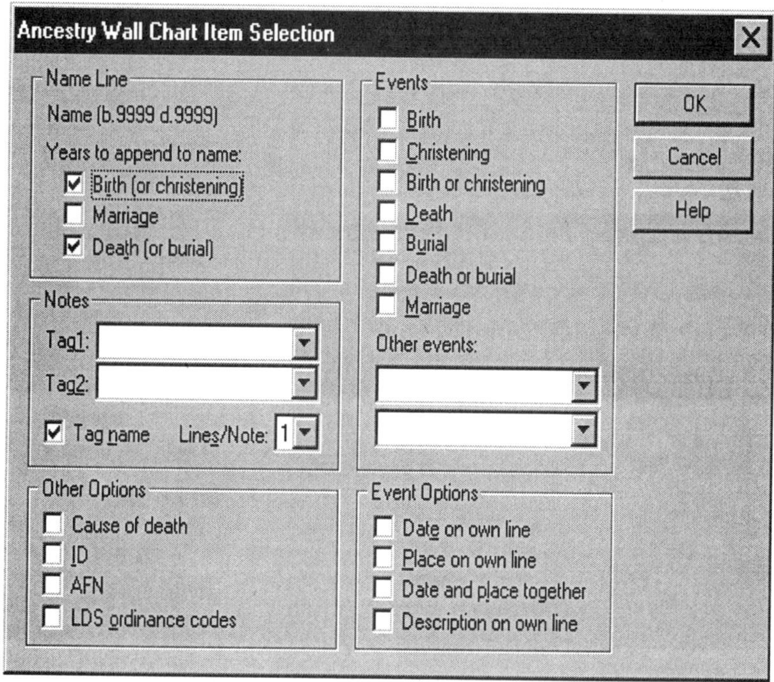

Figure 129

OPTION	DESCRIPTION
Name Line	Select the event years you want to print on the chart.
Notes	If you want to include tags with your notes, select the tags from the drop-down box. Click on the arrow to the right of the empty **Tag** field to access the drop-down menu of tags. You can select 1, 2, or 3 lines per tagged note.
Other Options	Select the options you want to include: cause of death, custom ID, AFN or LDS ordinance codes. **Hint: Use LDS data** option must be turned on for the LDS ordinance codes to appear under other options. From the toolbar, **Tools ➛ Preferences; General; Use LDS data**.
Events	Select the events you want to include on your chart. If you have selected other events on the individual record, PAF will allow you to select two of them using the drop-down box.
Event Options	Choose how you want your events to be formatted on your chart.

Box Styles

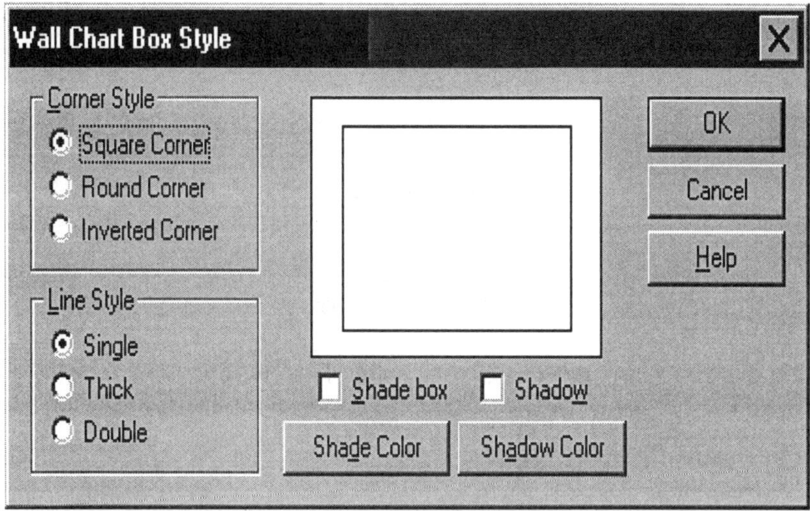

Figure 130

Hint: You must turn on the **Print** box under **Chart Options** to select **Box Styles.**

Both the wall charts and scrapbook pages give you an option of printing decorative boxes around the individual's information. As you select options, the window shows you what the box will look like. Choose from the following styles:

STYLE	DESCRIPTION
Corner Style	Select **Square**, **Round,** or **Inverted** corners.
Line Styles	Select **Single**, **Thick,** or **Double** lines to outline the box.
Shade Box	Select **Shade Box** to shade the interior of the box.

Shadow	Select **Shadow** to print a shadow behind the box, giving a three-dimensional appearance.
Shade Color	Select **Shade Color** to select the color of background shade.
Shadow Color	Select **Shadow Color** to select the color of the shadow behind the box. Keep in mind that colors will only print on color printers, so although these options are available, they are limited by the printer you use.

Title

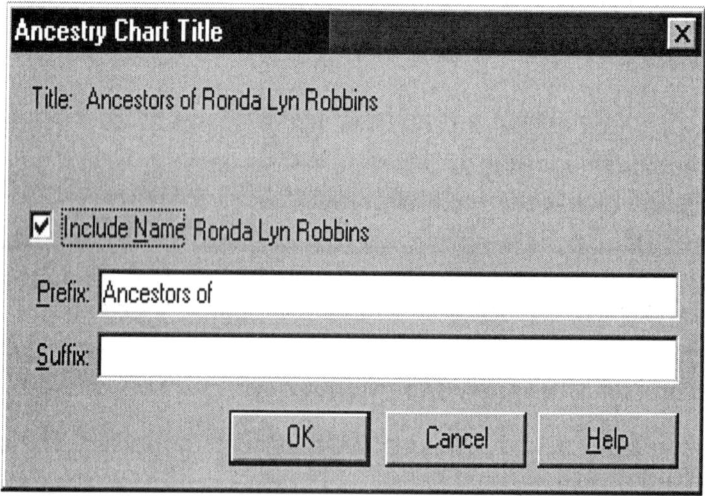

Figure 131

Select the **Title** button to record the title of your report. PAF displays **Ancestry Chart Title**. (Fig. 131)

Click on **Include Name** if you want the name of the Primary person printed on the report.

- **Prefix** - Enter some text to precede the name.
- **Suffix** - Enter some text to print after the name.

When you have completed your selections, click **OK**.

Descendants

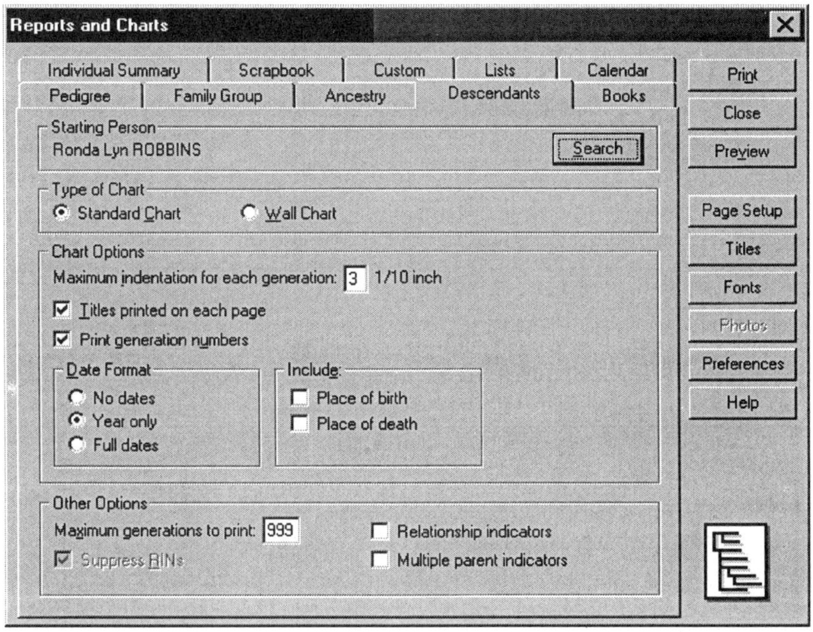

Figure 132

This chart has information about an individual and his/her descendants in a graphical format. As with **Ancestry Charts**, **Descendants** print in two formats: **Standard** and **Wall Chart**.

The options for this chart are the same as with Ancestry Charts. Please refer to **Ancestry Charts** for more detailed information.

Books

Books contain information pertaining to several generations of your family. The birth, christening, marriage, death, and burial information is printed in narrative form. You can organize your books in one of two formats.

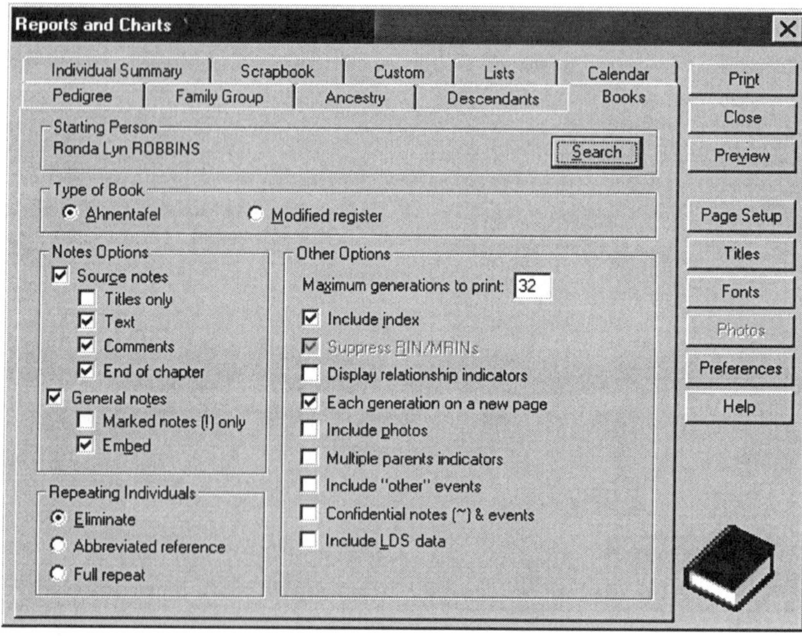

Figure 133

Ahnentafel

An **Ahnentafel** book is arranged according to generations of ancestors. Each person is assigned a number according to a specific pattern, which helps an individual to trace generations. It starts with a specified person and lists all of his ancestors. Each person is numbered. The first person is 1. The number of each father is calculated by multiplying 2 times the number of his child. The mother's number is 2 times the child's number plus 1.

Modified Register	A modified register book lists all the individual's descendants. The starting person is 1 and the other individuals are numbered sequentially as they are encountered. The **Modified Register** can print 1-199 generations which is more than is possible in recorded history.

Notes Options will be displayed for you to determine which notes you want to print on the report, and where the notes will be placed.

General Notes	Select **General Notes** to include your notes. If you select General notes, the following options become available. • Select **Marked (!) Only** to include notes where the first character is (!) • Select **Embed** to have the notes embedded within the body of the text. If you check this option your notes will be printed immediately below the other information pertaining to this individual.

Source Notes	Select **Source Notes** to print sources in your book. You have the following options for your sources: • Select **Titles only** to print only the title. If you choose this option skip the **Text** and **Comments** options. • Select **Text** to print the actual text you typed. • Select **Comments** to print the comments you typed about the sources. • Select **End of chapter** if you want the sources placed and printed at the end of each chapter rather than in an appendix at the end of the book.
General Notes	Select **General Notes** to include your notes. If you select **General Notes**, the following options become available: • Select **Marked (!) Only** to include notes where the first character is (!). • Select **Embed** to have the notes embedded within the body of the text. If you check this option your notes will be printed immediately below all of the other information pertaining to this individual.

Repeating Individual	Select how you want to print individuals who are linked to more than one family: • Select **Eliminate** if you want to print them only once. • Select **Abbreviated Reference** if you want to have a minimal amount of information in subsequent citations with a cross reference back to the full information. • Select **Full Repeat** if you want all the information to be printed every time the individual appears.

Other Options

Several other options are available that allow you to fine tune the layout of your book.

OPTION	**DESCRIPTION**
Index	Select **Include Index** to print an alphabetized list of all individuals in your book at the end of the book. Depending on how much horizontal space you have on the page, the index prints anywhere from a single column on a narrow portrait layout to three columns on a legal landscape layout. The default is two columns.
Suppress RINs/MRINs	Select **Suppress RINs/MRINs** to conceal these numbers in your book.
Display relationship indicators	Select **Display Relationship Indicators** to print the parental indicators relationship for each individual.
Each generation on a new page	Select **Each generation on new page** if you want a page break between each generation.

Include photos	Select **Include Photos** to print the attached photographs.
Multiple parent indicators	Select **Multiple parent indicators** if you want individuals who are linked to more than one set of parents to have {+} printed next to their name. If an individual has both a relationship and a multiple parent indicator, both are printed in the brackets.
Include "other" events	Select **Include other events** if you have typed additional or custom events for individuals and want to include them in your report.
Confidential notes (~) and events	Select **Confidential notes (~) and events** if you want the notes to print. Do not check this option if you want to keep these notes and sources private.
Include LDS data	Select **Include LDS data** to print the LDS ordinance information. **Hint: Use LDS data** option must be turned on for the **Include LDS data** option to appear under other options. From the toolbar, **Tools ➛ Preferences; General; use LDS data**.

Individual Summary

Use this report to print a summary of all information available for a specific individual. You can create a custom title and select the notes font for this report. If you have selected LDS data, LDS ordinance information will be included on this report. Use the **Search** option to place your starting individual in position. To print a single summary, verify that the **Use List** option is unchecked. However, if you choose to print a complete list of summaries, check this box.

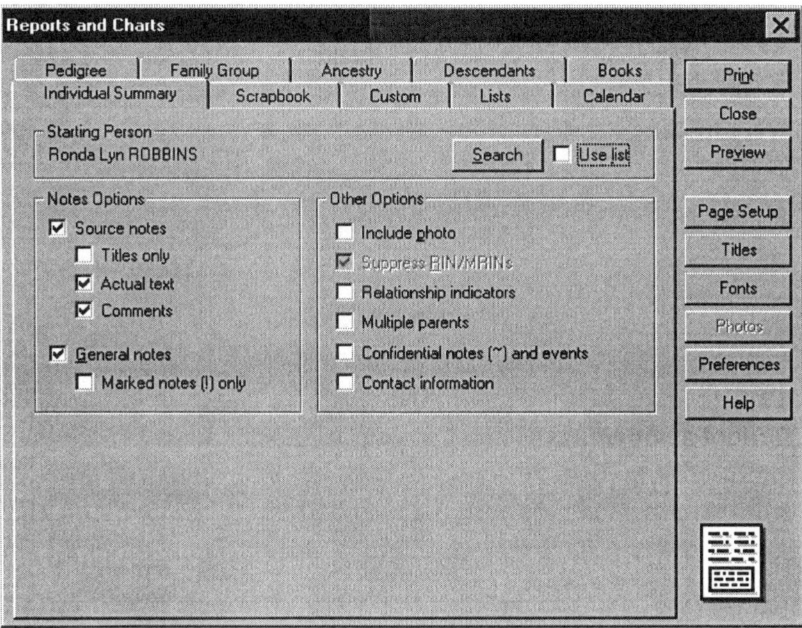

Figure 134

Select your print options from the following list:

OPTION	DESCRIPTION
Source Notes	Select **Source Notes** to include sources on your family group record. Your options are: • Select **Actual Text** to include the information typed in the **Actual Text** portion of the source. • Select **Titles only** to include only the source titles. • Select **Comments** to include information that you entered as comments in your source.
General Notes	Select **General Notes** to print notes included on the Family Group Record. • Select **Marked (!) Notes Only** if you want to include only the notes that have ! as the first character. If you used the (~) to mark confidential notes, select **Confidential Notes (~)** in the **Other Options** box to prevent them from being printed on the family group record.
Include Photo	Select **Include photo** to include the attached photos in your report. If you use this option, a space is reserved for each individual's picture although not all individuals have photos.
Suppress RINs/MRINs	Select **Suppress RINs/MRINs** to conceal these numbers in your report.

Relationship Indicators	Select **Relationship Indicators** to print the parent/child relationship for each individual. The relationship will appear as a code in brackets. An explanation of codes is printed on the bottom of the report. Select **Display relationship indicators** to print the relationships for the individual.
Multiple Parents	Select **Multiple parents** to print a (+) next to an individual who is linked to more than one set of parents. If this person has a relationship and a multiple parent indicator, both items are enclosed in brackets { }.
Confidential notes (~) and events	Select **Confidential notes (~) and events** if you type (~) as the first character in some notes to keep them private, and if you have events you want to remain private.
Contact Information	Select **Contact Information** to include the submitter's name, address, and an e-mail address.

Scrapbooks

The Scrapbook report will allow you to print all or part of the photos and scanned documents collected for an individual. If you don't want all the items to print use the **Edit Photo** window (Fig. 95). If you exclude a photo in a printed report, it is also excluded on the interactive scrapbook as well.

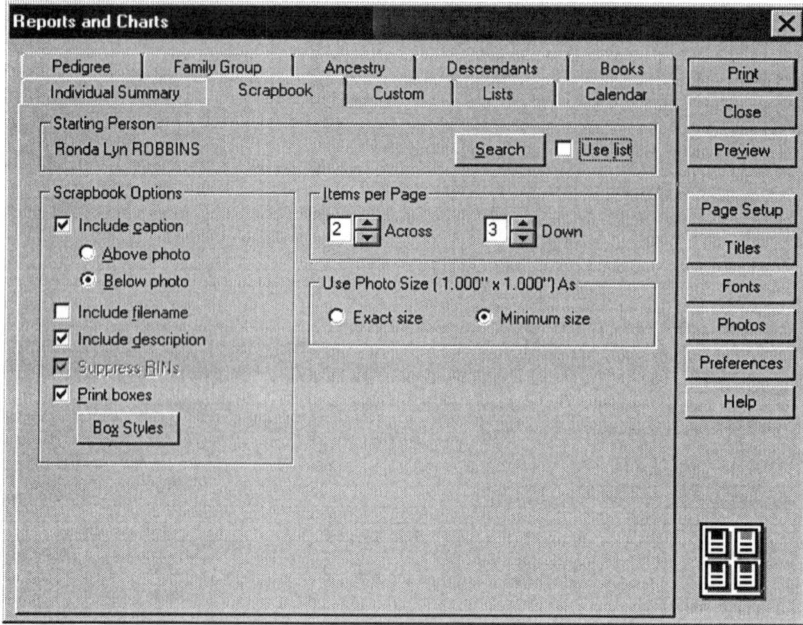

Figure 135

1. Check the **Use List** box to determine the number of individuals to include in your printed scrapbook.

2. Choose which pieces of information should be included in the scrapbook. Your choices are:
   - Caption. If you choose this option you must determine where to place the caption–above or below the photo.
   - File name (location of the photo).
   - Description.
   - Box Style. Choose the style of the box surrounding your information by clicking on **Box Styles.** (Fig. 135)

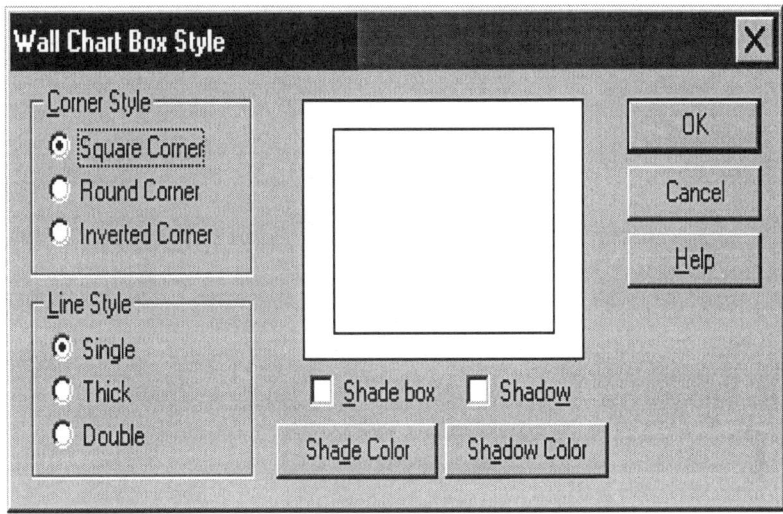

Figure 136

3. Items per page. You determine the layout of your photos, and the approximate size of each item in the **Scrapbook**, by indicating how many items are displayed across and down the page. The more items you display the smaller the size.

4. Photo Size. You can see the current size of the photos that will be used in the Scrapbook. If you want to adjust the size, use the **Photo** button to access that screen. Use this option to fine tune your pictures in your Scrapbook. If you choose **Exact Size**, PAF will size the photo to your specifications. If there isn't enough room on the page, it will be scaled down proportionately. PAF will attempt to provide at least one line for your caption, filename, and description if requested. If you choose **Minimum Size**, PAF will print the photo as requested, however, if there is more room available then requested the picture will be re-scaled to fit the larger space.

Custom Reports

The **Custom Reports** you create here are generally limited only by the extent of your understanding of the tools provided and by your imagination.

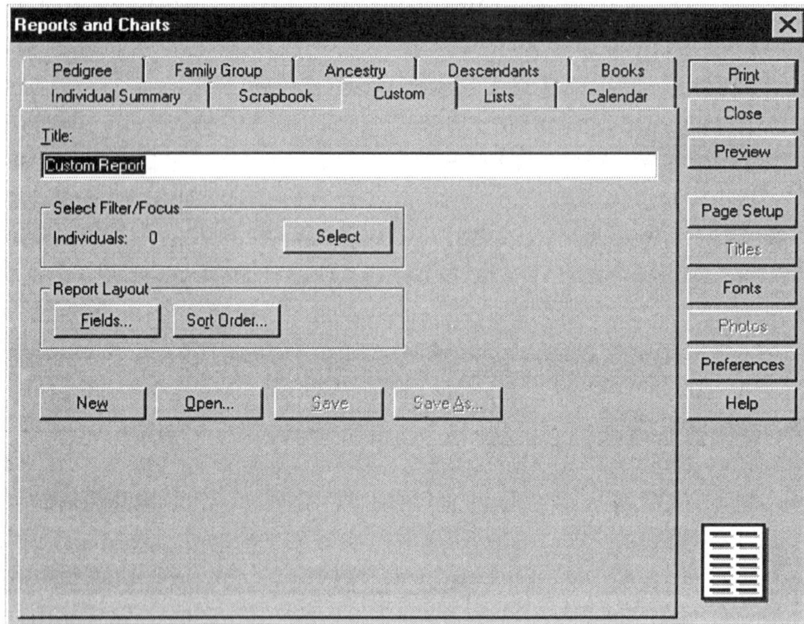

Figure 137

To create your custom report you must first do the following:

- Select the individuals that are to be included in your report. Use the **Advanced Focus/Filter** option to find these individuals.
- Choose the fields and column options that you want to see.
- Choose how the report should be sorted.

You can save custom reports for use in any of your PAF databases. You can also modify or delete a custom report that you have saved. After making your choices, view your report before printing to verify that the end result will be what you expected.

Hint: You can print custom reports or save them in a file in your word processor.

Select **Print Preview** to display your report on your screen.

Other options to consider:

- Title. Enter the name of the report.
- Filter. Put the power of the **Advanced Focus/Filter** to work here. Click **Select** to select the persons you want in your report. (See Chapter 9 for a more detailed explanation.)
- Fields. Click **Fields** to select the pieces of information you want to print in your report. **Fields** option will also allow you to define column headings and column widths. You can select the fields in two ways:
    1. Highlight the field, click > or double-click on the field.
    2. Highlight several fields using the CTRL+CLICK and SHIFT+CLICK on the first field, then CRTL+Click on all other desired fields. Then click on the > button to move all highlighted fields to the Columns list. To remove any of your choices, highlight the field and click (<) button. To remove all fields from the **Selected Columns** list, click the (<<) button. If you choose to print notes with any of the fields, you will be asked whether you want all notes or just those with a specific tag. To change the order of your columns, use the up/down arrow buttons next to the **Column Options** button.
- Sort Order. Select this button to tell PAF how you want to sort the data. To sort from the smallest value to the largest, select **Ascending**. To sort from the largest to the smallest, select **Descending**. If you decide to change the sort order for a field, highlight the field in the **Order List**, highlight the field and push the (<) button.
- New. Clear the previous selections to begin to define your new report.
- Open. This button allows you to retrieve previous definitions that have been created and saved.
- Save. Consider saving your **Custom Report**, as it might be an option you will want to use time and time again.
- Print Preview. Until you become comfortable with the options and with your ability to create exactly what you want in exactly the right format, use **Preview** before you use your ink and paper.
- Print. If you are satisfied with the look of the report, **Print**.

Lists

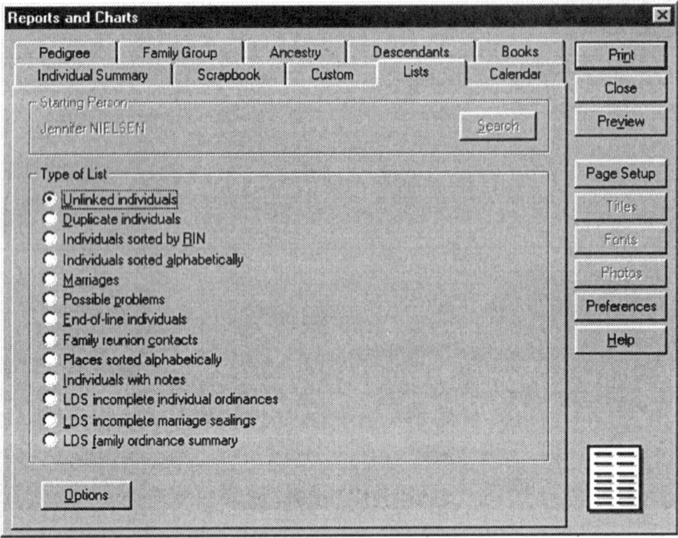

Figure 138

The **List** report allows you to select and print any of the following lists. If you select a list with an **Option** button, that button becomes active. Click it to specify how your list should be printed. (A couple of the **Option** windows are shown below.)

Choose your options from this list:

OPTION	DESCRIPTION
Places sorted alphabetically	A list of records sorted alphabetically by event places and the temple for LDS events.s
Individuals with notes	A list of individuals that have notes.
Unlinked Individuals	A complete list of individuals in your database who are not linked to any family or spouse.

Duplicate Individuals — A complete list of the individual records, which appear to be duplicated, sorted by RIN.

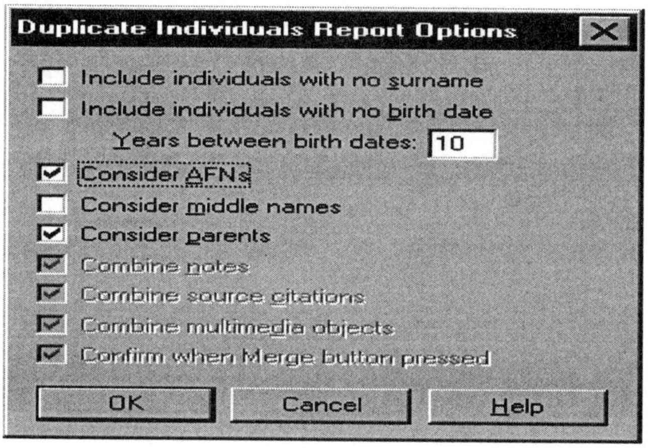

Figure 139

Use this window to select which criteria you want to consider when determining the validity of the duplicate records.

Individuals by RIN — A list of part or all of the individuals in your database, sorted by RIN.

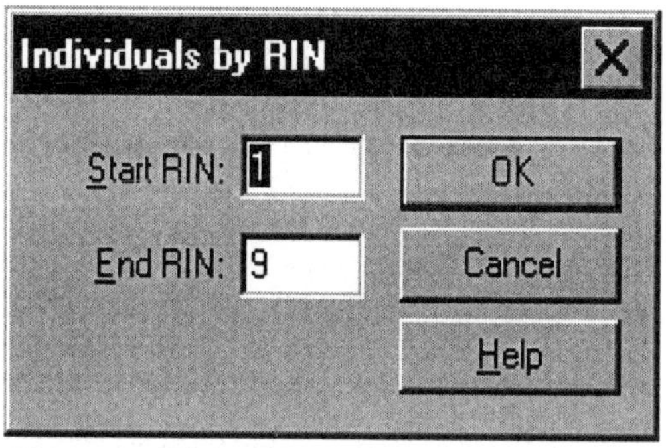

Figure 140

Use the **Option** button to select a starting and ending RIN for the report. The defaults are first and last RINs, which could produce a report with everyone in your database.

Individuals by Alpha — A list of all or some of the individuals in your database, sorted alphabetically by name.

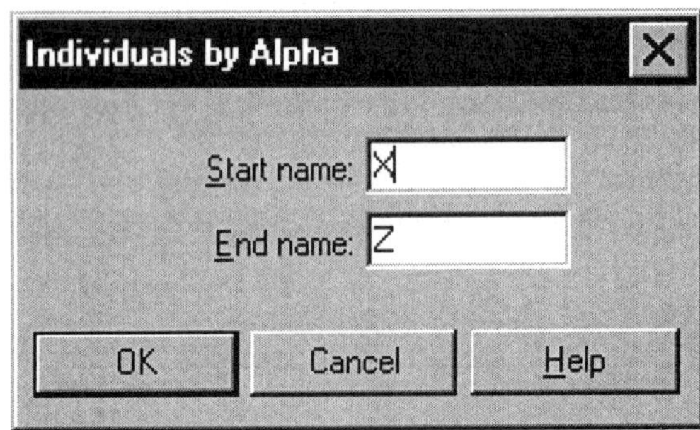

Figure 141

Use this option window to choose the starting and ending names for the report. By default, the report includes names that start with a space through 'Z'. This should be everyone in your database.

Marriages — A list of marriages. You can choose to sort the list by MRIN, husband's name or wife's maiden name. You can also limit the report to a range of MRINs or to a name range.

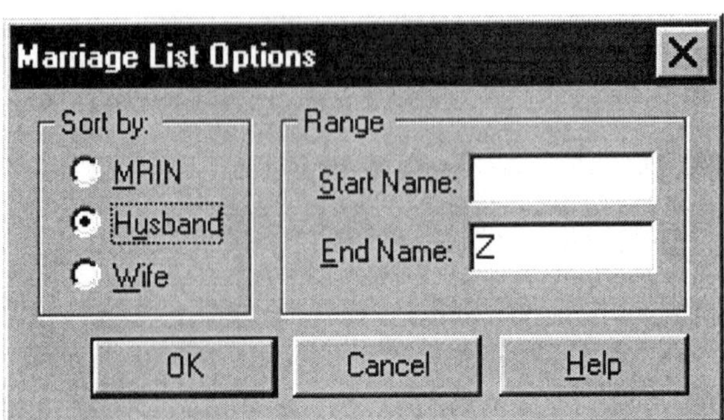

Figure 142

Possible Problems

A list of any data discrepancies, such as a death date prior to a birth date, or a birth date after the parents were too old or had died.

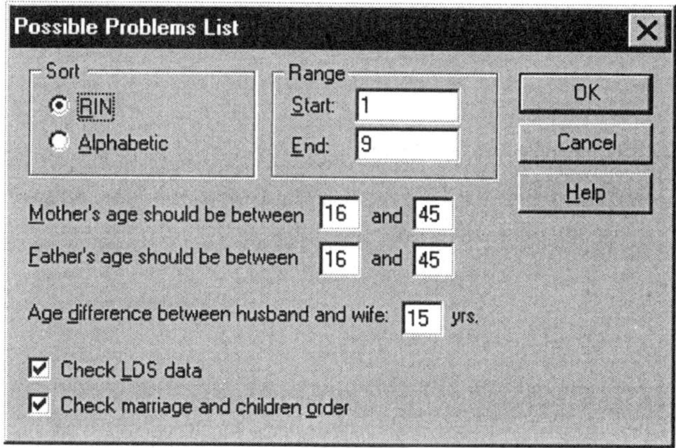

Figure 143

Sort

This option will allow you to sort by RIN or Alphabetically; select Range of records to print; select a range of years for Mother/Fathers age; determine the age difference of husband/wife; check LDS data; check the marriage and child(ren) order.

End-of-line Individuals

A list of individuals who are not linked to parents. The options menu will allow you to search for individuals without any links to parents or those with links to a single line.

End-of-Line Individuals Options

All Individuals without recorded parents

Individuals without recorded parents on a single line

Current selection: Ronda Lyn ROBBINS

OK Cancel Help

Figure 144

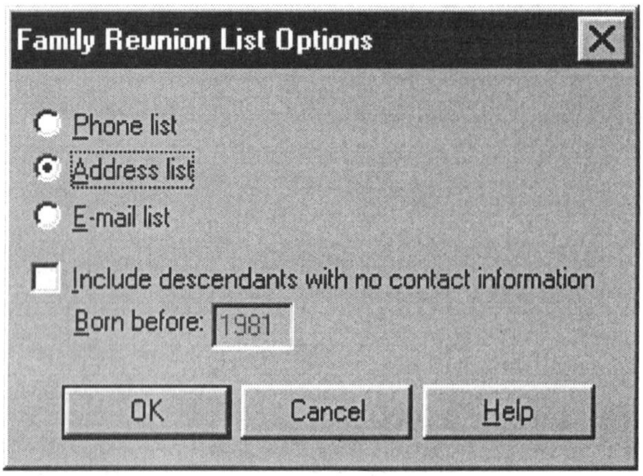

Figure 145

Family Reunion Contacts

A list of the contact information for people in your file. You cannot print this list, however you can export it to a word processor. Before you export you should be aware of the following:

- The starting person should be the patriarch or matriarch of the set of relatives you are interested in. By default the Primary person is the selected individual. To select another individual, select **Search**.
- By default, only those individuals whom you have entered contact information for will be included in the list. To change this select **Options**.
- Only living descendants will be included on the list.
- If the contact name is used for the person and has the value of **NC** or **No Contact** this person will not be included on the list.

Hint: If you enter an address for children still living at home, you will have a number of entries on your list with the same address. Because of the increased mailing costs, you will likely want to exclude these individuals from your list.

When you select the **Family Reunion List** option, the **Options** button becomes accessible. Click the button to open the **Family Reunion List Options** window. (Fig. 145) From this window you can select:

- A telephone list.
- An address list.
- Any mailing address.
- You can also include individuals that have no address, telephone, or e-mail address to your list.
- Specify a **Born before** date. If you would like to specify a calendar year before which you would like descendants to be listed, type that date in the correct field. Only descendants who have a recorded date of birth are listed.

LDS Incomplete Individual Ordinance	An alphabetic list of every individual that is missing at least one ordinance. All available ordinance information is displayed.

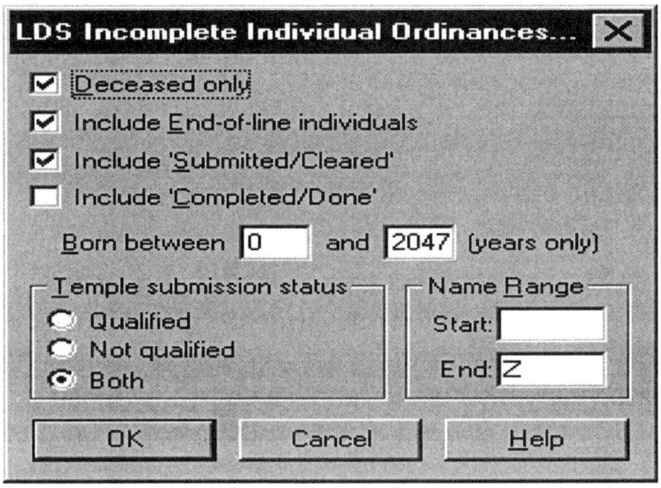

LDS Incomplete Individual Ordinances...
Deceased only
Include End-of-line individuals
Include 'Submitted/Cleared'
Include 'Completed/Done'
Born between 0 and 2047 (years only)
Temple submission status
Qualified
Not qualified
Both
Name Range
Start:
End: Z
OK
Cancel
Help

Figure 146

LDS Incomplete Marriage Sealings	An alphabetic list of marriages that are without a recorded sealing. This report is only available when LDS data option has been selected. It provides an Alphabetical list of marriages that have no recorded sealing date.

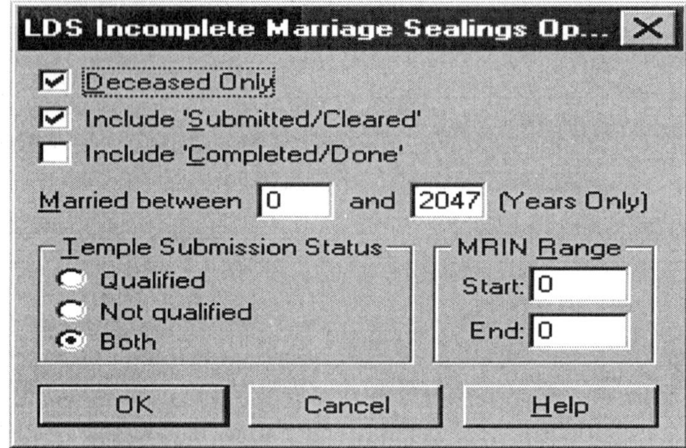

Figure 147

The following options are for **Incomplete Individual** and **Marriage** ordinances:

OPTION	**DESCRIPTION**
Deceased Only	Prints only deceased individuals without temple ordinance information.
Include End-of -Line Individuals	Since end-of-line individuals do not have parents, they are excluded from the **Seal to Parents** ordinance.
Include 'Submitted/ Cleared'	You may want to show individuals with an ordinance status of **Submitted** or **Cleared**, as the work is not yet done.

Include 'Completed/Done'	Although the status of these individuals indicate the ordinance work as complete, you may want a list of these to help you research the exact dates of the ordinance upon completion.
Born between	This range serves much the same purpose as **Deceased Only**, but can give you greater control when reviewing names.
Temple Submission Status	Choosing **Both** displays records that match the other options on this screen. Choosing **Qualified** displays those whose names you could now submit. Choosing **not qualified** limits the report to those few whom you need future research.
Name Range	This range enables you to look at a segment of your database names.
LDS Family Ordinance Summary	A report showing an individual, his/her parents and grandparent and their LDS ordinance information.

Event Calendar

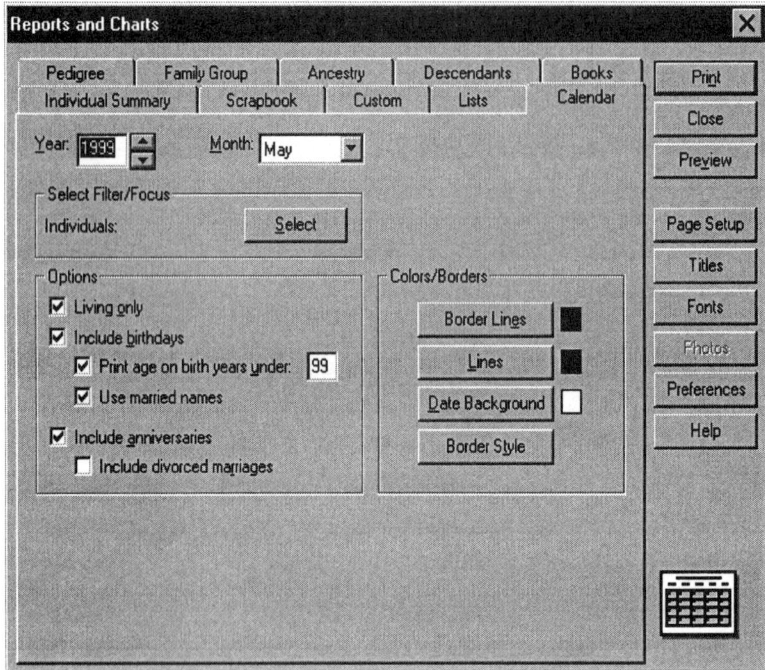

Figure 148

The **Event Calendar** is a great way to remind you of upcoming birthdays and anniversaries! You can print a calendar for any month between the years 1980-2100 by entering a year and selecting a month. If you want a year's worth of calendars, print the pages one at a time, selecting each new month as you go.

Select the **Event Calendar** options from the list below:

OPTION	**DESCRIPTION**
Filter Select	Click the **Select** button to choose the individual(s) that you wish to include on your calendar. If you select no one, PAF will create a blank calendar page for the month designated.

Living Only	Select **Living Only** to create a calendar with those individuals who are living.
Include Birthdays	Select **Include Birthdays** to include the birthdays of the individual(s) on the calendar. • Select **Print age on birth years** if you want to print the ages of the people on the list. Type the age you would like. • Select **Use married names** to use a woman's married name.
Include Anniversaries	Select **Include anniversaries** to include the anniversaries of the individuals on the calendar. • Select **Include divorced marriages** to include any anniversaries even if the couple divorced.
Border Lines	Select **Lines** to create or select a color for the lines around the days of the week.
Date Background	Select **Lines** to create or select a color for the background of the days of the week.
Border Style	Select **Border Style** to choose a style for the lines.

Photos

If you have opted to include photos in your reports, the **Photo** button will be present on each report menu. Clicking on the photo button will bring up the **Photo Options**... window, where you can specify (in most cases) the size of the photo, the placement, and whether to hold space for those individuals that don't have photos attached.

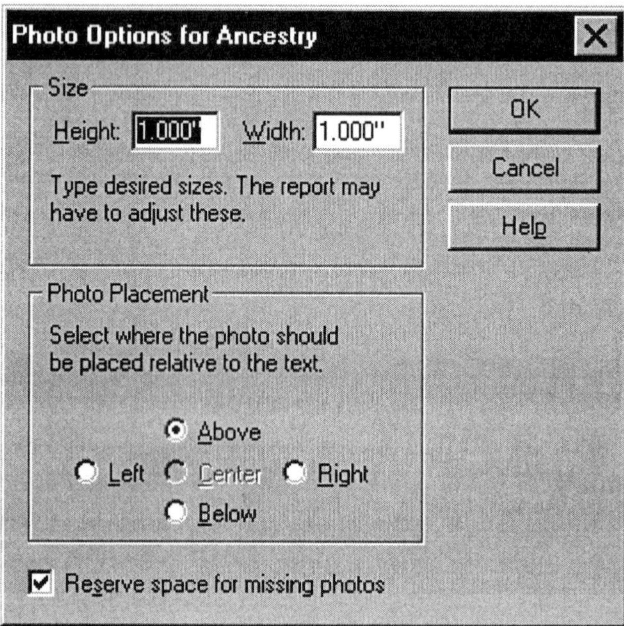

Figure 149

The following options are available:

OPTION	DESCRIPTION
Size	Use the **Size** section of the window to choose the height and width of the photos on the report. Depending on several factors, including the paper size, orientation, and margins, the reports will attempt to accommodate your specified dimensions.
Photo Placement	Use the **Photo Placement** option to place your photos relative to the other printed data for the individual. Each report has different parameters and where this option is not available the option will be faded.
Missing Photos	Use the **Missing Photos:Reserve Space** check box to leave room on the report for a photo to be attached at a later time. If you don't have a photo and don't want to save space for a future time, leave this box unchecked.

Preview

Before you begin printing any report, select **Preview** and see what your report will look like with the options you have selected. You can zoom in to a specific portion of the report, change your display from one to two pages, scroll through several pages, and even print the report directly from this screen. Keep in mind that some photos take longer to display than others. To expedite the process you can choose to place a gray place holder instead of the actual photo. From the toolbar, **Tools ➛ Preferences; Multimedia** to facilitate this change.

Page Setup

If you are attempting to generate wall charts, play with the larger paper size. Windows software now supports some plotters, and you may find you can print your wall chart on a single sheet of paper.

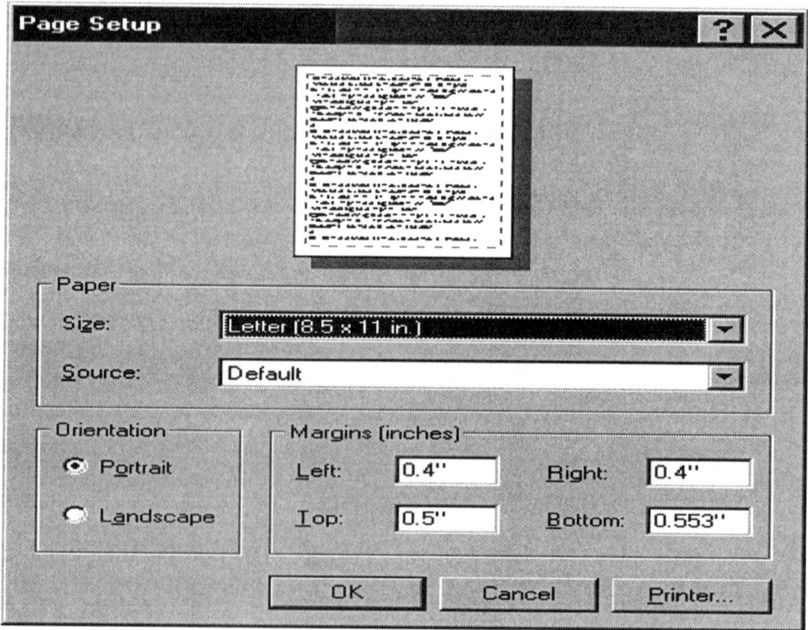

Figure 150

•	Printer	Make sure the printer you intend to use is selected correctly.
•	Paper	You can choose any paper size that your printer will allow.
•	Orientation	The default page is **Portrait** mode, however, if you want to print your reports sideways choose **Landscape**.
•	Margins	Choose any combination of left, right, top and bottom margins.

Printing

When you are ready to print, simply select **Print** in the **Reports** window. You can select a range of pages to print, or a complete report, depending on the printer you selected.

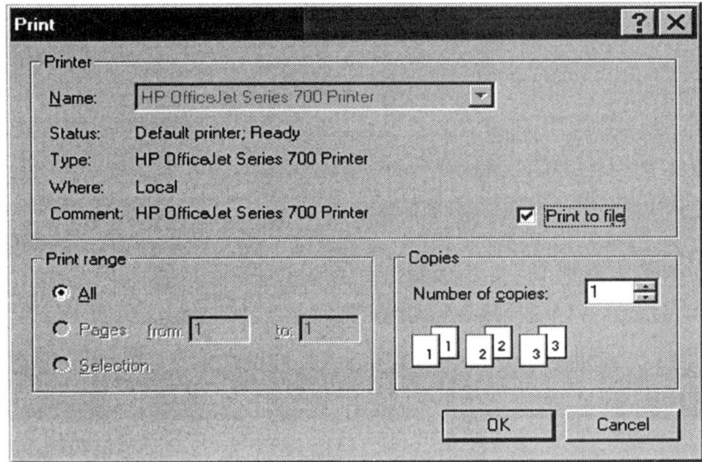

Figure 151

Print to File

There are two ways to send a report to a file, for two entirely different purposes.

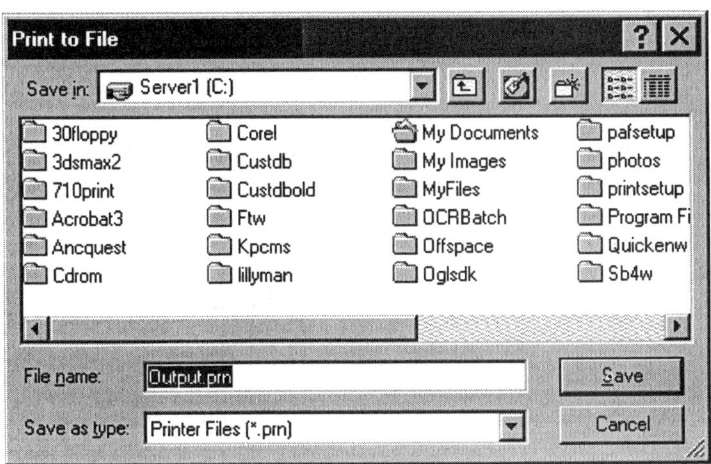

Figure 152

1. Use the **Print to File** option on the **Print** dialogue box that appears after selecting the **Print** button.

    - This will create a file that can be copied to a printer and will have all the codes embedded in it for generating the report later. You can use this option to print a report to a printer you don't have connected. Simply install the driver for the printer on your computer and print the report to a file. Copy the report onto a floppy disk and take it to the printers location where you will copy the file to a printer port using the command: **c:\copy a:myfile,prn lpt1.**

    - If you have access to a Postscript printer, you can print the file to an .EPS file using the above procedure. You then can copy the file to a document in a word processor.

2. This second option is only available for **Custom Reports**, and the **Family Reunion** lists.

    - For **Custom Reports**, select **Print** directly from the **Reports** screen. You will be given the choice of sending the report to a printer or to a file. If you choose the printer, you can still print to a file as mentioned above, or go directly to the printer. If you choose to print to a file from this screen, you will be asked for a filename, and the report will be printed to a text file that can be edited from your word processor.

    - The **Family Reunion Contact** list will only print to a text file. Because of this, the **Print** button changes to **OK** when working with the list.

Chapter 13

Generating Internet Web Pages

This chapter will guide you through the process of creating a web page that will allow you to share your genealogy, including the scrapbook, with relatives, friends or anyone else worldwide.

Web Page Creation

To create a Web Page:

1. Click on

Figure 153

or

2. From the toolbar select **Tools** ➛ **Create a Web Page**.

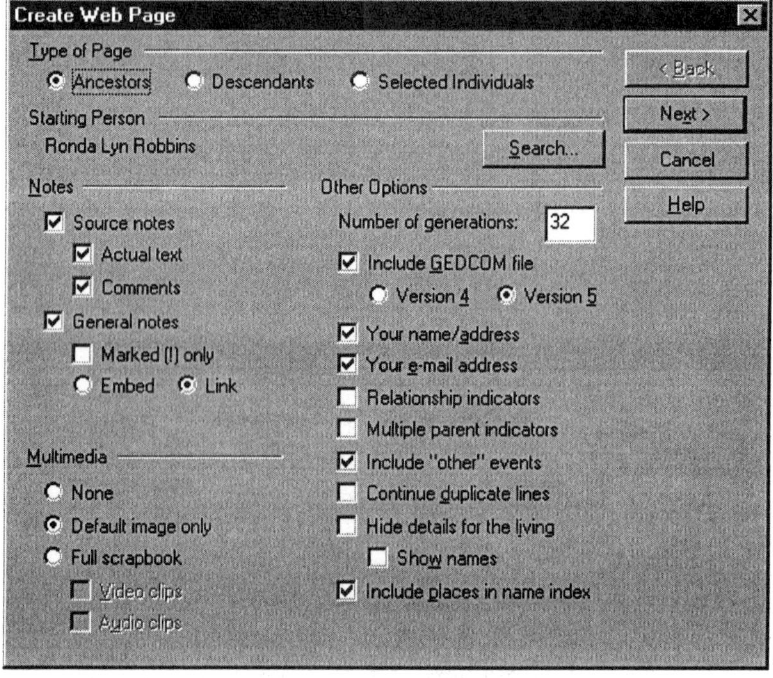

Figure 154

Type of Web Page

Page Type

1. **Ancestry** creates a Web Page that contains the ancestors of a starting person.
2. **Descendants** selects the descendants (children, grandchildren, etc.) of a starting person.
3. **Selected Individuals** allows you to choose which individuals you will display on your Web Page.

Start Person/Filter

This box displays the starting person on the Web Page. If you choose **Selected Individuals**, this box changes to a filter box. You can then click **Select** to choose the individuals you want to include.

Selected Individuals

NOTE: IF YOU ARE DOING A ANCESTOR OR DESCENDENTS WEB PAGE, SKIP THIS SECTION.

To choose a list of **Selected Individuals** click **Select**. PAF will display **Select Set of Individuals**. (Fig. 155)

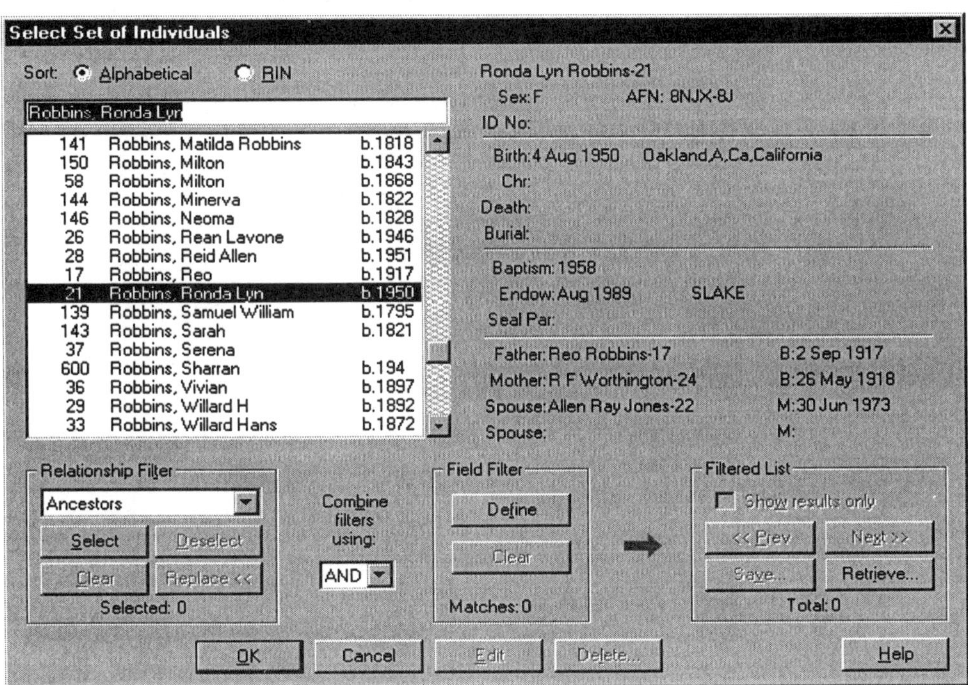

Figure 155

From this window you can select those individuals you want to publish to your Web Page. (See Chapter 9 **Advanced Focus/Filter** if you need to compile a list of individuals.) At **Relationship Filter** you are given a list from which you may narrow your list of individuals. Click the down arrow and make a selection. When you selection process is complete the count of individuals selected will be displayed on the **Create Web Page** window. Select **Next** to continue.

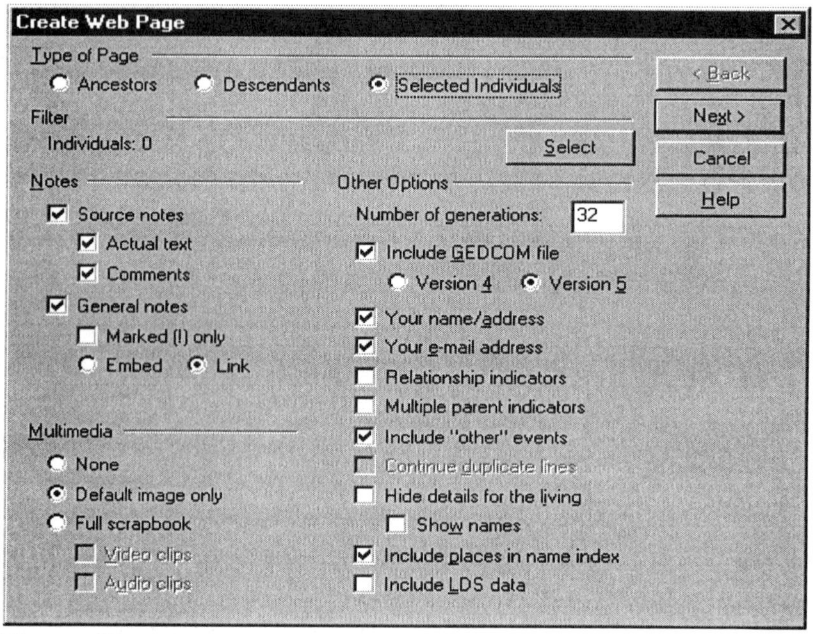

Figure 156

Search/Select — Select this button to choose the starting individual of an **Ancestry** or **Descendants** Web Page or to select the specific individuals you want to include.

There are many options for the design of your Web Page. Click on the box next to the line item to turn the option on or off. The options available are described below.

Notes and Multimedia

Source Notes — Select **Source Notes** to include all source records in your Web Page. If you select **Source Notes**, the following two options become available:

- Select **Actual Text** to include the actual text of your sources.
- Select **Comments** to include the comments in the sources.

General Notes	Select **General Notes** to include your notes. If you select general notes, the following options become available: • Select **Marked (!) Only** to include notes whose first character is (!) • Select **Embed** to embed the notes within the body of text. • Select **Link** to have the notes in a separate, but linked, HTML file.
None	Select **None** if you do not want your Web Page to include any multimedia files.
Default Image Only	Select **Default image only** if you want your Web Page to include each individual's default image.
Full Scrapbook	**Full Scrapbook** if you want your Web Page to include all items in each individual's scrapbook. If you choose **Full**, the following options become available. • Select **Video Clips** if you want to include each individual's video clips. (Available only if you choose Full) • Select **Audio Clips** if you want to include each individual's audio clips. (Available only if you choose Full)

Other Options

Use this section to determine which options, if any, you want to include on your Web Page.

OPTION	DESCRIPTION
Number of Generations	Type the maximum number of generations, from the starting individual, that you want to include.
Include GEDCOM file	Click here if you want to include a GEDCOM file of the individuals on your Web Page that others can download from your site. You can choose GEDCOM vers. 4 or 5. **Hint**: Version 5 is the same as 5.5, which is the version that PAF 3.1 and 4.0 use.
Your name/address	Click if you want your Web Page to include your name and address. This information will come from the **Prepared by** table in the **Preferences** option.
Your e-mail address	Click here if you want your Web Page to include your e-mail address. This information will come from the **Prepared by** table in the **Preferences** option.
Relationship indicators	Click here to display the relationship that each individual has with his/her parents. Relationship codes {A}, {G} and {S} will be included after the name of any individuals who have Adopted, Guardian and Sealed parent relationships.

Multiple parent indicators	Click here if you want an {+} to appear next to individuals who have more than one set of parents. If there is a relationship indicator and a multiple parent indicator they are both enclosed in brackets.
Include "other" events	Click here if you want to include other individual events.
Continue duplicate lines	If you use a descendancy-type of Web Page, line duplication is unnecessary. For the ancestry type of Web Page, duplication is also unnecessary. However you may want the duplicate lines to keep the Ahnentafel numbering pure.
Hide details for the living	Click here if you intend to publish your Web Page on the Internet. This option will hide all information about living individuals. A person who is living displays a designation of **Living** with no additional details or scrapbook items.
Include places in name index	Click here to include places in the name index to your website. This can be useful but might make the name index look a bit cluttered.
Include LDS Data	Click here to include LDS ordinance dates and places. Available only if the LDS Option was turned on under the **Preferences** ➛ **General** window.

Scrapbook Options

Use this section to specify which type of scrapbook items, if any, you would like to include.

None	Select **None** if you do not want your Web Page to include any multimedia files.

Default image only	Select **Default image only** if you want your Web Page to include each individual's default image only.
Full scrapbook	Select **Full scrapbook** if you want your Web Page to include all of the items in the individual's scrapbook. If you select **Full Scrapbook**, the following options become available. • Select **Video Clips** to include video clips. • Select **Audio Clips** to include audio clips.

When you are finished with **Scrapbook**, click on **Next**. PAF will display **Preparer's Address** (Fig. 157) and/or **E-mail Address**. (Fig. 158)

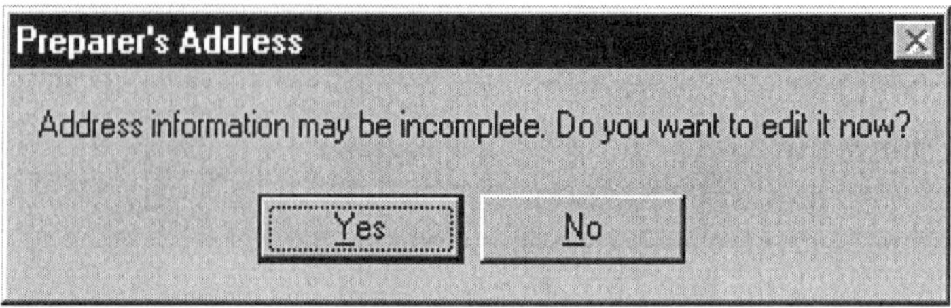

Figure 157

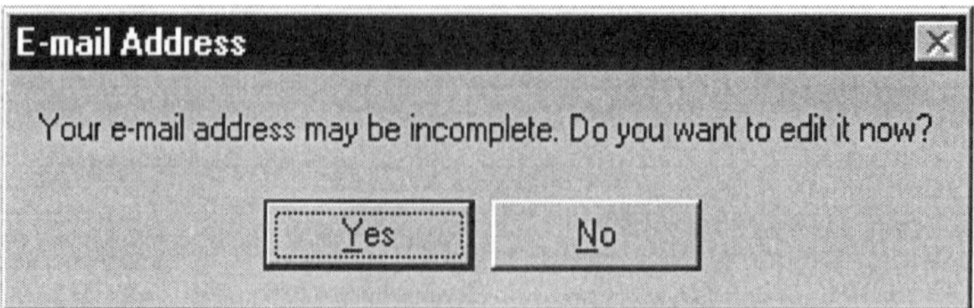

Figure 158

If you are sure this information was entered in the **Preferences ➛ Prepared by**, select **No**. If you are not sure select **Yes**. PAF will display the **Preferences ➛ Prepared by** window. (Fig. 159) Enter the information you want to supply for display on your Web Page.

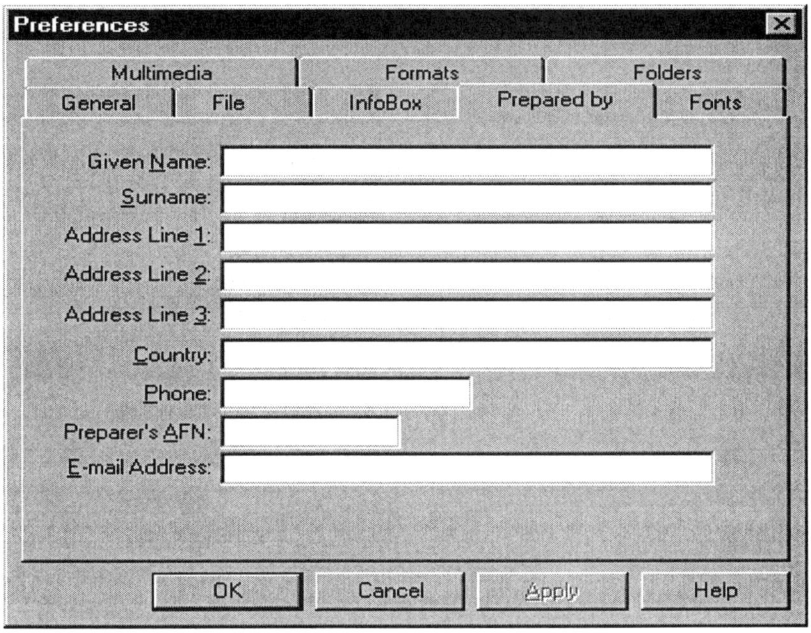

Figure 159

Hint: This information is published to your Web Page and has the following implications:

- Your name is available.
- Your address is available.
- Your telephone number is available.
- Your e-mail address is available.

NOTE: UNDER **OTHER OPTIONS** YOU CAN TURN, **INCLUDE YOUR NAME/ADDRESS**, AND/OR **INCLUDE YOUR EMAIL ADDRESS**, ON/OFF. HOWEVER, TO TURN ON THE INFORMATION YOU MUST FIRST ENTER THE INFORMATION.

When you finish entering the information, click **OK**.

PAF will display **Create Web Page**.

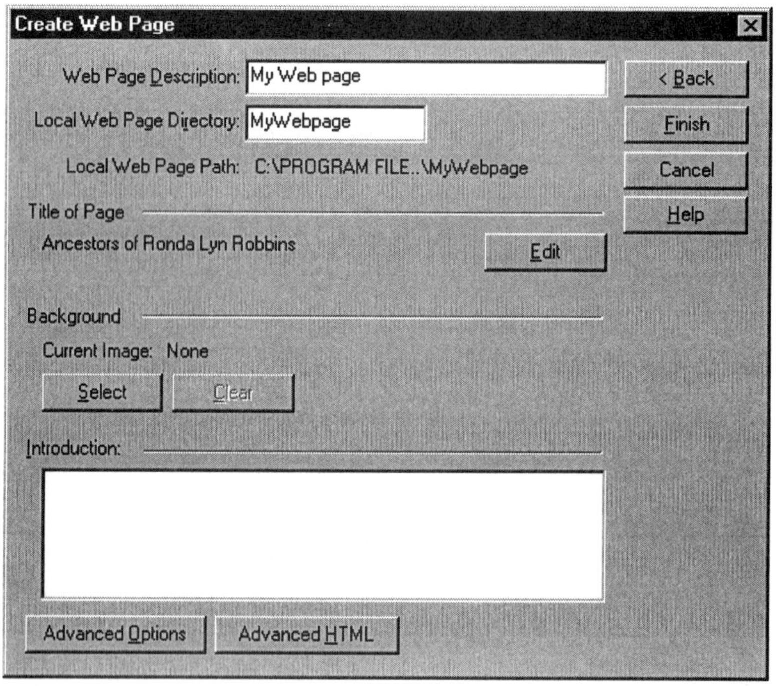

Figure 160

If you choose to publish your Web Page to the Internet you will need to provide a description of your Web Page. The following are options which you must choose.

- **Web Page Description**. Enter a brief description of your Web Page. For example, My Web Page.

- **Local Web Page Directory**. Enter the folder where the Web Page will reside. You can create a new directory with a name of up to eight characters in length. If you type in a description, a folder name will be suggested after the first few characters. (Fig. 160)

- **Local Web Page Path** will display the folder or subdirectory name where the Web Page will be constructed on your hard disk prior to uploading to your Internet site.

- **Title**. You can modify the title that will appear on your Web Page. Push the **Change...** button to access this option.

- **Background Image** allows you to **Select** or **Clear** the background image of your Web Page. (See Chapter 7 - **Multimedia Collections** for the list of formats that are supported by PAF 4.0) Click **Select**. PAF will display **Open Photo File for Web page Background Image**. (Fig. 161)

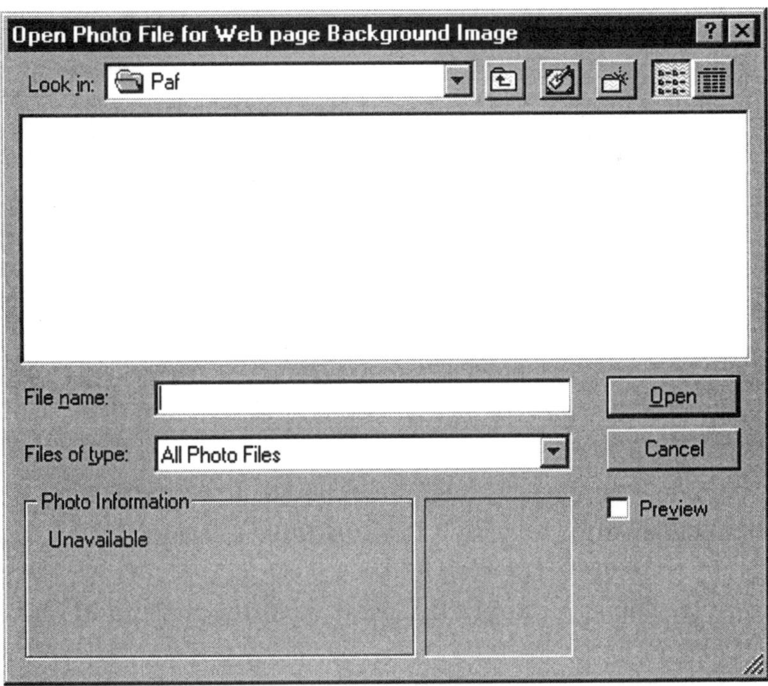

Figure 161

If you scanned photos, a list of files will be displayed. Select the photo you wish to use. To view any of the items listed, highlight the file name and select **Preview**.

Introduction is any additional text you want to appear on the top of the index page. PAF will store the first few hundred characters for use in later pages, but if the description becomes too long, you will find you have to reenter some of it each time you generate a Web Page.

For those individuals that understand HTML, the **Advanced HTML** button allows you to specify a link to a parent page, along with header and footer HTML code to appear on the top and bottom of each page. This is useful if you have a family logo or copyright notice you want to appear on each page.

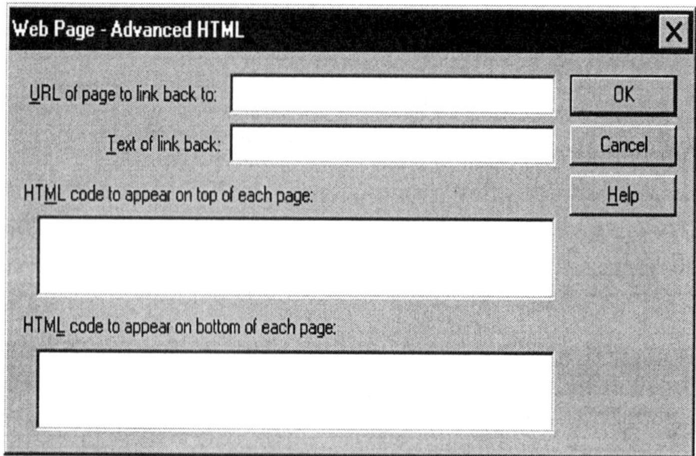

Figure 162

Advanced HTML Options

OPTION	DESCRIPTION
URL of page to link back to	Enter the URL of the page for which you want this page, created by PAF, to link .

Text of link back	Enter the text you want the user to see for the link back to a **master** or **parent** page. If you don't have a master or parent page, leave this option blank.
HTML code to appear on top of each page	You may a logo, slogan or other text or image you want to include as a header on each page. Enter the HTML code for that header.
HTML code to appear on bottom of each page	If you have a copyright notice or other information you want to include in the footer, enter the HTML code for the footer.

Advanced Options

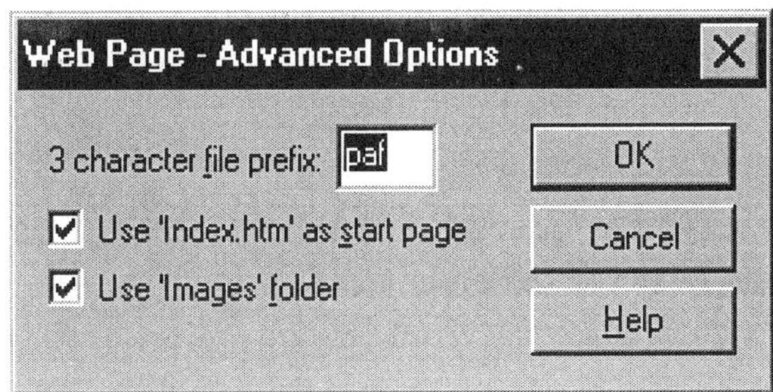

Figure 163

OPTION	DESCRIPTION
3 Character file prefix	If you intend to place several Web Pages in the same directory of your website, you need to assign a different three-character prefix for each to keep them from trying to use the same name.
Use 'Index.htm' as start page	PAF creates the start page with the name **index.htm**. If you have another primary page, or if your Internet Service Provider (ISP) requires a name other than Index.htm, you can change the name of the start page.

Use ‘Image’ Folder	A sub-folder named Images includes any graphics (scrapbook images or a background image or even the standard navigation icons for next, previous, etc.). Some ISPs do not allow users to have sub-folders, so you can override this default.

If you need to go back to the previous screen, select **Back**. To complete your Web Page, Select **Finish**.

PAF will display **Create Web Page**. (Fig. 164), immediately replaced by **GEDCOM Export**. Fig. 165)

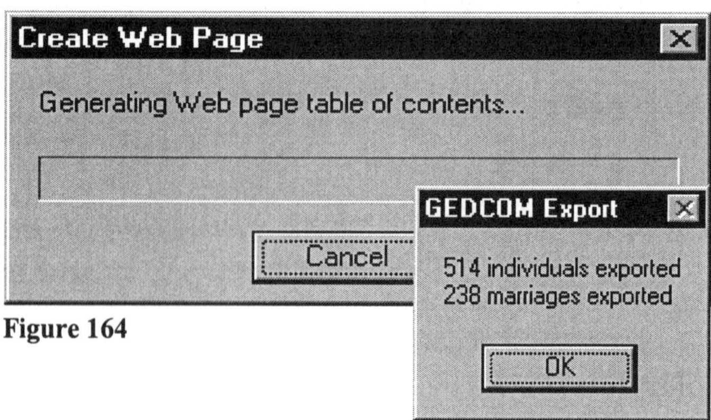

Figure 164

Figure 165

The **GEDCOM Export** window will display a count of individuals being included in the GEDCOM file. When the count is complete click **OK**. PAF will return to **Create Web Page**. (Fig. 165). **Generating Web Page** will display and the field window in the center will begin to fill as the Web Page nears completion. Upon completion, a pop-up window will be displayed. (Fig. 166) This window will show the location of your Web Page and brief instructions.

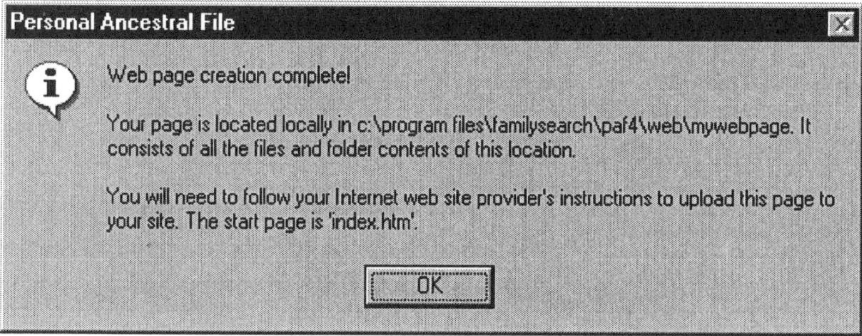

Figure 166

PAF will then ask if you would like to view your Web Page. Select **Yes** or **No** . If you select yes, your Web browser will open and your new Web Page will be displayed.

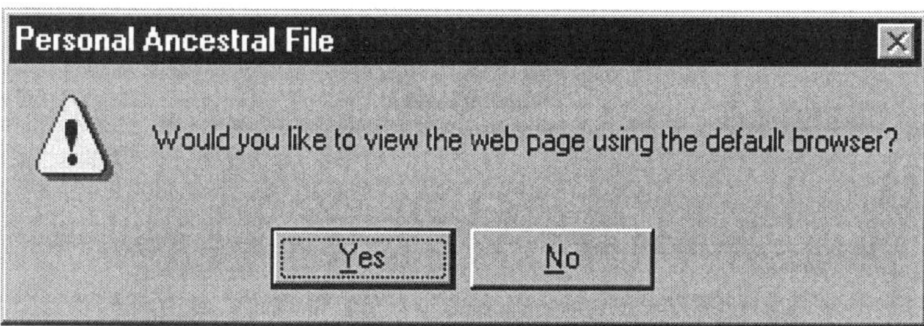

Figure 167

You will need to follow instructions provided by your ISP, or contact your ISP for instructions, to upload your page to the Internet.

A Note about Uploading Your Web Page
PAF will create a local copy of a Web Page on your hard disk in the directory specified by Local Web Page Path near the top of this screen. In order to make this page available on the Internet, you must follow the instructions of your Internet Service Provider to upload this page. YOU WILL WANT TO UPLOAD ALL FILES, FOLDERS, AND FILES IN SUBDIRECTORY FOLDERS TO YOUR INTERNET SITE.

Appendix A

Tagged Notes

Tagged notes contain a specific kind of information. The information is "tagged" using a descriptive word or unique character. Previous versions of PAF allowed you to record dates and places of only a very few events: birth, christening, death, burial, and marriage. The notes were then used to record information concerning other types of events.

Tags can serve many useful purposes. You may want to use them to identify Events, Subjects, or Relationships. You can use them as a reminder that Research needs action or follow-up. You can use LDS or Tags representative of other religions to identify notes about events in the lives of family members.

There are two unique tags used in PAF 4.0. Notes marked with an explanation point (!) are referred to as **Marked Notes**. Notes marked with a tilde (~) are referred to as **Confidential Notes**. These two tags are used primarily to allow the user certain printing options. You may elect to print:

- All Notes
- All Notes less Confidential Notes
- Only Marked Notes

(See Chapter 12 **Printing Charts, Reports & Lists** for a more detailed treatment.)

PAF 4.0 provides a number of pre-defined tags for your use. However, you can add an unlimited number of your own tags as well.

The **Notes Selector** will allow you work with all of the notes for an individual at once or with the notes with a particular tag.

A number of useful tags are listed below.

Event Tags:

Adoption	Divorce	Birth
Emigration	Christening	Marriage
Immigration	Cremation	Naturalization
Death	Probate	Burial

Research Tags:

Action	Name (variations)	AKA (also known as)
Comment	Note	Nil (no information located)
Conflict	Dead end	Place
Error	Question	Researcher
File	Update	

Subject Tags:

Biography	Land	Cemetery
Military	Census	Obituary
Citizenship	Occupation	Court
Organizations	Education	Relationship
Honors	Religion	Hospital
Residences		

Relationship Tags:

Child	Parents	Siblings
Children	Father	Spouse
Half-(relative)	Step-(relative)	Mother

LDS Tags:

Baptism	Mission	Blessing
Patriarchal_Blessing	Confirmation	Priest
Deacon	Sealing_Parents	Elder
Sealing_Spouse	Endowment	Seventy
High-Priest	Teacher	

Appendix B

PAF 2.x File conversion

If you have used PAF 2.31 you must convert your databases before using them.

From the toolbar select **File** ➛ **Open**. At **Files of Type** click on the down arrow and select **All *.*; Search**. This action will find all PAF, .DAT and .GED files. This action will allow you to view all of your genealogy files at once.

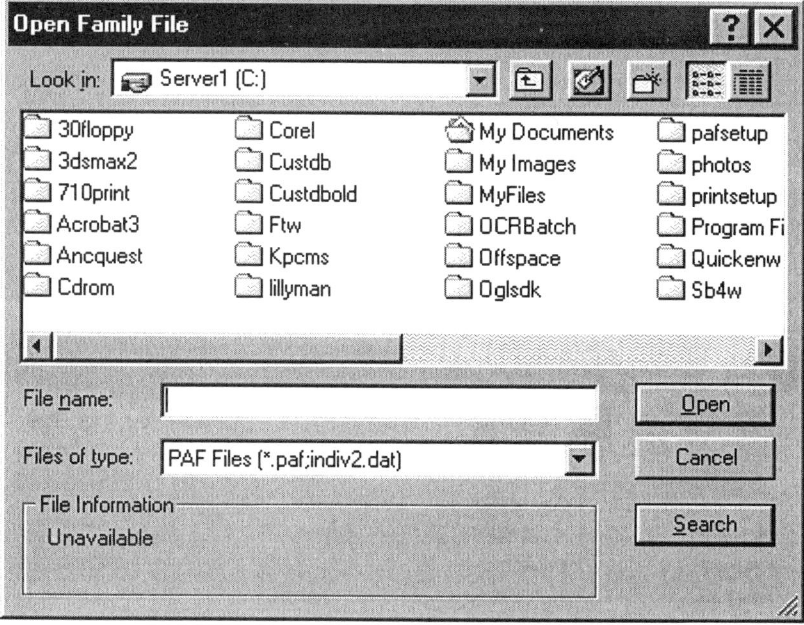

Figure 168

PAF will display **Open Family File**. (Fig. 169) Highlight the INDIV2.DAT file to convert.

Open Family File

Files:	Name:	Individuals:	Marriages:
c:\PAF3\DATA\HANSEN.PAF	HANSEN	0	0
c:\PAF3\DATA\HESTERMN.PAF	HESTERMN	0	0
c:\PAF3\DATA\JOHNSON.PAF	JOHNSON	3510	1575
c:\PAF3\DATA\LUKE.PAF	LUKE	918	386
c:\PAF3\DATA\RICHARD.PAF	RICHARD	376	142
c:\PAF3\DATA\ROGER.PAF	ROGER	14741	5961
c:\PAF3\DATA\ROSEMARY.PAF	ROSEMARY	312	199
c:\PAF3\DATA\SPEIRS.PAF	SPEIRS	10600	5857
c:\PAF3\DATA\TOMST.PAF	TOMST	25	7
c:\PAF3\DATA\WEBLAWRE.PAF	WEBLAWRE	0	0
c:\PAF3\DATA\WEBSITE.PAF	WEBSITE	14731	5959
c:\PAF3\WILCKEN.PAF	WILCKEN	0	0
c:\PCOMP\FARREN.PAF	FARREN	85	30
c:\PRACTICE\indiv2.dat	Untitled	0	0
c:\WINDOWS\F146\INDIV2.DAT	Untitled	0	0

Open Cancel

Figure 169

Click **Open**. PAF will display the **PAF 2.x File Conversion** window. (Fig. 170) There are three options that allow you to customize the conversion process.

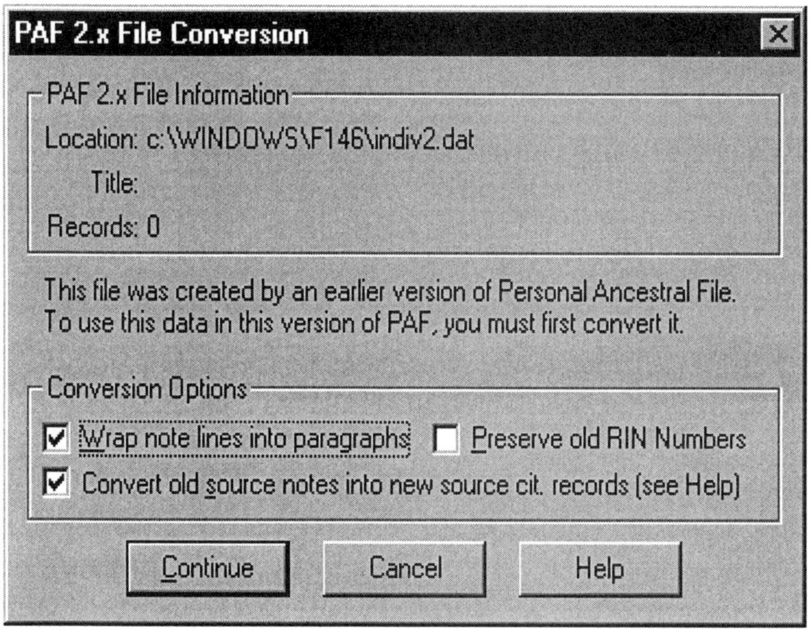

PAF 2.x File Conversion

PAF 2.x File Information

Location: c:\WINDOWS\F146\indiv2.dat

Title:

Records: 0

This file was created by an earlier version of Personal Ancestral File.
To use this data in this version of PAF, you must first convert it.

Conversion Options

Wrap note lines into paragraphs
Preserve old RIN Numbers
Convert old source notes into new source cit. records (see Help)

Continue
Cancel
Help

Figure 170

OPTIONS	**DESCRIPTION**
Wrap note lines into paragraphs	Before version 3.0, the notes in PAF did not wrap. This meant that you had to press ENTER after each line which was 79 characters. You pressed ENTER twice to separate paragraphs. Select this option to remove the line breaks within notes. The conversion process will maintain the double line breaks between paragraphs. **Hint**: If you do not select this option, your notes will print only about 2/3 of the way across the page.
Preserve old RIN numbers	Select this option if you are used to the RIN numbers used in your previous database and would like to keep them.

Convert old source notes into new source citations records.

If you used the source guidelines from Silicon Valley PAF users group (SVPAFUG) or from the PAF 2.31 manual to type your sources into notes, you can choose to have these converted into sources. Each time the conversion process finds such a source, it pauses and shows you how the information will be converted. You can then indicate whether or not you want it to be converted. All of your notes that are not sources will be transferred to notes.

Hint: If you are not sure if you followed these guidelines, select the option and see what happens. It will probably be faster than transferring the notes manually. If you do not like how a note would be converted, you can indicate that PAF should not convert it.

When you are finished click **Continue**. PAF will then display the **Save As** window. (Fig. 171) Give your file a name and select **Save**.

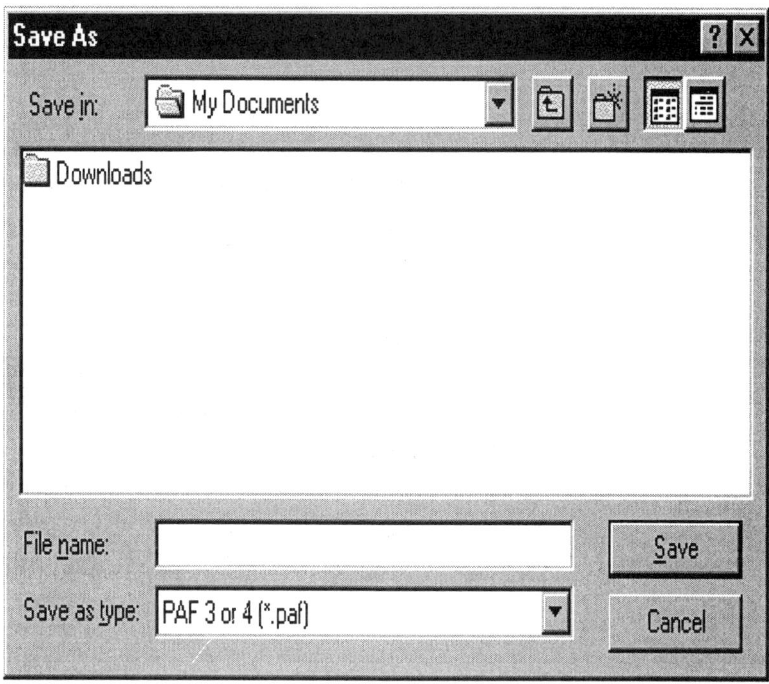

Figure 171

PAF will then complete the conversion process. Depending on the speed of your computer and the size of your file, you might see a new window on your screen, **File Converter**. (Fig. 172)

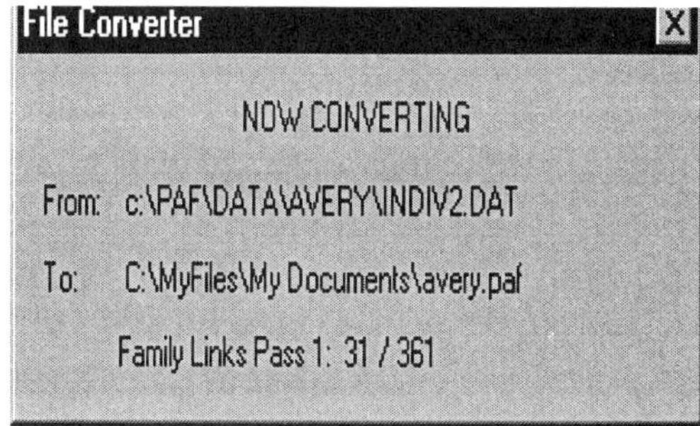

Figure 172

If you did not have any sources to convert, PAF will display the **Family View** window with your newly converted file in place.

If you have sources to convert, PAF will display **Convert Source Notes for...**(Fig. 173) PAF will display this window for each source you have in your database.

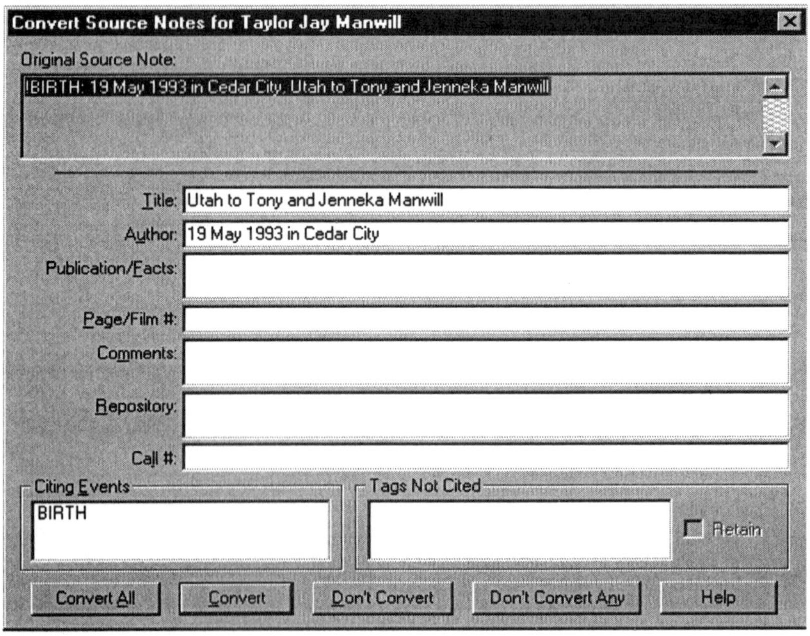

Figure 173

The conversion process follows these conventions:

- It identifies source notes as those that have an exclamation point (!) as their first character.
- It uses semicolons (;) to determine when one piece of information ends and the next starts.
- It uses tags to determine which pieces of information to transfer into which fields in a source. The tags themselves are not transferred.
    - It puts the title in the **Source Title** field.
    - It puts the author in the **Author** field.
    - It puts the years covered in the **Comments** field.
    - It puts the series, volume, and publisher information in the **Publication Facts** field.

- It puts page numbers in the **Film/Volume/Page #** field on the citation detail.
- It adds the repository name and address to a list of repositories, and adds that repository to the source record.
- It adds text and comments to the **Comments** field.

Hint: If the information does not get transferred onto the source record as you would like, you can edit the source record and use cut, copy, and paste to move information to the fields you want.

Appendix C

Temple Names Preparation

To submit your names to Temple Ready™, you must first prepare and qualify your documentation. Upon completion of the preparation and qualification process you then take your files to a family history center or The Family History Library, located in Salt Lake City, Utah. There you can use Temple Ready™ to verify that you have provided enough information for ordinance work and verify completed ordinances. Temple Ready™ will qualify and prepare a file for submission to any LDS Temple.

Guidelines for submitting names for temple ordinances.

- Do not submit names for individuals to whom you are not related.
- A person whose name is submitted must have been dead at least one full year unless permission from their Bishop is obtained.
- If the person was born within the past ninety-five years, permission should be obtained from a living relative before submitting the name.
- Ordinances are not necessary for children who are stillborn. However, if the possibility exists that the child lived after birth, the sealing to parents should be completed. Unless, of course the child was born in the covenant. (The child's parents were sealed before the birth.)
- Children who died before their eighth birthday and were not born in the covenant should be sealed to the parents. No other ordinance work is necessary.
- Clearance must be obtained from the First Presidency before temple ordinances may be performed for deceased persons who, at the time of their death, were excommunicated or had their names removed from Church records.

Information Required for Temple Ordinances

This list shows the minimum information needed to perform ordinances. Some information can be estimated. The information should be as accurate as reasonably possible. PAF will automatically check each name you select to verify the necessary information.

Baptism and Endowment
- Name
- Sex
- Event date, such as a birth date (at least the year is required)
- Event place, such as a birthplace (at least a country is required)

Sealing to Parents
- Information under Baptism and Endowment
- First or last name of the father

Sealing to Spouse
- Name of the husband
- Marriage date
- Marriage place

Using the Temple Names Submission Options Screen

OPTION	DESCRIPTION
Submit only qualified individuals	Select this option to check the individuals you selected to verify they have enough information to qualify for temple ordinances. PAF will then include only those names that qualify in your submission.

Option	Description
Submit all selected individuals	Select this option to submit all individuals you select, regardless of whether they have enough information to qualify. **Hint:** Use this option if you want TempleReady™ to verify that an individual has enough information to qualify for temple ordinances.
Put the word *Submitted* in ordinance fields to indicate names sent to the temple	Select this option to add the word *Submitted* to the ordinance date fields. **Hint:** You may want to use this feature if you are submitting a large number of names. It will help to track which names have been submitted. When the individual ordinance work is complete you can replace Submitted with the date.
Produce a submission report	Select this option to produce a submission report. The report will list the people and ordinances that were submitted. It also contains the reasons some ordinances were not submitted. **Hint:** This report will be displayed in NotePad after the export process is complete.

Export Information for TempleReady™

From the toolbar, select **File** ➛ **Export**. Select **TempleReady™**. (Fig. 174)

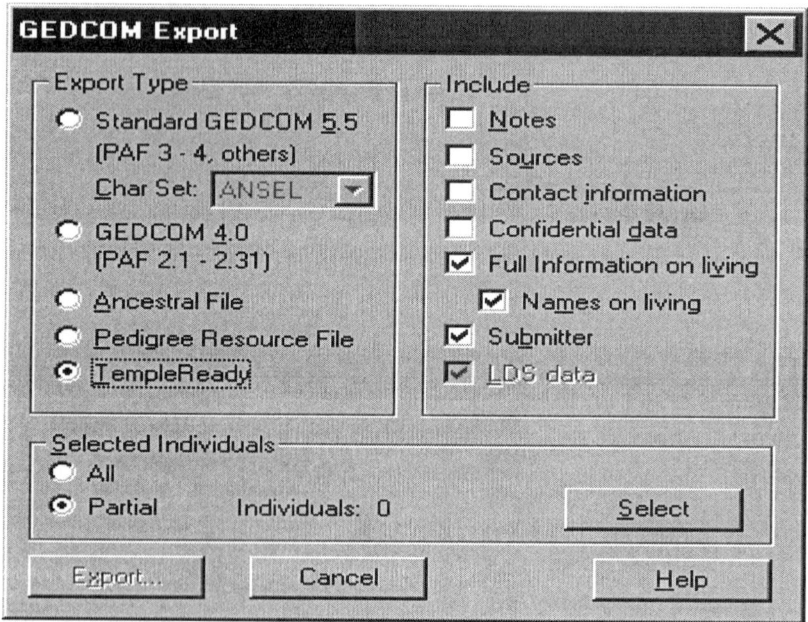

Figure 174

Include All Individuals

1. Select **All** (includes all individuals).

2. Select the **Include** options. (See Chapter 5 **Maintaining Your Database** for a detailed description of each feature)

3. Select **Export**. PAF will display **Temple Names Submission** window. Read this and click **Continue**.

4. Select the **Submission** options from **Temple Names Submission Options**. Click **OK**. (Fig. 175)

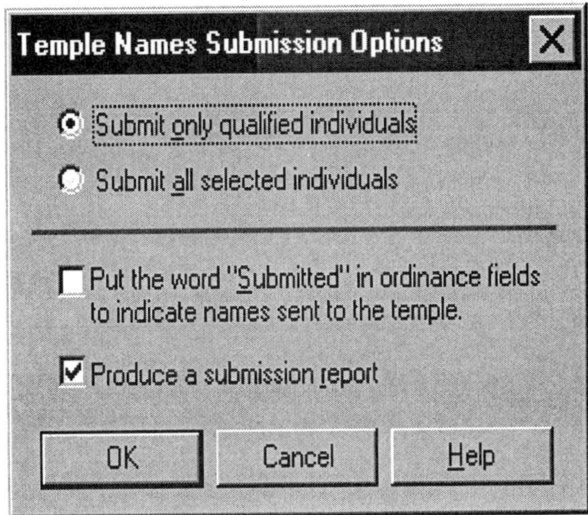

Figure 175

5. PAF will display the window **Export GEDCOM file as.** Enter the name of the file. Select **Export**.

6. PAF will display two windows. (Fig. 176 and 177) The top smaller window displays how many names were exported. Click **OK**. You will then see **TempleReady™ Instructions**. Read these instructions. Click *OK*.

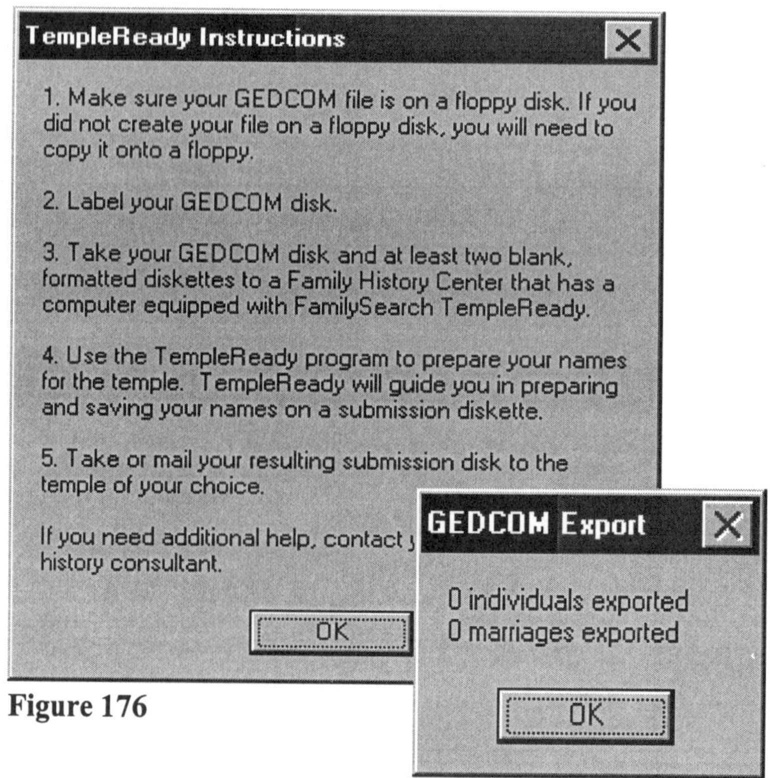

Figure 176

Figure 177

Hint: If you requested a printed report, PAF will display that report in NotePad, where you can read, print, or edit. When you have finished, select **File ➤ Exit**.

Export - Selected Individuals, Partial

From the **GEDCOM Export** window, (Fig. 167) Select **Partial; Select**. PAF will display **Select Set of Individuals -Temple Names Preparation**. (Fig. 178)

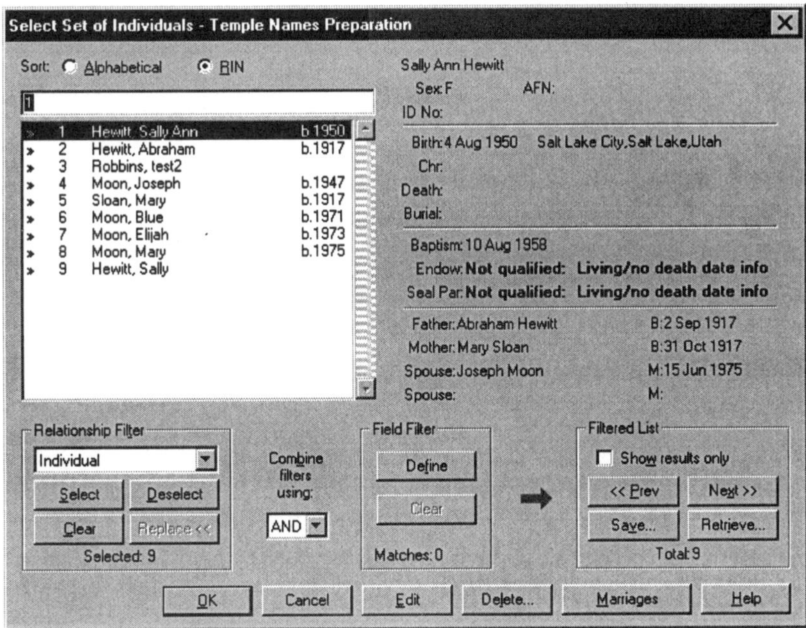

Figure 178

Use the relationship and field filters to select specific individuals. (See Chapter 9 **Advances Focus/Filter**) If you select **Marriages** on the bottom of this window a new window, **Temple Names Preparation-Seal to Spouse Status** will display. At this window you can edit a couple's marriage information. If you find the record is missing marriage information, select **Edit**, and add the data. This step allows PAF to qualify a record that otherwise would not have qualified.

Hint: If you click **Select**, PAF will display the ordinances for which the individual qualifies. PAF will allow you to edit the individual and marriage record.

1. Select the **Include** options.

2. Select **Export**.

3. PAF will display **Temple Names Submission** window. Read this and click **Continue**.

4. Select the **Submission** options from **Temple Names Submission Options**. Click **OK**.

5. PAF will display the window **Export GEDCOM file as**. Enter the name of the file. Select **Export**.

6. PAF will display two windows. (Fig. 176 & 177) The top smaller window tell you how many names were export. Click **OK**. You will then see **TempleReady™ Instructions**. Read these instructions. Click **OK**.

Hint: If you requested a printed report, PAF will display that report in NotePad, where you can read, print or edit. When you have finished, select **File ➤ Exit**.

Appendix D

Understanding the Log

As you make changes to your database, PAF records a log with all the changes made. The log contains a time and date of the change. A code indicates what changed. To turn the log on/off: From the toolbar select Tools ➛ Preferences; File. PAF will display **Preferences**. To turn the log on, select **Log Changes**.

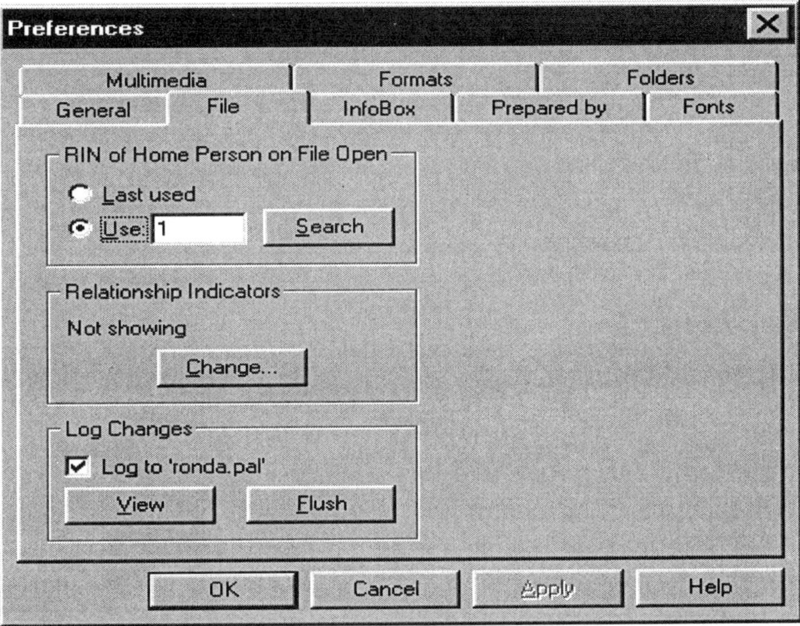

Figure 179

Keeping a log of your changes is useful if you have wondered if you made a mistake or if you are coordinating research efforts with someone else.

Examples of log entries are as follows:

LOG ENTRY	MEANING
3-12-97 11:29 Mod Ind 1	This entry indicates that on 12 March 1997, the record with RIN 1 was modified.
3-12-97 11:35 Mod Nts 15	This entry indicates that on 12 March 1997, the notes for RIN 15 were modified.
3-12-97 11:41 Unl Ch 62 10	This entry indicates that on 12 March 1997, the RIN (child) 62 was unlinked from RIN 10.
3-12-97 11:41 Unl Sp 63 10	This entry indicates that on 12 March 1997, that (spouse) RIN 63 was unlinked from RIN 10.
3-12-97 11:41 Del Mar 10	This entry indicates that 12 March 1997, that RIN 10 was deleted.

View the Log

From the **Preferences** window (Fig. 179) select **View**. (This option is only available if a log exits.) PAF will display ….**pal - Notepad**. (Fig. 180)

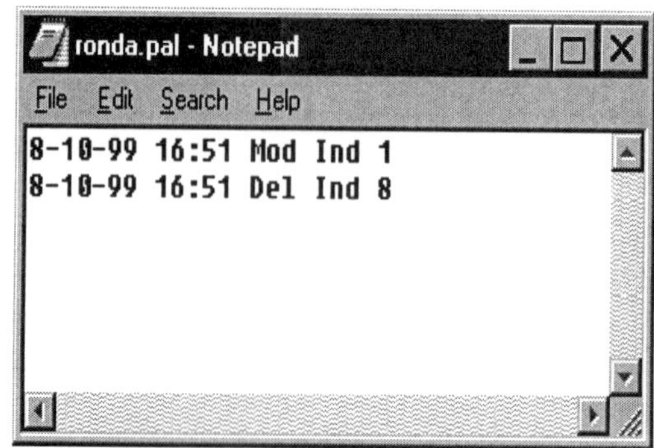

Figure 180

Flush the Log

From the **Preferences** window (Fig. 179) click **Flush**. The **View** and **Flush** will become light gray meaning those options are now longer available.

From time to time the log should be flushed or deleted.

Appendix E

Pedigree Resource File

Submitting Information to the Pedigree Resource File

The Pedigree Resource File is a computer file that contains names, family relationships, birth, marriage, and death information for millions of people. The information in this file will appear as it was originally submitted and will not be merged with information submitted by others.

You can both obtain information from the Pedigree Resource File and contribute information. You are responsible for the accuracy of the information you provide. Please verify the following provisions:

- Your records are accurate and, if possible, documented.
- Your records **do not** contain information that may confuse, mislead, hurt, or embarrass other people.
- Your records contain information about living people only if they have granted permission for use.

The Pedigree Resource File is maintained by the Family History Department of The Church of Jesus Christ of Latter-day Saints.

You are invited to contribute your information to the Pedigree Resource File. You can contribute through the Internet at *www.familysearch.org*. If you don't have access to the Internet you can submit your information using a floppy disk. Mail the disk to:

Family History Department
Ancestral File Operations Unit
50 E. North Temple St.
SLC, Utah 84150-3400
USA

Copyright and the Pedigree Resource File

To protect Pedigree Resource File contributions from misuse, the file is copyrighted by Intellectual Reserve, Inc.

As part of the file, information you contribute may be available to the public in the Family History Library located in Salt Lake City, Utah, family history centers worldwide and in other LDS Church facilities. In addition, copies of the file will be available for sale. The indexes may eventually be available on the Internet.

If you do not want to give permission to have your information published, or if you are not authorized to give permission, please do not contribute to the Pedigree Resource File.

Including your information in Pedigree Resource File does not limit your right to publish the information yourself or to give it to others.

Conditions for Submitting to the Pedigree Resource File

To submit your genealogy to The Church of Jesus Christ of Latter-day

Saints, you must agree to these conditions:

1. You must get permission from all living persons named in your submission.

2. You give the LDS Church permission to publish your name and address as the contributor of the information you submitted. This helps others coordinate research with you.

3. You give the LDS Church permission to use, copy, modify, and distribute any of the information included in your submission without compensation and in any form the LDS Church feels appropriate. You also give the LDS Church permission to use the information from your submission to create new databases.

4. You affirm that you have the right to give the LDS Church permission to use the information in your submission, as described in these conditions. You agree to indemnify the LDS Church for any legal claims resulting from the use of the information in your submission.

5. The LDS Church is not responsible for any alteration, loss, damage, or corruption to your submission.

6. Once you submit your genealogy to the LDS Church, it becomes the property of the LDS Church and cannot be retracted or returned. However, this does not limit your right to publish, sell, or give the information to others.

To Export Information for the Pedigree Resource File

From the toolbar, select **File** ➛ **Export**. PAF will display **GEDCOM Export**. (Fig. 181)

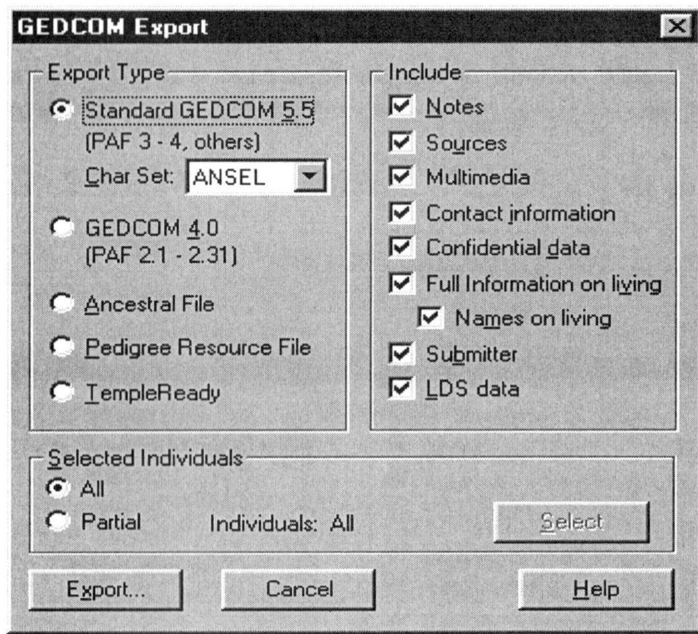

The procedure for this option is exactly the same as those for TempleReady. Go to Appendix C - **Export Individuals for TempleReady™**. Follow the guidelines provided to create and export a GEDCOM file to submit to the Pedigree Resource File.

Appendix F

Source Citations

Name of Publication: ______________________________
(The full title of the source or record.

Add'l Information: ______________________________
(Record may contain other information–name of the compiler, translator, etc.)

Publisher: ______________________________
(Include name of publisher, place, and date of publication.)

Call No.: ______________________________

Vol./Film # & Page ______________________________

Repository: ______________________________
(Name, address and telephone number of the repository where record may be found, if applicable.)

Notes about Source: ______________________________
(Is the book indexed? # of pages in the book/source. # of pages copied. Condition, etc.)

Appendix G

Decimal Numbers for Diacritics

DECIMAL	CHARACTER	DECIMAL	CHARACTER
0138	Ŝ	0221	Ý
0140	Œ	0222	Þ
0154	ŝ	0223	ß
0156	œ	0224	à
0159	Ÿ	0225	á
0161	¡	0226	â
0192	À	0227	ã
0193	Á	0228	ä
0194	Â	0229	å
0195	Ã	0230	è
0196	Ä	0231	ç
0197	Å	0232	è
0198	Æ	0233	é
0199	Ç	0234	ê
0200	È	0235	ë
0201	É	0236	ì
0202	Ê	0237	í
0203	Ë	0238	î
0204	Ì	0239	ï
0205	Í	0240	õ
0206	Î	0241	ñ
0207	Ï	0242	ò
0208	Đ	0243	ó
0209	Ñ	0244	ô
0210	Ò	0245	õ
0211	Ó	0246	ö
0212	Ô	0247	÷

0213	Õ	0248	ø
0214	Ö	0249	ù
0215	x	0250	ú
0216	Ø	0251	û
0217	Ù	0252	ü
0218	Ú	0253	ý
0219	Û	0254	þ
0220	Ü	0255	ÿ

Personal Ancestral File Glossary

Ahnentafel chart	A table that lists the name, date and place of birth, marriage and death for an individual and specified number of his/her ancestors. The first individual on the list is number one, the father is number two, the mother is number three, the paternal grandfather is number four, the paternal grandmother is number five, and so forth. *Ahnentafel* is a German word meaning ancestor chart or ancestor table. This chart is also called a continental pedigree.
Also known as	A field on the individual screen where you may type the other names by which a person was known.
Ancestral File Number (AFN)	A number used to identify each record in Ancestral File.
Ancestral File	A computer file containing names and often other vital information (such as date and place of birth, marriage, or death) of millions of individuals who have lived throughout the world. Names are organized into family groups and pedigrees. To allow you to coordinate research, the file also lists names and addresses of those who contributed to the file. Ancestral File, which was created by The Church of Jesus Christ of Latter-day Saints, is available on compact disc and on the Internet.
Ancestry chart	A pedigree chart that contains only names and limited information about the people on it.

ANSEL character set	A set of characters used in computers. ANSEL contains the characters in the ASCII character set as well as many non-English and other characters. Personal Ancestral File uses the ANSEL character set rather than the ANSI, which uses a different technique to define the non-ASCII characters.
ANSI character set	The set of characters that are used in Windows. This set of characters includes the standard ASCII characters as well as math symbols, non-English diacritics, and special characters.
ASCII	A very basic standard set of letters, numbers, and other symbols used in computers. ASCII is the most universal set of characters for a computer, but it is also the most limited.
Baptism Type	A field on the Individual screen used for recording whether a person was baptized into The Church of Jesus Christ of Latter-day Saints while they were alive or by proxy.
Baptism	An introductory ordinance in many religions, including The Church of Jesus Christ of Latter-day Saints.
Books	An option that allows you to print Ahnentafel charts or modified registers.
Browse List	A button that displays the Individual List. **NOTE**: THIS MAY CHANGE TO INDIVIDUAL LIST, IN WHICH CASE THIS COULD BE DELETED.

Calendar	An option that allows you to print calendars showing names, birth dates, and other information about individuals in your database.
Call number	The number used to identify a book, microfilm, microfiche, or other source in a library or archive. Library materials are stored and retrieved by call number.
Caption	Text that briefly describes a multimedia file.
Cascading pedigree	An option that allows you to print pedigree charts for a specified number of generations. Each page is numbered, which allows you to keep the pages in order.
Cascading family group record	An option that allows you to print family group records for a specified number of generations in a family.
Cause of death	A field on the Individual screen where you may type the reason that a person died.
Char set	An abbreviation for character set, the numbers, letters, and other symbols available for use in a computer.
Character map	A screen that displays all of the numbers, letters, and symbols available in a given font or for a given program.
Check/Repair	A feature on the **File** menu that allows you to scan a file for database problems. You can select whether or not Personal Ancestral File should fix any problems it finds.
Child	An option on the **Add** menu that allows you to add a child to the highlighted individual.

Citation Detail	The part of a source citation that contains the information needed to find a particular piece of information within the source. For example, it might contain a page number of a book or a page and line number of a census.
Confidential data	Information in a database that should be kept private. Confidential data includes both events that have been marked as confidential and notes that have (~) as the first character of the paragraph.
Contact information	Information used to identify a person to contact about a record in your database. For living individuals, the contact information may list the individual in your database. For deceased individuals, it might be the person who gave you the information or a close living relative. You can type the name, address, telephone number, e-mail address, and website address. Type this information on the **Contact Information** screen.
Create Web Page	A feature on the tools menu that allows you to create a Web Page containing the information in your database.
Custom ID	A field on the **Individual** screen where you may type an identification number for an individual. This field is used mainly by genealogists who use a specific numbering system to identify each individual in a database. Do not use this field for Social Security numbers or any other information that should be kept confidential. In previous versions of PAF, this field was called the ID number.

Custom reports	An option that gives versatility when designing reports.
Date calculator	A feature on the **Tools** menu that can determine the days, months, and years elapsed between two dates or to determine a date based on the amount of time elapsed before or after a date.
Date entry	An option on the **Preferences** screen where you select how the computer interprets dates that are typed as all numbers. U.S. style (3/4/99 means 4 March 1999) versus European style (3/4/99 means 3 April 1999).
Delete Individual	A feature on the **Edit** menu that removes all information about the highlighted individual from your database.
Descendancy chart	A report that lists an individual and his/her children and their spouses and children.
Descendancy List	A feature on the **Search** menu that displays an individual's descendants and allows the selection of an individual to display.
Description	Text that describes a multimedia file. The description is generally longer than the caption.
Duplicate Individual	In match/merge, the record that is the same as another record in your file. If you merge the records, the record of the duplicate individual will be deleted from your file.
End of line	The last known person in a line of ancestry. An end-of-line person has no parents in the database.

Endowment	A priesthood ordinance performed in temples of The Church of Jesus Christ of Latter-day Saints. The endowment explains the purpose of life and Heavenly Father's plan for the exaltation of his children.
Export	A feature on the **File** menu that saves information to use in another genealogical program, to submit to Ancestral File or the Pedigree Resource File, or to submit for temple ordinances.
Family	A feature on the **View screen** menu that displays an Individual and his/her spouse, children, and parents. The **Family View** window is one of the main screens in Personal Ancestral File.
Family History SourceGuide	A computerized reference library of information about how to do family history research. SourceGuide is produced by The Church of Jesus Christ of Latter-day Saints.
Family group record	A printed form that lists a family--parents and children–and gives information about dates, places of birth, marriage, and death. Also called a ***family group sheet***.
FamilySearch Internet Genealogy Service	A search service on the World Wide Web that helps people find and share family history information. This service is provided by The Church of Jesus Christ of Latter-day Saints.

FamilySearch	A term that refers to computer products created by the LDS church that help people learn about ancestors. FamilySearch products currently include (1) a DOS-based version that includes Ancestral File™, International Genealogical Index®, Military Index, Social Security Death Index, Scottish Church Records, Personal Ancestral File®, and the Family History Library Catalog™, and (2) a search service on the World Wide Web that helps people find and share family history information.
Father Field	A feature on the **Add** menu that adds an individual's father.
Field	A place on a computer screen where you can type or view information.
Field filter	An option on the **Advanced Search/Focus** screen that allows you to select individuals who have similar information in fields in the individual record, marriage record, notes or sources.
Find by RIN/MRIN	A feature on the **Search** menu that finds an individual in your file by typing the RIN or MRIN.
GEDCOM	The acronym for GEnealogical Data COMmunications. GEDCOM is a computer data format created by The Church of Jesus Christ of Latter-day Saints for storing genealogical information so that many computer programs can use it. Personal Ancestral File® and FamilySearch® both use GEDCOM.

Gregorian calendar

The calendar system used in most of the present-day world. Pope Gregory XIII introduced this calendar in 1582 to correct the Julian calendar, which, because of miscalculated leap years, no longer matched the solar year. In the Gregorian calendar, the year begins on 1 January and has 365 days. Years that are divisible by four have an extra day in February, called a leap day. The year of a new century, however, has a leap year only if it is divisible by 400. Various counties adopted the Gregorian calendar at various times. England and the American colonies adopted it in 1752.

Home

A feature on the **Search** menu that returns to the person with RIN 1. You can change the home person by changing the RIN to **Display on File Open** feature in **Preferences**. The term home can also refer to the first person in a database.

Import

A feature on the **File** menu that brings the information stored in a GEDCOM file into your database.

Individual Summary

A printed version of an individual record.

Individual

A feature on the **Edit** menu that edits the highlighted individual. Also a feature on the **Add** menu that adds an unlinked individual to your file.

Individual List

A feature on the **Search** menu that provides a list of the individuals in your file and displays them on the **Pedigree** or **Family View** window. You can sort the list alphabetically or by RIN.

Individual record	The computer record that contains a person's name and birth, christening, death, burial, Latter-day Saint ordinance, and other information.
InfoBoxes	An option on the **Preferences** screen that allows you to select how much information you want to display in the **Pedigree View** window. **Pedigree View** displays information in two ways (1) in a floating box that appears only when you place your cursor over the name of an individual, or (2) in a locked box that appears only when you click the name of the individual.
Julian calendar	A calendar introduced in Rome in 46 B.C. This calendar was the basis for the Gregorian calendar, which is in common use today. The Julian calendar specified that the year began on 25 March (Lady's Day) and had 365 days. Each fourth year had a leap day, so it had 366 days. The year was divided into months. Each month had 30 or 31 days, except February which had 28 days in normal years and 29 days in leap years. This calendar was used for several centuries but was eventually replaced by the Gregorian calendar because leap years had been miscalculated.
Latter-day Saint data	Latter-day Saint baptism, endowment, and sealing information stored on individual and marriage records.
Link	The process of defining family relationships between individual records. The term link can also refer to the process of attaching a source to an individual or marriage record.

Listing file	Information from a GEDCOM file that did not fit in an individual record, marriage record, or source. You can put this information into the notes for an individual or marriage, or you can copy it into a separate file.
Lists	An option that allows you to print various lists.
Living	A person who is still alive. PAF defines a living person as someone who was born within the last 110 years whose individual record contains no death or burial information. This term is also an option available for the **Baptism Type** field on the Individual screen. It is used to indicate that a Latter-day Saint baptism was performed by the individual while he/she was still alive.
Log Changes	An option on the **Preferences** screen that tracks any addition, modification or deletion made to the individual and marriage records in your data.
Marriage	An option on the **Edit** menu that allows you to edit the marriage record of the highlighted individual.
Marriage list	A feature on the **Search** menu that displays a list of all couples in your database.
Marriage record	The computer record that contains a couple's marriage date, place, Latter-day Saint sealing, and other marriage information.
Married Name	A field on the **Individual** screen where you may type the name a person adopted after marriage.

Match/Merge	A feature on the **Tools** menu that finds duplicated records in your database and combine them into one record.
Media	A term used to refer to electronic pictures, sound clips, and video clips. Also called Multimedia.
Media collection	A feature that displays all of the multimedia files that have been linked to an individual, source, or marriage.
Merge on AFNs	A feature on the **Tools** menu that automatically merges records that have the same Ancestral File numbers.
Modified register	A report that lists an individual and his/her descendants in a narrative form. The first paragraph identified the individual and explains birth and other event information in complete sentences. The next paragraph describes the person's first spouse. Their children and their spouses are listed next. If the person had more than one spouse, those spouses and any children appear after that.
Mother Field	A feature on the **Add** menu that adds the mother of the primary individual.
MRIN	An abbreviation that stands for Marriage Record Identification Number. PAF assigns each marriage record a unique MRIN and uses it to distinguish one marriage record from another.
Multimedia	A term used to refer to electronic pictures, sound clips, and video clips.
Multiple parent indicator	A symbol used on reports that indicates that a person is linked to more than one set of parents.

Nickname	A familiar form of a person's name or a descriptive name given to an individual in addition to his or her given name.
Notes	Information about an individual, marriage, or set of parents that does not fit in the individual record, the marriage record, or sources. Notes can contain additional information, research notes, or other narrative information.
Notes Selector	A feature that lists tags used in your notes and allows you to view all of your notes or only the notes with a particular tag.
Order Spouses	An option on the **Edit** menu that can change the order of an individual's spouses. You can put spouses in chronological order according to the marriage date or in any other order. The spouse listed as number one will be the spouse who appears by default each time the database is opened.
Order Children	An option on the **Edit** menu that can change the order of an individual's children. Generally, you will put the children in chronological order by birth dates.
Other events	An event that does not appear by default on the **Individual** and **Marriage** screens. You can choose from a predefined set of events or add your own.

Parent Link	The type of relationship selected for an individual and his/her parents. The options are biological, adopted, guardian, sealing, challenged, and disproved. If a person is linked to only one set of parents, the relationship is assumed to be biological unless you change it. On the **Family** screen, the parent link appears only if it is something other than biological.
Parents Marriage	An option on the **Edit** menu where you can edit the marriage record of the parents of the highlighted individual.
Parents	An option on the **Edit** menu that allows you to add a new set of parents to an individual, change the order of the parents, change the **Relationship to Parents** code, unlink a person from a set of parents, make a certain set of parents the primary parents, add notes about a set of parents, and add Latter-day Saint sealing-to-parent information.
Password	A set of characters that you can use to prevent inadvertent changes to your database.
Pedigree Resource File	A computer file that contains names, family relationships and birth, marriage, and death information for millions of people. The information in this file will appear as it was originally submitted and will not be merged with information submitted by others.
Pedigree	A feature on the **View** menu that displays a pedigree chart of 5 generations of a person's ancestry. This term can also refer to a pedigree chart or be used as a synonym for lineage or ancestry.

Pedigree chart	A chart that shows an individual's direct ancestors-parents, grandparents, great-grandparents, and so forth. A pedigree chart may contain birth, marriage, and death information.
Physical description	A field on the **Individual** screen where you may type the information about a person's appearance.
Preferences	A feature on the **Tools** menu that customizes how PAF operates.
Prepared by	An option on the **Preferences** screen where you can type your name, address, telephone number, Ancestral File number, and e-mail address. PAF uses this information when it exports and prints information from your database.
Primary individual	On the Family screen, the person in the top, left position. On the Pedigree screen, the person in the first generation position. On the Merge screen, the record displayed on the left side of the screen that will remain in your database after a merge. Also called the primary position.
Print Reports	A feature on the **File** menu that can send information to a printer. You can print pedigree charts, family group records, individual summaries, and many other types of reports.
Properties	A feature on the **File** menu that allows you to display statistics about your database, such as the number of individuals, marriages, sources, and so forth.

Proxy	An option available for the **Baptism Type** field on the individual screen. It us used to indicate that a LDS Baptism was performed by an individual acting on behalf of a deceased individual. An individual who acts on behalf of a deceased individual to receive a temple ordinance.
Relationship filter	An option on the **Advanced Search/Focus** screen that allows the selection of individuals who are related.
Relationship to Parents Link	The type of relationship selected for an individual and his/her parents. The options are biological, adopted, guardian, sealing, challenged and disproved. If a person is linked to only one set of parents, the relationship is assumed to be biological unless you change it. On the **Family** screen, the parent link appears only if it is something other than biological. Also called the Parent link.
Relationship Indicators	Words that show the relationship of everyone in the database to the selected individual in the database.
Relationship calculator	A feature on the **Tools** menu that can determine how two individuals are related.
Relationship codes	A symbol used to represent parent links on reports.
Repository List	A feature on the **Edit** menu that allows you to add, edit, or delete repositories from you database.
Repository	The place where records are stored. In PAF, you can record a repository's name, address, and telephone number.

Restore	A feature on the **File** menu that uses a backup copy to return your database to its state when the backup was made.
RIN	An abbreviation that stands for Record Identification Number. PAF assigns a unique RIN to each individual record you enter. This number is used to distinguish that individual record from others in your database.
Root person	The person who has RIN 1. PAF uses the term root person when you turn on the **Relationship Indicators** in **Preferences**.
Scrapbook	A report that shows the photographs and other scanned images that are associated with an individual. Each image can be accompanied by its file name, caption, and description.
Sealing to parent	A term referring to priesthood ordinances performed in temples of The Church of Jesus Christ of Latter-day Saints, that make it possible for the relationships between parents and children to continue after death.
Sealing to spouse	A term referring to priesthood ordinances performed in temples of The Church of Jesus Christ of Latter-day Saints that make it possible for a husband's and wife's relationship to continue after death.
Selection file	A file that PAF creates when you choose the records you want to import into your file.

Soundex	A type of index that groups together surnames that sound similar but are spelled differently. Each surname is assigned a code that consists of the first letter of the name. The next three consonants are assigned a number. Vowels are ignored as are duplicate letters. The Soundex has been used to index the 1880, 1900, 1910, and 1920 U.S. censuses and some other types of records, such as naturalization records and passenger lists.
Soundex calculator	A feature on the **Tools** menu that calculates the Soundex code for a surname.
Source Description	The portion of a source citation that describes the source as a whole. A source description is stored as a separate record in your database. After you type a source description once, you need only to select it from a list to cite it in another place in your database.
Source	Information that describes the book, certificate, periodical, record, or other place where genealogical information was found.
Source List	A feature on the **Edit** menu where you can add, edit, or delete sources from your database.
Spouse	A feature on the **Add** menu that allows the addition of the highlighted person's spouse.
Status bar	A feature on the **View** menu that will hide or display the status bar (the bar along the bottom of the **Pedigree** and **Family** screens that displays instructions, the file name, and other information about your file).

Tag	A word or phrase used to classify the information in a note. Tags appear in all uppercase letters at the beginning of the word and are followed by a colon.
Tagged notes	A type of note that uses a keyword to identify the type of information contained in a note. The keyword is typed in all uppercase letters at the beginning of a paragraph and followed by a colon. For example, *NAME,* this person changed her name, *NAME*: is the tag.
Temple ordinances	A religious ceremony performed in a temple of The Church of Jesus Christ of Latter-day Saints by one having priesthood authority.
TempleReady	A computer program that helps members of The Church of Jesus Christ of Latter-day Saints prepare the names of their ancestors for temple ordinances.
Title (prefix)	A field on the **Individual** screen used for information that should appear before a person's name. It can be used for titles of nobility, scholarship, clergy, etc.
Title (suffix)	A field on the **Individual** screen used for information that should appear after a person's name. It can be used for information such as Jr. Sr., III, etc.
Toolbar	A feature on the **View** menu that displays or hides the toolbar (the row of buttons along the top of the screen).
Truncate	To shorten a long personal or place-name, PAF sometimes truncates names so they will fit on a screen or report.

Unlink Individual	A feature on the **Edit** menu that allows the removal of the family relationship between individuals.
Unlink	The process of removing the family relationship between two records. When you unlink records, the records stay in the database, but they no longer appear as family members.
Wall chart	An ancestry chart that can be taped together to form one large pedigree chart.

INDEX